VM and Departmental Computing

VM and Departmental Computing

Gary R. McClain

Intertext Publications
McGraw-Hill Book Company
New York, N.Y.

Library of Congress Catalog Card Number 87-83101

10 9 8 7 6 5 4 3 2 1

ISBN 0-07-044938-4 (Hardcover)
ISBN 0-07-044939-2 (Paperback)

Intertext Publications/Multiscience Press, Inc.
McGraw-Hill Book Company
11 West 19th Street
New York, NY 10011

VM/PC, VM/XA SP, VM/SF, VM/SP, VM/IS, VM/HPO, MVS, DOS,
VSE, PROFS, NetView, RSCS, VTAM, SNA, CP, CMS, 9370 Information System, IUCV, ACI, REXX, EXEC, EXEC2, DDR, and SQL/DS
are trademarks of International Business Machines Corporation. IBM
is a registered trademark of International Business Machines Corporation.

VMCENTER II is a trademark of VM Software, Inc.

V/ is a trademark of VM Systems Group.

VM/SP Single System Image, RAPID, CMAP, and FAST Checkpoint
are copyrights of VM/CMS Unlimited, Inc.

Composed in Ventura Publisher by Context, Inc.

Table of Contents

Acknowledgements

Without the support and guidance of many individuals, writing *VM and Departmental Computing* would not have been possible.

Richard Moore, Vice President, Corporate Communications at VM Software, Inc. initiated this project and gave advice and encouragement throughout the research and writing process. Rich's perspective on what makes a good book was invaluable.

Robert Cook, VM Software's founder and Chief Executive Officer, offered his extensive insight into both the future of VM and the implications of Departmental Computing. Bob is one of the original proponents of the VM operating system, and his interest and support were key elements in the book's completion.

Others who contributed both through providing extensive technical information as well as exhaustive chapter reviews include Todd Margo, Carris Vondal, Steve Drill, Jon Rutherford, Robert Wheeler, Kevin Golden, Richard Rooney, Peter McManus, Nancy Zuiker, Charles Waser, Byron Vranas, Janet Gobeille, Mary Woodward, Julie Tray, Mitch Hsu, Tim Reid and Michael Mooney. Ronald Kral, Chief Technical Officer at VM Software, provided invaluable input into my understanding of managing the technical considerations of Departmental Computing. In addition, Richard Smith offered patient proofreading while Alison Keeter turned my scribbles into illustrations. There are many others at VM Software, too numerous to mention, who provided encouragement and assistance as well as tolerance for my sometimes "driven" behavior. William Mee contributed extensively to the content of Chapter 6, "Monitoring for Performance," particularly in the areas of "CPU Utilization" and "Tuning the VM CPU."

I owe a special debt of gratitude to my parents and family, who believe in me no matter what. It is to them that this book is dedicated.

Preface

VM and Departmental Computing was written to achieve two goals. The first is to enhance the reader's understanding of IBM's VM operating system, and the second is to explain the role of VM in Departmental Computing. As a strategic operating system, VM is extensively documented by IBM at the technical level. However, there is a large gap between technical specifications and practical applications. *VM and Departmental Computing* bridges the gap by taking a comprehensive look at real day-to-day issues — issues which remain relatively constant across VM product variations as well as being common among various organizations using VM. These issues, such as disaster recovery and system security, provide a framework upon which to "hang" technical concepts. The structure of the VM directory, for example, is discussed in light of system security, while paging and input/output control are discussed in relation to performance monitoring. Thus, the description of the functions of "native VM" unfolds gradually, in support of the issues.

The secondary goal of *VM and Departmental Computing*, to provide a perspective on VM's role in Departmental Computing, addresses a major need. Changes in technology have direct implications upon the way in which organizations function and, therefore, upon the way in which individuals within organizations perform their daily tasks. By placing users more in control of the information that they use in their job functions, Departmental Computing will have effects which include making large organizations more decentralized and users more powerful. This book clarifies the role of the VM operating system as a vehicle for ushering in these changes, as well as outlining the technical considerations associated with using VM in a departmental situation.

VM and Departmental Computing is addressed to three audiences: managers, system programmers and others with a technical focus, and users. Managers, of both technical and non-technical backgrounds, are often in the position of making major decisions that affect both users and the technical staff, though they may not actually have the technical skills to carry out these decisions. It is important that managers have available as much information as possible concerning the implications of their decisions, including the technical considerations. Those responsible for the technical concerns of VM may be in the position of carrying out management directives regarding, for example, system security, and reconciling system requirements and limitations with the needs of the organization. Technical knowledge must be balanced with an understanding of the "larger picture." Users have their own specific job functions to carry out and may feel that the environment either facilitates or interferes with these functions.

The needs of these three groups are addressed through an integration of the technical perspective with the practical considerations that are critical to successful implementation in the organization. To accomplish this, concepts and issues are presented to clarify how the VM operating system works, how to get the most from VM, and how VM contributes to the Departmental Computing scenario. Information resource strategies in organizations are becoming increasingly multidisciplinary, with diverse groups working together to discover, and subsequently operationalize, practical solutions. This trend towards cooperative decision-making, with an increased focus on the user, is most evident in the rapidly increasing momentum of Departmental Computing. The VM operating system, combining flexibility and ease-of-use with technical sophistication, is the ultimate foundation for applications that truly enable the organization to compete in the dynamic global community.

1

Introduction

The information industry is entering yet another new era, that of Departmental Computing. A major impetus to this movement is the introduction of IBM's 9370 Information System, a series of midrange computers, which was announced in October 1986. These machines bring the power of the mainframe to the departments and remote sites of large organizations, as well as to smaller shops for whom this resource was previously unaffordable. The 9370 will help to make Departmental Computing a reality by providing users with more control over their own information, with hardware and software resources within their departments, while maintaining the availability of the needed information and support from the central site.

VM is clearly the strategic operating system for the 9370 and, by inference, for the realization of Departmental Computing. Because of VM's flexibility, interactivity, and networking capabilities, it provides the essential framework for departmental solutions. VM is uniquely qualified to meet the demands of multiple online users, as well as provide the foundation for communication between the central site and remote sites.

The purpose of this book is to provide an in-depth look at the design of the VM operating system, with a particular focus on the practical aspects of the day-to-day management and operation of VM. In addition, as the title implies, features of VM which make it particulaly adaptable to the Departmental Computing environment will be expanded.

For many years, users perceived that VM was being treated as an "unwanted stepchild" by IBM. Recent trends, including the Information Center and end-user computing, led to an increased interest in VM on the part of users and, subsequently, IBM. As a result, VM is now considered to be a strategic operating system and, as such, is being aggressively enhanced by IBM. These enhancements, at the purely technical level, are well-documented. However, there is a large gap between technical specifications and the reality of practice. The contents of these pages is written to bridge this gap.

Though the features and capabilities of VM are improving with each new release, the basic design, and consequently considerations such as security and accounting, remain relatively constant across the VM variations (VM/SP, VM/IS, etc.). Managers and technical people are often in the role of making major decisions about these issues, and the technical documentation does not provide the crucial real-world perspective. Technical experts are available to carry out these decisions, but even decisions of a technical nature must be made from an organizational perspective.

Furthermore, changes in technology have direct implications for the way in which organizations function and, therefore, for the way in which individuals work. By placing users more in control of the information that they use in their daily job functions, Departmental Computing will have effects which include making large organizations more decentralized and users more powerful. Yet because of easier to use software, users may at the same time become less computer literate and technical people may have a less defined role. The book will clarify the role of the VM operating system as the vehicle for both ushering in and managing these changes.

There is much more involved in the management of VM than installation and maintenance considerations. For example, managers must make decisions concerning the need for disaster recovery plans, and the level of security needed. These decisions, in turn, affect users and therefore the organization as a whole. Many chapters take a comprehensive look at what VM offers, in its "vanilla" form, and, in the process of outlining the important considerations, provide suggestions for better control of this environment.

Why VM?

Computer industry watchers have been predicting a "shift in power" in the management of information resources within organizations. This power has, in brief terms, shifted from almost dictatorial control by corporate Management Information Systems (MIS) to a situation in which the users themselves have a much greater voice in the decision-making process. Though the voice of the user is stronger in some organizations than others, it is clear that, overall, the power balance is shifting toward shared responsibility between the two groups.

In conjunction with these shifting powers is a demand for applications that are more "user friendly"; it is also felt that the resources of the computer should be more accessible in general. The VM operating system has been the clear frontrunner among IBM operating systems in providing the foundation for meeting these demands. VM was not developed because of the need for providing more resources for users, but it has certainly grown and developed as a response to this need. Among the features of VM is its ability to accommodate multiple on-line users at the same time, so that users can interact with the computer, posing queries and receiving information, as if each was in control of a real machine. This is a sharp contrast to more traditional, batch-oriented systems in which users are responsible for designing "jobs" which are then sent off to be completed at a later time.

VM's strong user orientation, as well as ease of use, have made it a mainstay of the Information Center environment. As the industry moves toward decentralizing information resources even further, through Departmental Computing, VM will continue to provide a flexible foundation for growth.

Departmental Computing: A Brief Definition

Departmental Computing provides a means to use all of the data in an organization without regard for where it was generated. It means that data stored in the central mainframe and data generated within individual departments can be used up, down, and sideways throughout the corporate structure. For years there has been a concern within organizations that a central repository of data, with controlled access, was necessary in addition to more specialized sources within departments. Isolated departmental solutions, through unconnected midrange machines and personal computers, have been attempts to provide this capability. The results have been unsatisfactory and, at times, chaotic.

The significance of the announcement of the 9370 machine is that it is the midrange solution that is essentially the missing link in this scenario. Based on 370 architecture, it is compatible with IBM's largest machines. This means that the central repository can now be a reality, connected to smaller departmental machines, sharing data for specialized departmental functions. The key to this capability is 370 architecture, which serves as the basis for this compatability between machines.

As has been the case with concepts such as Office Automation and the Information Center, there are many interpretations of the meaning of Departmental Computing. These definitions will be explored throughout the pages of this book. However, as a means of departure, the basic definition of Departmental Computing begins with a hardware configuration in which one or more large mainframes, in a central site, are connected to midrange machines located within individual departments. The central mainframe serves as a repository of corporate data while the departmental machines contain specialized applications and data that are relevant to work groups within those departments. Some departmental machines may be dedicated to one function alone; some may be connected to personal computers as well.

The role of VM as a basis for Departmental Computing will be established in the chapters that follow.

Chapter Overview

The following is an overview of the chapters in *VM and Departmental Computing* with a brief description of content.

Chapter 2. An Overview of VM

Chapter 2 discusses the history of the VM operating system, from its early development and use to its current status. In addition, the basic design of VM is outlined, including the major components, CP and CMS, and communications within the VM environment. The variations of VM are also briefly described.

Chapter 3. The Emergence of Departmental Computing

The movement toward the decentralization of computer resources is described in Chapter 3. Trends in the management of information in organizations are chronicled, including Distributed Processing, the Information Center, and Office Automation. Departmental Computing is contrasted against changes that are occurring in organizations in general, and the role of the user is further described.

Chapter 4. VM Installation and Maintenance

The installation of the VM operating system is presented, focusing on the elements necessary in getting a basic system "up and running." The maintenance process, including the management of new product releases and the application of "fixes" is described. The issue of system modifications is discussed.

Chapter 5. Security in VM

Security is a critical component in any VM system, whether a single processor or multiple processors are involved. This chapter begins with further discussion of the role of the CP directory, with a focus on potential "security holes" in VM. This is followed by guidelines for solving VM security problems. Security in the remote sites is also discussed.

Chapter 6. Monitoring for Performance

Performance monitoring is presented with further analysis of VM internals. The major performance management areas, CPU utilization and I/O, are considered, with a discussion of problem and supervisor states and paging. The monitoring capabilities of VM, and how to expand these capabilities are described. Monitoring in the departmental scheme is discussed.

Chapter 7. Balancing the Workload

Because VM is interactive, many users will be accessing the system at the same time, with the risk of subsequent system degradation. VM's capabilities for balancing workload are discussed, followed by alternatives for managing workload through scheduling. Departmental implications are included.

Chapter 8. Managing DASD

DASD is further defined in this chapter, with a perspective on its role in a user environment. Methods of allocating VM DASD are included, with a perspective on DASD management for Departmental Computing.

Chapter 9. VM Applications

A practical overview of CMS is provided with examples of applications within native VM. EXEC 2 and REXX are also discussed. Major application trends for VM are outlined.

Chapter 10. Disaster Recovery

The need for system backup, in case of natural or other kinds of disasters, is presented, as well as VM system backup capabilities. Alternatives to providing backup capabilities are provided, including disk and tape storage, and the use of a hotsite. A departmental perspective is included as well.

Chapter 11. Tape Storage in VM

It is often necessary to store outdated information on tapes, and with limited computer sizes, this issue has many implications for the multi-user environment. Native VM tape capabilities are described, followed by guidelines for tape management and alternatives to the use of tape, including DASD. Suggestions for tape use at the departmental level are provided.

Chapter 12. VM Accounting and Chargeback

With departmental users, the chargeback and accounting issue becomes both a corporate and a departmental problem. The accounting capabilities of VM are described, with an in-depth look at CP accounting. Methods of chargeback and guidelines for setting up the resource accounting system are included. The departmental accounting issue is discussed.

Chapter 13. Planning for Capacity

The importance of capacity planning is presented, focusing on capacity issues in VM, and the use of performance monitoring data as a basis for this process. Modeling as a forecasting method is discussed, as are capacity planning considerations in the departmental scenario.

Chapter 14. Making Departmental Computing Work

Control in the Departmental Computing environment is an important issue in making this concept work. This chapter looks at the management issues, including the roles of MIS, users, and department managers. Guidelines concerning the central site, and the use of system software, are also presented.

Chapter 15. Conclusions

Future perspectives regarding the VM operating system and Departmental Computing are discussed.

2

An Overview of VM

VM has a variety of features which have contributed to its success in such diverse environments as engineering laboratories, manufacturing plants, and Information Centers for end users. Chapter 2 takes a closer look at VM's roots, followed by a discussion of CP and CMS functions.

Why Operating Systems?

The purpose of the operating system is most basically to take the place of what in the early days of computing was the line in front of the computer operator's desk. When programs were run serially, users took their program and data, contained on a stack of punch cards, walked to the building that housed the computer, and stood in line to have their programs executed. The operator placed the cards in a reader. When the "button" was pushed, the computer read the cards and executed the program. Following this, the next user in line was serviced. This was inefficient for many reasons. Obviously, it was a drain on the time of the users, not to mention a strain on patience. But it was also inefficient for the CPU, because it was also in a wait state between users, waiting for the operator to load the next deck of cards and "push the button."

Operating systems are programs that control and balance the work of the CPU, making sure that it is never idle when there is work to be done. Users may not feel that their programs are running fast enough, but because of the operating system, the CPU is being effectively utilized so that even if users are not getting instant interactive responses, they are at least able to concentrate on other tasks while the work is being performed. When in the past programs were run serially, perhaps one program would require 15 seconds of CPU time while another would require 20 seconds. If both run at the same time, with the help of the operating system, each may require a few more seconds. But because of the "fancy, esoteric and scary" things accomplished by the operating system, both programs are essentially being run at the same time.

The operating system is, in effect, the "foundation" software of the computer, mediating the demands of users, and generally controlling the use of the hardware. The operating system should be distinguished from applications software, such as accounting packages, and system software, which in effect helps the operating system to work more efficiently.

VM: The First PC

The VM operating system can support varied hardware and software environments on a single machine. For example, programmers can be involved installing, generating and testing new releases of an operating system, subsystems, and program products. They can be applying and testing preventive and corrective maintenance to one copy of VM, or another operating system, while another copy of VM is being used as the production system. All this is happening while users are going about their daily work, using applications and storing information as if each was in control of his or her own dedicated machine.

The VM shop could in many ways be considered the forerunner of what the personal computer (PC) has accomplished in the arena of end-user computing. The level of user control that VM offers, to the point that a user can basically do whatever he wants in his own machine without interfering with other users — this level of control, outside of VM, is only available on an individual personal computer on which the user is totally in control.

The timesharing industry is a particularly good example of VM's similarity to the PC environment. Timesharing with VM provided companies, and in turn their users, with dedicated computer resources without the expense and maintenance concerns of owning a mainframe. Organizations were able to rent a "piece" of the computer, load their own software, register their users, and then compute at will without being aware that the same "box" was shared not only by other users but by other organizations.

VM's unique ability to simulate a real machine, combined with its interactivity, makes it a solid solution for a user-oriented environment, including Departmental Computing. VM's compatibility with 370 architecture further reinforces its role in Departmental Computing. IBM's decision to make the 9370 a 370 machine was not without practical considerations. It is estimated that there exists over $150 billion worth of programs in the U.S. market today which are 370-

oriented. Some of these programs will be usable at the departmental level, while others may be used in part at this level. In addition, the largest universe of applications and systems software in the marketplace is estimated to be oriented toward 370 architecture.

Essentially, IBM didn't have a choice but to base the 9370 and Departmental Computing on 370 architecture. The precedent was already there. VM in turn runs on the widest range of machines, from the high-end 3090 to the AT/370 Personal Computer. In this respect, VM is even more flexible as IBM's most "extensible" operating system.

The Orphan that Made Good

The VM operating system was developed during the mid-1960s in IBM's Research and Development Center in Cambridge, Massachusetts, by a team led by names that are now famous in the VM world, including Norman Rasmussen and Robert Creasy. The goal for the initial development of VM was simply to create a virtual system that would appear to each user as a dedicated machine. At the beginning, the term "end user" was unknown, and users were hardly a consideration in any data processing environment. VM's virtual machine capabilities were designed for the purpose of providing a testing and development environment for system programmers.

Originally referred to as CP/CMS, the basic operating system functions were provided by the Control Program (CP) while the user-friendly capabilities were provided by the Cambridge Monitor System (CMS). In VM's early development, much of CP/CMS was moved to the 360/67 machine, and it became known as the CP/67 operating system. CP/67 quickly gained a following of users, due in part to its adaptability in the growing timesharing market. Many organizations were involved in timesharing during this time, and the predominant operating system, TSS (Time Sharing System), was not particularly popular among users. Timesharing users were quick to take advantage of CP's ability to manage diverse users and provide the dedicated machine illusion, while CMS provided more user-friendly capabilities.

In 1972, IBM announced the System/370 series of machines, and real memory was featured on each model in this series. VM/370 was announced simultaneously with the 370 machine, with features that included CP, CMS (which was now referred to as the Conversational, rather than Cambridge, Monitor System), and RSCS (Remote Spooling Communication System), which provided enhanced communications with remote subsystems. VM/370 and 370 architecture were natural complements to each other, and VM began to amass more and more users. In addition, Release 2 of VM/370 also included support for DOS language compilers, enhancing its role as a host for DOS, and as an aid for sites migrating from DOS to OS (now MVS).

Even with VM's growing popularity during the 1970s, IBM was slow to give it extensive support. During this time, VM remained a Type III product, which means that it received little attention from either developers or sales representatives. It seemed unnecessary, considering that IBM was offering other mainframe operating systems, including MVS, DOS, and VS1. For example, efforts to bring VM into the SNA (System Network Architecture) were delayed. This meant that customers using both VM and another operating system were forced to use two networks.

The introduction of the 4300 series in 1979 was a major boon for VM, due to the concurrent emphasis on the Information Center and end-user computing. As a consequence, VM became a fully supported product.

VM's Essential Elements: CP and CMS

VM provides each user with a "virtual machine," the illusion that he or she is in sole control of the computer. By simulating this real machine within each user's virtual machine, an environment is created where each user is protected from the activities, as well as the potential invasion, of other users. End users need transparency in the computer environment; that is, they don't care where the data is coming from and they don't care about the internals of the machine. VM provides this transparency through the virtual machine concept. For example, 200 users may be using the system concurrently, each interacting with the same mainframe computer, while also having the ability to send messages and files to each other, all through the use of very simple commands.

VM provides these capabilities with two separate components, CP, the Control Program, and CMS, the Conversational Monitor System. The discussion of the functions performed by these components begins in this chapter. CP and CMS will both be discussed in much more detail throughout subsequent chapters.

Overseeing the Virtual Machine

The Control Program is a tremendously complex set of programs which enable VM to oversee the resources of the computer, balancing the needs of both multiple online users as well as other operating systems. More about its design, maintenance, critical modules, and how it works will be discussed where appropriate.

The major functions of CP can be summarized as follows:

• User scheduling and dispatching

- Real storage management
- Virtual memory management
- Spool management
- CP command processing
- Error recovery and recording

CP is essentially a system program whose function is to "construct" individual 370 computers through the creation of the virtual machine environment that is responsible for this illusion. These resources include the physical equipment such as the computer itself as well as the peripheral equipment like tape drives, printers, and Direct Access Storage Devices.

CP controls computer resources by mapping virtual resources to real resources, acting as an interface between the hardware and the user, facilitating what the user is able to accomplish in the virtual machine and see on the terminal. The terms virtual and real are critical to an understanding of not only CP, but the VM environment itself. Because of CP's ability to manipulate the memory of the machine and balance multiple users, the resources of the machine can in effect be overcommitted. For example, users can be assigned much more memory than is actually available in the computer. This is because CP is able to balance user requests, giving each request just enough actual, or real, memory to satisfy it and then keeping everything else in virtual storage (i.e., on disk storage). So a user who thinks he or she is controlling 1 megabyte of real memory may only be using a fraction of that; the rest is in virtual memory, to be called in as needed. This process, called paging, is described in more detail in the discussion of CPU utilization in Chapter 6.

Figure 2-1 illustrates the relationship between the user, CP, and the machine resources. CP acts as the gatekeeper for these resources, providing each user with a virtual machine, and as a result, "virtual" control of the CPU.

A typical scenario that demonstrates how CP functions would be a situation in which two users are logged on to the system at the same time. Suppose the first user's virtual machine is 1 megabyte, and this user is involved in using a database search. Another user also has a 1-megabyte virtual machine, and she is using CMS to develop a program. Each may feel in control of the total machine memory, or at least 1 megabyte of it, but most likely CP is allocating each user only enough real memory to satisfy individual requests. So each user is virtually in control of 1 megabyte of memory, but most likely not in reality.

CP is basically in an interceptor role in its control of machine resources, not only in the control of real memory but also of peripherals. When a user requests the use of a device such as a printer or a tape drive, CP also intercepts this request. Thus the user

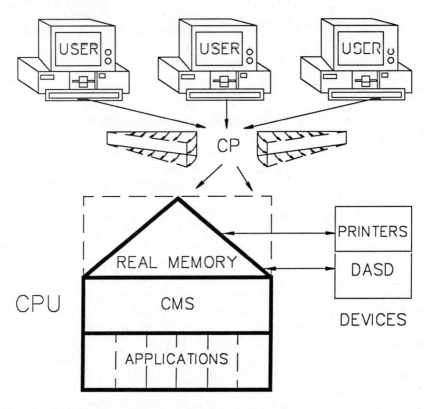

Figure 2-1 The control program in the role of gatekeeper

has the illusion of being directly in control of this device but CP is actually performing this operation, balancing it with the requests of other users, on the user's behalf. Again, these requests are balanced in conjunction with the competing demands of other users. A user feels in control, for example, of his own printer but CP is simulating this control. His usage is being emulated by CP.

Much of the virtual machine concept is rather esoteric at first glance. With further understanding of CMS and the issues critical to VM, CP's interceptor role as the provider of the virtual illusion will become clearer.

The CP Directory

CP does not simply exist as an amorphous entity, floating around the computer. It uses real space on Direct Access Storage Devices (DASD), just like other information that is stored in the computer. One storage requirement for CP is its Directory, and this is also a key to understanding how CP operates.

The directory is a database that is maintained by CP, and it does just as its name implies: It is a guide to the users in the VM environment. The directory is described in much more depth in the chapter concerning security in the VM environment; a brief description is necessary for understanding the function of CP. The directory performs the following:

- Defines the virtual machine configuration, including the attributes and privileges associated with each virtual machine. Thus, information about each user and what he or she can do in the system is stored in the directory.
- Defines permanent storage, the DASD space that is available to a virtual machine (a user) for storing data.
- Stores LINK and LOGON passwords, which control the user's ability to log on to the virtual machine or to access data stored on DASD.
- Specifies data sharing privileges, or the ability for a virtual machine to share data with another virtual machine, one user to another.

The directory is maintained on a special formatted area of DASD, and is accessed by CP when a user logs on, as well as at other times when a user's privileges must be verified. Each user must be associated with an entry in the directory. This in effect sets up the user's environment, with restrictions of what can and cannot be done, how much storage space (DASD) the user has, where this is located, and what other users are allowed to access the user's data. This information may be called the user's virtual machine configuration. This is the term given to the overall set of definitions and privileges given to each user, and by inference, each virtual machine. VM sites have the ability to specify a basic configuration for the virtual machine of each user, for example, allocating each user the same amount of storage space and the same basic privileges. This provides a means of defining and enforcing organizational standards, with site-specified options in turn becoming part of each user's virtual machine configuration. The virtual machine configuration can also be assigned on an individual basis, depending on the unique needs of the users. The virtual machine configuration is key to VM's flexibility.

A user's virtual machine also contains other information that facilitates the overall effective functioning of the VM environment. This includes the setting of virtual storage limits, which is the amount of main storage that can be used by a virtual machine for executing programs or maintaining data files. These limits are critical for assuring that the computer's main memory is not overloaded with competing requests. Virtual machine configuration also contains a priority setting. This is a ranking assigned to the virtual machine. With multiple users all making demands on the computer, this ranking allows CP to determine which virtual machine should receive system resources next. With requests being executed in milliseconds, the user is generally unaware of his or her priority setting, unless the system is attempting to operate beyond its capacity due to excessive demands.

Other information associated with the virtual machine configuration includes an account number, which is an eight character identifier that is recorded in the directory. Accounting data, in the form of CP accounting records, may be generated by CP whenever resources are consumed by a virtual machine. These accounting records are identified and discussed in the accounting chapter.

CP has been described as being in control of the machine's real devices, such as printers and tape devices. Again, direct access to these devices is only available to CP. The virtual machine configuration generally includes a virtual card reader, a virtual printer, and a virtual punch. These are vehicles for sending data or receiving data from other virtual machines (other users) and are virtual devices that are simulated for the virtual machine by CP. In other words, when a user sends a file to "his" printer in order to generate hard copy, he is actually sending the file to a virtual printer. The command is intercepted by CP who in turn chooses a real printer and, based on the user's priority, places the file in a queue at the real printer for execution of the command. Again, the user has the illusion of being in control of his own printer, but CP has intercepted the command and maintained control over the real devices of the machine.

CMS: Providing the Interactivity

The Conversational Monitor System, CMS, is an interactive operating system that operates under the control of CP. The virtual machine component of VM is CP; CMS provides user-friendly facilities that allow users to work interactively within the VM environment. Referring to CMS as an operating system may at first glance seem confusing, but it really is. Because of the ability of CP to mediate the demands of various operating systems, CMS functions at the level of these other operating systems, such as MVS, in providing standard operating system functions to users.

When VM is referred to as the first personal computer operating system, it is because of the capabilities of CMS. CMS is a one-user operating system, with each user having his or her own "copy" of CMS at the moment of logging on to the system. This single-user design is what provides the interactivity that VM is known for. With a combination of a copy of CMS, a storage area that is not shared with anyone else, and the mediating abilities of CP, a user is able to interact with the computer with no interference by other users. In fact, a user can "crash" his or her own virtual machine and still not affect the other logged-on users.

CMS is not only single-user oriented but also single-task. Through CMS, the user does one thing at a time such as, for example, creating a document and then performing a search of a database. Though VM allows many users to be logged on at the same time, including multiple CMS users, CMS itself performs one task at a time for each user. The user initiates a task, completes it, and then moves on to another one.

CMS users store their data in files on minidisks which have been assigned to them in the CP directory. These minidisks are not real devices, rather they are portions of real DASD which CMS treats as actual disks. In other words, DASD is allocated in pieces — minidisks — of various sizes. Users are assigned one or more of these minidisks on which to store their files, or data. A minidisk is "owned" by the user, without having to be shared with other users, and the user may manipulate data contained on this minidisk as desired. In conjunction with the user's "own" copy of CMS, the single-user illusion is maintained.

As the most user-friendly of operating systems, the CMS role has expanded with the growth of end-user computing. This has lead to its use in Information Centers and Office Automation. IBM's Professional Office System (PROFS) is an example of a mainframe office system which runs under VM, using CMS capabilities in providing document creation and storage, and messaging between users. These applications-oriented capabilities have contributed to VM's pivotal role in Departmental Computing as well.

CMS is not without its benefits outside of the realm of the end user. It is also a good application development tool, being easy to use, to learn, and to maintain, with fewer systems programmers needed than other operating systems. In addition, CMS supports many more interactive users than, for example, the more batch-oriented MVS/TSO. By developing within CMS, developers can test and debug under VM, then transport programs either to a production VM environment (production referring to day-to-day operations) or transport the programs to another operating system, such as MVS, which makes use of the same FORTRAN and COBOL compilers.

The attractiveness of CMS as a program development tool actually preceded, historically, its popularity with end users. Early in VM history, VM was heavily used (heavily being a relative term, of course) in educational and research establishments due to their attraction to the program development facilities of CMS, particularly for testing, debugging and migration without interfering with the production environment, as well as the overall ability of VM to support large numbers of terminal users compared with other systems. CMS was attractive in spite of its lack of facilities, at this time, for running batch jobs.

Often a guest operating system, such as VS1, was used for batch work. (VS1 was an early operating system; guest operating systems are explained later in this chapter).

CMS has been greatly enhanced since its first availability, but as it has evolved IBM has allowed for upward compatability. Even with these enhancements, the basic components of CMS have remained the same. These components include:

- Editor
- EXEC processor
- Debug environment
- OS simulation
- Commands, e.g., COMPARE, SORT, COPYFILE

Because CMS was not originally developed as a product, many modules were added as "quick and dirty" solutions as needs arose. These modules, and the ways in which they interface, were modified with time. Again from a historical perspective, a design element in early CMS that has contributed to its success is its high performance. In early CMS development systems support code had to occupy as small an amount of memory and use as few CPU cycles as possible due to limited machine sizes. It had to accommodate several users on a very limited computer system. The result was that its design had much in common with the early DOS operating system, streamlined to require as few system resources as possible.

With VM program product versions based on VM/370 Release 6, the CMS file system was one of the first components to be significantly revised. The original file system was designed for small systems with disk drives of an older technology, such as the Model 2311 and 2314 drives. The design of these drives limited both the size of the mini-disks and the size of the files. This restriction was balanced by a simple user interface with direct access and high performance. IBM improved the file system in this release with an evolutionary design that preserved the more desirable features of the conventional system, as well as continuing to support the original user interface. Thus, streamlined development in CMS has evolved without compromising, and even improving, its ease of use.

CMS itself is maintained on a CMS system disk, shared in read-only mode by all CMS users. This provides the illusion to users that they are in control of their own copies of CMS. Larger installations often use multiple CMS system disks because of heavy CMS use. The efficient design and high performance of CMS facilitates both of these arrangements.

When VM/SP (System Product) was introduced, it included two new major CMS components — XEDIT and REXX (in Release 3). To illustrate the importance of these components, it is estimated that the two of them constitute almost one-third of the code in VM/SP Release 4. Both XEDIT and REXX were developed by one person, separate from the CMS development group. Perhaps as a result of this, each has an end-user orientation, with capabilities that are relevant to users of varying levels of sophistication.

As discussed, CMS has a file orientation. In other words, users store groups of data in files, which are given names for ease of identification. For example a program, which would constitute a file, might be identified by a filename of PROG, or simply by a number, such as 1. Subsequent versions of the program, if the user wants to keep them separate, might be identified by PROG1, PROG2, and so on. The same user might also store a letter for future reference, identified by the filename LETTER, or by the name of the purpose of the letter, such as COMPLAIN. Each item that the user is storing is referred to as a file, and identified by a filename, which may be up to eight characters in length. File is also a CMS command, used to initiate the storing of a file.

XEDIT is simply a means of creating and editing files. Users use XEDIT subcommands to initiate a file, name it, and then subsequently store information. XEDIT can be used to edit a file that contains any kind of information, including programs that are subsequently compiled and executed. REXX, as well as EXEC, are essentially CMS "job control languages" which allow a user or an installation the ability to combine subcommands to meet specific needs. Writing something in EXEC or REXX provides a faster way of performing various tasks which are performed repeatedly. An EXEC statement, for example, might be used to archive and then retrieve program listings, or to prepare documentation for printing, or to perform a financial analysis.

Following the introduction of REXX and XEDIT, enhancements to VM/SP have been focused increasingly on user productivity, with improvements to both end-user components as well as programmer interfaces. Release 5 of VM/SP, for example, provided for enhanced CMS session services through full-screen CMS, including windowing and scrolling.

In spite of its user-friendliness, CMS is not without its difficulties for the user. For example, a user involved in editing a file may enter the XEDIT FILE subcommand, to store the file. However, if another user has sent a message previous to this, upon pressing the ENTER key the screen will suddenly clear, the terminal will "beep" at the user, and the message will be displayed with the message "MORE ..." at the bottom of the screen. The user may not understand that he is supposed to clear the screen at this point, or even know how to clear the screen. Upon first using CMS, interruptions such as this will seem confusing. In turn applications that rely on CMS are subject to these same limitations.

Communications in VM

There are numerous communications features available within VM and, with the departmental orientation of the 9370, communications and networking capabilities are being enhanced aggressively. Distinguishing between the various methods of communications, and understanding the situations in which they are used, is at first a difficult process. However, the communications capabilities that are most relevant to the focus of this book are outlined below.

Systems Network Architecture (SNA) is a key to communicating within the VM Departmental Computing environment. SNA provides a means of sending data through a network, the term itself referring to the rules and formats used to accomplish this communication. Basically, SNA allows the tasks of the main CPU (main computer) to be spread throughout a network — a set of interconnected locations — so that the work of the main CPU is distributed. SNA would provide a basis for the communications between the central mainframe and departmental machines, sharing resources on the network through teleprocessing facilities.

Virtual Terminal Access Method (VTAM) works within SNA. It is an access method that allows VM terminals to make use of the SNA network. In other words, VTAM makes it possible to take advantage of SNA capabilities under VM.

Capabilities provided by VTAM include:

- Allowing users to use resources on the system, such as terminals and lines, without knowing where these resources are located (their addresses)
- Allowing the sharing of resources between applications programs
- Managing the resources of the network
- Controlling the smooth flow of data between the resources of the network

The Remote Spooling Communications Subsystem (RSCS) is an important communications facility within VM. RSCS provides a means of transmitting and receiving messages, commands, and files within a VM system. For example, it is used to send data to another user or to a printer. RSCS works within SNA, for organizations involved in networking machines, or it works within a single-processor situation to handle the transfer of files.

A critical piece of hardware within the SNA network is the 3705/3725 Remote Communications Controller. The 3705 is an older version of this hardware, while the 3725 is more currently used. The 3725 is a front-end processor, which in conjunction with its "operating system," the Advanced Communications Function/Network Control Program (ACF/NCP), manages and supports the network. The

ACF/NCP sends data to other parts of the network and controls line traffic, among other capabilities.

Another key to Departmental Computing connectivity is IBM's Net-View network management software, an IBM licensed program. NetView runs under VTAM, and serves to automate network operations, by troubleshooting network problems and gathering network management data, and provides a set of SNA host network management services. Recent enhancements to NetView include network configuration aids and software downloading for the 9370 line. NetView includes a command facility that serves as an operator's interface to VTAM in a data communication network, controlling, recording, and automating various operator tasks. It includes a session monitor for the SNA network that assists in identifying any network problems, as well as a hardware monitor.

For organizations with a small number of networked machines, such as two or three machines, and not taking advantage of SNA, IBM's Pass-Through Facility will allow remote machines to communicate with a host.

There are other facilities in VM which handle a facet of communications. Another facility, the Inter-User Communications Vehicle, is described under System Security in Chapter 5.

Welcome Guests

VM, because of the capabilities of CP, is often referred to as the perfect host. Though it is debatable at what level guest operating systems will be needed in a Departmental Computing environment, many organizations will be relying on these capabilities as they undertake the conversion process with both applications and even operating systems in the process of adopting a Departmental Computing approach. An understanding of the role of guest operating systems is important in gaining an overall perspective on VM.

A myriad of different operating systems can coexist in the same machine under the umbrella of VM's Control Program. The only real limitations are based on the size of the machine. An example of this might be a site with 185 userids, 160 of these actual users with the rest representing guest operating systems. This would not be a strange arrangement for an installation heavily involved in various levels of program development. From a technical standpoint, most operating systems run with somewhat coordinated tasks, some synchronous and some asynchronous (independent). The CP component of VM, to manage multiple on-line, yet independent virtual machines, tends to do this in an asynchronous mode, with everything independent of everything else. The result is that VM is extremely powerful as a multitasking machine, allowing these diverse systems to coexist on a single CPU. Under VM, for example, both development and production copies of MVS can be contained on one machine.

There are many reasons, other than program development, to run guest operating systems. Many organizations have applications which have locked them into using DOS or MVS, even though VM may be used for other applications. VM allows them to continue this use through guesting. Other sites do not have this history, and are primarily VM/CMS shops. Yet there is also a strong need for batch processing at a level not provided for in VM. Batch facilities can be provided by running a batch-oriented system as a guest. Batch facilities within VM, through the use of system software provided by IBM and other vendors, is increasingly able to meet this need without requiring a guest system.

Testing, and then conversion, is a major consideration that VM has historically solved better than other operating systems through providing an environment where multiple copies of an operating system can be run. For example, a version of one operating system, including a new release of VM, can be tested on one virtual machine without affecting the day-to-day functioning of users in the production environment. When the testing is complete, the transition can be accomplished relatively painlessly, without creating the need for bringing the system down and interrupting users. Some organizations use VM solely for the testing and conversion process, bringing it up long enough to accomplish this purpose, and then subsequently shutting it down until the next product release.

Under VM, conversion can be accomplished progressively. If, for example, batch-oriented applications are being converted from DOS to MVS, some production can be run simultaneously under both operating systems, with applications being converted one at a time to MVS. This makes the process easier to live with both for the staff involved in the process as well as for users who may also have a learning curve to overcome. In addition, applications development does not have to be frozen during a gradual conversion, as development can continue under DOS while conversion is taking place under MVS.

VM handles guest operating systems in much the same way as multiple online users. As the driver of a computer, VM can oversee everything that goes on in the system, acting as a "super supervisor," or hypervisor. Through CP, guests are run in what is called "problem state." Each time a guest system attempts to issue a privileged instruction to the hardware, CP intercepts this instruction, checks to see how the hardware will be affected, and then allows the program to continue. Problem state, which is also the state in which CMS users operate, causes VM to actually simulate the affect of the instruction issued by the guest operating system.

Privileged instructions are those which are executed directly, without mediation by CP. VM can't allow multiple operating systems direct control over the real hardware, such as real memory and tape

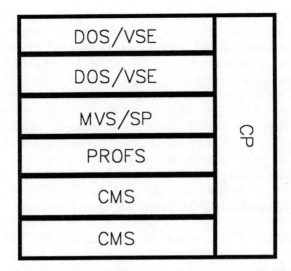

Figure 2-2 Guest operating systems under CP

drives, because the result would be chaos, with operating systems working independently and accomplishing nothing. By handling guest systems as other users, these demands can be simulated.

Though on the surface running a guest operating system is the same as mediating the demands of other users, the resultant impact on overall system performance can be negative. Because of the need to handle guest operating systems in problem, or non-privileged state, there is an addition of system overhead. This has implications both in terms of cost and response time. In addition, each guest system requires a certain amount of disk space. Some of this space can be shared, but there is still additional impact on the system. Through tuning, giving some guest systems priority over others, the impact can be lessened.

It is still necessary to consider the fact that with guest operating systems, there is further competition for sometimes scarce system resources. Operating systems are generally designed such that activities that have the lowest impact on the CPU are given preferential treatment. CP is designed to give preferential treatment to interactive users, CMS users in particular, because they basically sit at a terminal and occasionally press the ENTER key. This generally causes minimal system impact. Someone using a guest operating system is also, technically, an interactive user. because she presses the ENTER key and begins her job. But the internal activity that results from this action can be extreme. Thus, system tuning by a system programmer can determine which kinds of applications and activities receive prime time in the system.

Performance considerations aside, guest operating systems under VM can not only run efficiently, but performance can even improve. Figure 2-2 illustrates a CPU with guest operating systems under VM.

There is much vacillation concerning whether or not DOS is being discontinued, with reports changing almost from year to year. It is still used a great deal, however, to run IBM's transaction-oriented CICS system. This has helped to perpetuate the existence of DOS/VSE. This is a limited environment, however, with a DOS/VSE operation allowing only a certain number of devices, and other restrictions that include memory limitations. Organizations with heavy DOS/VSE use may be forced to run multiple copies in order to add more users and hedge software and hardware limitations. VM provides this capability. VM handshaking, for example, is a special feature of VM which enhances communication between VM as the host and DOS/VSE as a guest. When using the VM and DOS/VSE handshaking capability, DOS/VSE often runs with better throughput and less operator interaction than when running alone on a real machine. DOS/VSE takes full advantage of VM's paging facility, with little or no overhead penalty.

MVS, though not providing the interactive capabilities of VM, is often used for batch production as a guest under VM. In addition, IBM tends to encourage DOS/VSE shops to convert to MVS. Under VM/HPO, the MVS operating system has been estimated as running at 80 to 90% efficiency, and this is improving. MVS does not recognize VM paging functions, and consequently does its own, so there is a duplication of results. MVS is compared with VM later in this chapter.

Guesting in the Departments

Whether guest operating systems will be a need in Departmental Computing is a debatable issue. As with many other Departmental Computing decisions, it really depends on the needs of the organization. VM is capable of handling about anything that users need to do, and if the applications that users need have been provided, the need for guest systems should be precluded.

There are also some limitations in this environment which have effects on the ability to even make use of guest operating systems. Though an extremely capable machine, the smaller models of the 9370 do not make use of the capabilities of MVS, and, further complicated by the issue of CPU size, attempting to run MVS as a guest is not feasible. And considering the specialized needs of departmental users, it will seldom be necessary. In some cases, running DOS under VM on specified departmental machines would allow for batch processing to be offloaded to these departmental machines from other departments. For example, each department might use a copy of the corporate data during the day and then, at night, the master copy updated as a batch process under DOS. With adequate networking capabilities, some departmental machines could be designated as batch processors only, and used for the purpose of keeping the online processors offloaded. In many cases, however, adequate batch capabilities can be provided without the need for a guest operating system.

Absent networking, guest operating systems either send information to their own disks, or to a printer. VM can communicate with the guest operating system, but the return communication is a problem. This problem can be summed up with "Now what?" Without modifications, a guest operating system cannot close the printer, let alone tag a file and send it to the correct user. Guest operating systems in a departmental environment aren't going to work unless the operating system has a networking package in it that ties in the host VM operating system. Though not impossible, many organizations will question the need for doing this, and will, instead, ship data back and forth by tape and avoid the communications costs.

VM and MVS

With industry experts generally considering DOS/VSE to be on the decline as a strategic operating system, VM and MVS are the IBM mainframe operating systems which are most strategic for future growth. MVS, which is an abbreviation for Multiple Virtual Storage, is a batch-oriented operating system. MVS does not offer the interactivity that VM offers, though TSO (Timesharing Option) does offer some CMS-like interactivity under MVS. Many larger organizations, particularly those with heavily transaction-oriented tasks, such as banks, do find that MVS meets their needs as a production environment. MVS is particularly strong, as discussed previously, in managing a large number of CICS users as well as for large databases.

MVS architecture is such that each user does not have his own "playpen" as in VM. Instead there is more sharing between the storage space of individual users and that of the system. MVS also has Extended Architecture (XA) available. The chief advantage of XA is that it allows you to address units of memory larger than 16 megabytes, allowing for the use of extremely large databases and heavy transactions. In a transaction-oriented, rather than single user-oriented, environment, there is often very large amounts of data in memory at a time for the purpose of performing quick transactions. XA also has significant I/O improvements over MVS/370. VM has traditionally not had this large amount of memory (over 16 megabytes) available. This memory needs to be available for large transactions because reading data from a tape, or retrieving it from disk, is more time-consuming. VM is rapidly developing sophisticated XA capabilities, including for CMS.

The MVS "answer" to the interactivity of VM has been TSO. However, the command language between TSO and VM is much different, and the MVS file structure intrudes much more into the realm of the user, through TSO. The command structure of MVS, and in turn TSO, is much more oriented toward the data processing professional than is the command structure of CMS. IBM has attempted to lessen some of these problems, for example, TSO provides defaults for things that the MVS file structure does not, but TSO has still not provided the same level of usability as VM/CMS.

TSO is an interactive facility, and users can do many of the same things that they can do in CMS. However, CMS response time is much quicker. In fact, various studies have shown that on the same hardware configuration, it is possible to support anywhere from two to four times as many users in CMS as in TSO. CMS is much more extendable and user-friendly than TSO, allowing more user interfaces to be built in which increase this ease of use even more. And because of the virtual machine concept, the CMS user is always an isolated user, whereas in TSO, it is much more a possibility that simultaneous on-line users can interfere with each other.

Unlike MVS, in VM the software really takes over much more of the drudgery, particularly with regard to the file structure. In CMS, creating a data file and then having it be useful is relatively easy. The VM operating system is tuned for this. In MVS, much more has to be indicated to the operating system in the creation and use of a data file. For the general user, VM's handling of the administrative drudgery is a definite plus.

VM Variations

Because of its strategic importance, VM is being rapidly enhanced by IBM. Each new VM release — and releases are being announced at a dizzying pace — is in one or many respects a dramatic improvement over the last. Requirements vary among organizations of different sizes. Because of this, there are different variations of VM to better meet these needs. These variations, though offering differing levels of features and functions, are all based on the standard architecture of VM.

To complete the perspective on VM, these variations are briefly described in terms of their functional capabilities.

VM/IS

VM/Integrated System (VM/IS) is the entry level VM system, designed specifically to run on the 9370 Information System. It is particularly useful for installations that are just getting started with VM, and who do not have extensive systems programming staffs. VM/IS is preconfigured, meaning that many of the decisions normally made during installation, concerning how and what the operating system will do, have already been made. There are both positive and negative aspects to this preconfiguration, as is discussed in the chapter concerning installation and maintenance. Using VM/SP as its base, VM/IS supports guest operating systems.

With the announcement of VM/IS also came an announcement concerning the availability of SolutionPacs. These are "canned" applications targeted for specific industries such as education and banking, as well as cross-industry applications such as expert systems and software engineering. SolutionPacs are similar to VM/IS in that they require little or no technical expertise and are simple to install and maintain.

VM/SP

VM/System Product, or VM/SP, is really the "vanilla VM." It provides the same VM capabilities as VM/IS but without the added applications. Running VM/SP requires system programmer expertise for both installation and maintenance, but provides the flexibility needed to manage the shifting information needs of dynamic organizations. Organizations adopting a Departmental Computing strategy should consider VM/SP for departmental machines, including the 9370.

VM/HPO

VM/High Performance Option, VM/HPO, is oriented toward organizations with extensive system demands, such as both heavy CMS use as well as guest operating systems. VM/HPO is the required VM on larger IBM machines (308X and above) because of its ability to support the architecture and increased memory capacity of these machines.

VM/HPO has the same functional and interactive capabilities as VM/SP with added modifications that increase performance in critical areas. It supports machines with memory sizes greater than 16 megabytes, while VM/SP is limited to machines with 16 megabytes or less of memory.

VM/XA/SF

At the high end of VM variations is VM/XA/SF (System Facility). VM/SF was referred to as VM/XA (Extended Architecture) in its first release, then became VM/SF in Release 2. The only use for VM/XA/SF is for converting from MVS/SP, VS1, or DOS/VSE to MVS/XA. For major operating system conversions on a large computer, VM/SF is required. IBM has recently announced XA support for VM/SP, including CMS, and this will enhance VM capabilities for high-end machines.

VM/PC

VM is also available for the personal computer through VM/Personal Computer (VM/PC). It is particularly useful for program development. Application development and testing can be very CMS-intensive, and through VM/PC these tasks can be offloaded to the microcomputer, thus maintaining response time for mainframe CMS users. New uses for VM/PC are in development.

Chapter Summary

The following points were discussed in Chapter 2:

* VM was first developed as a testing and development environment, and later adapted for the user.
* Major components of VM include CP, which provides the virtual machine capabilities, and CMS, providing ease of use and interactivity.
* VM is also distinguished as an operating system through the ability to serve as a host to other operating systems, mediating the demands made on the hardware by both multiple users and operating systems.
* The variations of VM, which are being rapidly enhanced, are all based on the standard VM architecture.

3

The Emergence of Departmental Computing

Technological change does not occur in a vacuum. It is both an end result of changes that are occurring in society as well as a catalyst for further change. This chapter provides an overview of the IBM's 9370 and a definition of Departmental Computing, as well as a perspective on the relationship of Departmental Computing to recent trends in information management.

An Evolving Scenario

Before delving into a discussion of Departmental Computing, it is appropriate to look at an example of what a departmental strategy might mean in an organization. This is best described through before and after scenarios.

The standard large business organization is typified by characteristics that have an effect on both overall productivity as well as employee morale. The overriding atmosphere stifles both organizational and individual growth, with lengthy meetings attended by the same department managers discussing different angles of the same problem. Taking action requires numerous telephone contacts, and much of this time is spent with individuals leaving messages for each other requesting that the call be returned. Information is funneled through various layers of management, beginning at the corporate level down to the doers in the departments.

Information management in this setting reflects the bureaucratic structure. Data is stored on a large central mainframe, with users throughout the organization accessing this information through applications that are also focused at the central mainframe. New applications are added only at the end of an extensive approval cycle, regardless of how immediate the need might be for the group requesting the application. System response time is often slow as users compete for limited resources. The ability of a work group to respond to a new business opportunity is severely hampered if new applications and information access must be approved. To complicate the scenario, the operating system may be batch-oriented, causing further delays as jobs are sent off into the "black hole," for processing at a later time.

Departmental Computing provides the basis for a much more responsive environment. Users have computer resources and specialized applications within their own departments. When a new application is desired, it is evaluated in contention with the other demands within the department itself, rather than being based on the diverse needs of the total organization. System response time is faster because users are not competing on an organizationwide basis for the resources of a single machine. With VM as the operating system, users can take advantage of its ease of use and interactivity, while gaining further control of their own computing needs through VM's virtual machine capabilities.

The central mainframe continues to serve as a central repository of corporate information in a departmental strategy. Departments have more flexibility in accomplishing their goals, including responding to new business opportunities, without having to fight through the layers of the organization for needed resources. Information becomes decentralized. Thus, fewer meetings and telephone calls are needed. The organization as a whole is in a much better position to mobilize needed resources for competition in the dynamic business environment.

Departmental Computing is by no means a panacea for organizational sluggishness. However, it does provide a basis for a much more streamlined approach to information management, with the applications and resources that are relevant to the tasks of a specific department localized within that department.

In Search of a Definition

If there is one thing generally agreed upon in a definition of Departmental Computing it is that there isn't a definition. Some see it as a hardware concept, others define it in terms of software applications, and still others look at it as an organizational development trend. In many ways, Departmental Computing is all these things. But even at that, confusion remains.

Departmental Computing implies that computing is occurring in departments, that users have information and applications available to them where they work, rather than having to go off to a "glass house" or even to an Information Center to access information. Furthermore, the information and applications in the department are there primarily to support the goals of the members of the department. This is a nebulous definition, but it at least might be one which would result in, if not agreement, at least some affirmative headshaking.

Departmental Computing is both reality and fantasy. The increasing power, and decreasing prices, of minicomputers and microcomputers, accompanied by greater availability of software options, have increased the feasibility of distributing resources into the departments of organizations to serve user groups. But there are many implications inherent in spreading these resources around, one of them being confusion over control. Not all organizations are ready for this. And for those that are, the question of whether all these diverse resources can be connected enough that this distribution doesn't result in chaos is still a concern, with differences of opinion concerning how this should be accomplished. Departmental Computing is on its way, but whatever it is, it is not here yet.

At both the hardware and software levels, Departmental Computing is a language with many regional dialects. These include LANs, microcomputers, supermicros, superminimainframes, micro-to-mainframe links, and multiuser systems. Other more obscure terms include intelligent workstations and communications platforms. Thus, there is not only lack of agreement on how to make Departmental Computing work but also lack of agreement on the necessary tools.

Departmental Computing can be described as being closer to a philosophy than to a well-defined set of rules. It represents a commitment by management to provide users with technological resources where they can best use these resources: in their own departments. This is in contrast to the traditional approach to information management in which resources are centralized in one location forcing users to leave their work areas to seek out these resources. Departmental Computing is also a means for central MIS to regain control of the information resources of the organization.

The Empire Strikes Back

The control issue, particularly with regard to central MIS, is important to an understanding of Departmental Computing. Having computer resources in the departments is not unknown. In spite of user-oriented trends in computing such as the Information Center, the need for more timely response to departmental needs has led work groups to find their own solutions. The problem is that user groups have found their own solutions without coordinating either with MIS or other departments. As a result, Departmental Computing has a negative connotation to many MIS people, with the older term "dis-

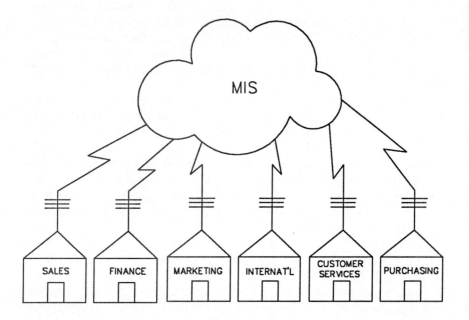

Figure 3-1 Departments in competition for MIS services

tributed processing" or a new term, "End-User Enterprise" computing, substituted. These alternate terms imply that the departmental resources are connected with, and coordinated through, central MIS.

The independence of departments has arisen from the lack of responsiveness from the central MIS group in their organization, as well as from the proliferation of departmental solutions, including the minicomputer and the personal computer. In the 1960s and 1970s, as users became more comfortable with using computers, they started going to their central MIS group to ask for applications. They were placed on a long waiting list, with backlogs running 2 years or more, because many user applications were considered by MIS to be superfluous. When an application was finally considered, users were told what they would get; they were not part of the implementation process. By the time applications were completed, users' needs had changed. This problem was further complicated by having to access strained central mainframe resources from remote terminals, using unfriendly software and having to accept poor response time. This was the classic MIS situation with the computer in the basement, running applications like the payroll.

Figure 3-1 illustrates this situation, with central MIS off in its own world, with little responsiveness to users. It is this lack of responsiveness by central MIS that, in most organizations, gave birth to the need for Departmental Computing. Larger departments, because their

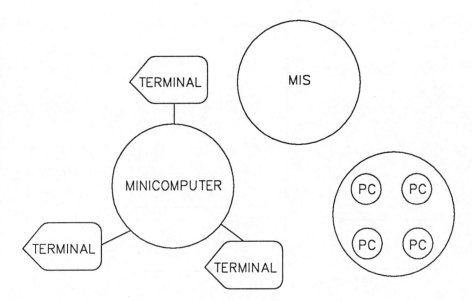

Figure 3-2   Configurations unconnected to MIS

immediate needs could not be answered by MIS, found their own solutions. Some groups became involved with timesharing situations and
this industry flourished during the 1970s. Others purchased minicomputers to service departmental needs. Corporate finance departments,
for example, bought a departmental minicomputer with easy-to-use
software packages to perform tasks such as accounts payable. As the
personal computer became more available in the early 1980s, users
flocked to these low-cost solutions. Individual users began using these
for their own "personal" databases.

   Figure 3-2 shows the end result of these departmental solutions,
from the organizational level: Departments, having gone off in their
own directions, quickly realized that there existed information on the
central corporate mainframe that was needed for some of their applications. Also, departments with minicomputers wanted to share
this information with other departments. Microcomputer users
wanted corporate information as well as the ability to share on an organizational basis. Because of departmental independence, and quick
solutions, this communication was not possible. Nor was support from
MIS.

   Perhaps it is a function of human nature that when users find
something that works, they want to share it with others. With
microcomputers, there is a point at which they become an indispen-
sable utility to the user, such that other users involved in similar applications want to start exchanging data between each other. This
desire led to the development of personal computer networks which at
least provided departmental solutions. This is also true with minicom-

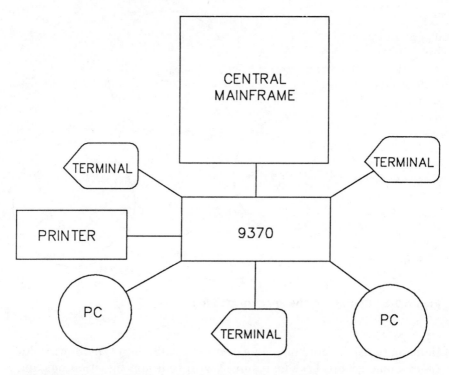

Figure 3-3 A configuration organized around the 9370

puters, which often lead to a desire for sharing data at the organizational level. For example, providing a regional branch with the ability to do sales analysis is a step in the right direction, but soon there is a need to make comparisons with other branches. At this point, individual and departmental solutions begin to look very inadequate.

The end result of the proliferation of a helter-skelter approach to computing in the departments is that both users and central MIS lost something in the process. Central MIS lost control over these valuable resources, weakening and blurring the role of MIS in the organization, and users lost the valuable expertise that is available from MIS.

Departmental Computing, as it is developing, is a means of reconciling these two groups. MIS has in many ways already started to regain some influence over the information management of the organization. For example, users have recently begun to rely on MIS for help in making bulk purchases of personal computers, as well as assistance from the Information Center in using them. Nevertheless, with the potential for networking of resources offered by the current and near-future technology, this control will be even more solidified. In addition, MIS has learned to work better with users, and has realized the control that the user has over the MIS budget.

Thus, from an organizational perspective, the Departmental Computing environment might look like the diagram shown in Figure 3-3. This scheme allows for communication with the central mainframe as well as with other departments, while still allowing for relative independence within the department. With the unique needs and applications of departments, this independence is necessary to streamline the day-to-day computing activities of professionals. The basic demand in Departmental Computing is for a two-tier processing network, with a central mainframe connected to minicomputers in the departments. The departmental processors are connected to terminals, and in some cases, microcomputers to add yet a third level. Data flows back and forth between all levels.

For the purpose of this book, the above is the model of Departmental Computing that is used as a basis for further discussion. Of particular concern regarding the role of VM are the central mainframe and minicomputer levels.

Enter the 9370

IBM's midrange processor, the 9370 Information System, is a key element in understanding Departmental Computing because it provides the needed departmental hardware link which makes this strategy possible.

A critical feature of the 9370 is indicated in the numbers 370. All models of the 9370 are fully compatible at the architecture level with the other machines in IBM's System 370 series of computers. This means that operating systems and applications that run on the central mainframe will, almost without exception, also run on the 9370. From the smallest 9370, the Model 20, to IBM's large 3090-600 mainframe, there is a 160 times increase in horsepower, with virtually unlimited opportunity for growth. The investment in software and training is preserved throughout the organizational structure. In addition, IBM's 370 architecture provides a mechanism for interdepartmental communication.

Within the 9370 family of processors (IBM introduced four models at the time of the original 9370 announcement), there is a fivefold increase in processing speed from the smallest Model 40 to the largest Model 90. The Model 20 is the low-end 9370, with 4 to 16 megabytes of memory and the ability to support both VM and DOS/VSE operating systems. The Model 40 is a midrange 9370, with 8 to 16 megabytes of memory. The Model 40 is more easily upgraded and expanded than the Model 20, and supports VM, DOS/VSE, and UNIX under VM (IX/370). The Model 60 supports not only 8 to 16 megabytes of memory, but also additional memory. The Model 60, at the time of IBM's announcement, supported VM, DOS/VSE, IX/370, as well as MVS/SP. The Model 90 is the closest to the mainframe in capabilities, with extra expansion and storage options, and the ability to support large numbers of real devices.

With the 9370 IBM announced new I/O devices which were a departure from classical packaging. Tape and DASD (Direct Access Storage Devices for storing data) I/O devices are rack mounted in the CPU frame of the 9370. This reduces or eliminates the need for undertaking the detailed and highly complex task of cable planning. Rack mounting not only makes installation easier, but also eliminates one of the reasons for the raised computer room floor, where cables are generally stored. Departments do not have their own computer rooms, and these facilities are not needed for the 9370. Device control units, which sit between the CPU and I/O devices, are also eliminated. Instead, feature cards function as control units, interfacing between the CPU and the devices.

With devices that are either rack mounted or available as feature cards, the Model 20 is indeed similar to a two-drawer filing cabinet. This machine will also tolerate a standard office environment, with minimal air-conditioning, and makes very little noise. IBM indicates that when fully equipped with tape, DASD, printer and operator console, the 9370 uses 86% less floor space, 60% less electricity, and 40% less air-conditioning than the low end System 370 machines that were previously available. The Model 20 can even be plugged into a standard wall socket.

The 9370-oriented variation of the VM operating system, VM/IS, was announced at the same time as the 9370. This was an indication by IBM that the VM operating system was a key component in the 9370 strategy. The 9370 environment is one in which minimal operating staff assistance is required to perform the tasks generally associated with a large mainframe, including mounting tapes and monitoring system performance. In addition to being user-friendly and an excellent base for applications, VM is also a good match with the CPU size and DASD devices of the 9370.

The 9370 provides not only the hardware capability to extend mainframe resources into departments, it also has features, in conjunction with VM, which will enable users to manage these resources. It is clear that the needs of the user are a key element in the positioning of the 9370.

The Ascendency of the End User

The industry experts, in discussing Departmental Computing, are careful to point out the key role of the user in driving the direction of Departmental Computing. Lest Departmental Computing be viewed merely as a means of distributing hardware, it is important to look at it as being a user-driven phenomenon, which it is. The Information Center was the first visible overture by MIS to directly serve the needs of the end user, and whether this has helped to further fuel the desire of users for more direct control over their information resources or as simply a sign of this desire, is debatable. Users, especially professionals, have become more comfortable with using the computer and want even more access to this resource. In addition, corporate officers have become aware of the strategic edge that information can provide.

INPUT, a research organization in Mountain View, California, has conducted research in the trends associated with departmental systems and software. INPUT defines the department as an entity within the organization that is headed by a manager and composed of one or more work groups performing interrelated tasks, with departmental systems being computer processors with multiuser facilities, dedicated to specific department needs. INPUT estimates that departmental systems will have increased sixfold during the 5-year period between 1986 and 1991.

A major factor in the growth of Departmental Computing, according to INPUT, is grassroots demand from users who, having become PC-literate, are now looking both for increased power as well as easier access to the information and computer resources of the organization. The department is the next step in this increased automation, serving in many ways as a gateway to the corporate data. Further impetus to this growth is a top-down demand from corporate management for systems that will provide major strategic payoffs. Increased flow of information among previously isolated work groups is typically a requirement of these systems.

Sunday Lewis, president of Techvantage Research, a market research group in New York City, also looks to the end user as a key to the success of Departmental Computing. Lewis foresees that organizations will develop departmental strategies that revolve around the needs of the users in each department, with an approach centering around specialized machines: "A department that does a lot of spreadsheet work would have a machine dedicated primarily to that function; another departmental machine might be used for database management. I'm not talking about specialized hardware, but machines dedicated to specific functions. This is what end users need in their jobs."

Lewis stresses the importance of resources that accommodate the end user, rather than expecting the end user to accommodate the resources. "End users are not DPers and they do not wish to be. The terminal must be similar to a telephone or a copy machine, sitting on their desks to be used like other office equipment. But telephones cause frustration when you need to transfer a call and you can't figure out how; copy machines break down in the middle of big jobs. Computer resources need to maintain themselves without requiring technical sophistication, or at least support must be readily available when the user needs it."

Consequently, Departmental Computing becomes an issue of integrating man with machine. Merely getting the machines out into the departments is a start, but the issues go beyond steel, wires, and tape.

Rick Martin, an analyst with Sanford C. Bernstein and Company, Inc. in New York City, was formerly with IBM as product manager for the 4300 series of computers and, in his own words, has been "fighting the VM battle since 1972." Based on his years with IBM, Martin states that Departmental Computing is really based on a "grand plan" by IBM that revolved around sustaining mainframe growth through expanding the number of potential users to the professional user, who would integrate the computer into his daily job functions. Previous to this, the professional had not yet adopted the computer as a tool. He describes IBM's plan for Departmental Computing as involving extensive user interfaces that protect the user from the technicalities, allowing, for example, both menu- and command-driven applications that accommodate the skill levels of the users. The IBM plan includes extensive online documentation, online helps, and "behind the scenes" aids, including automated problem reporting and, as Lewis also discussed, machines that are able to perform a high level of self-maintenance.

Martin stresses the role of the personal computer in Departmental Computing to the extent that he includes it in his definition: "We view Departmental Computing as the integration of the PC, for the professional user, with larger computers, whether they be located in the departments or at some remote locations. It doesn't really matter in our view. Obviously, we feel that a certain amount ought to be done in the department itself and a certain amount should be done upstream." Martin cites IBM research, based on a survey in 1986 of 200 of their largest customers, with half of these respondents reporting that they would be basing their Departmental Computing strategy on minicomputers located in the departments, and half stating that they planned to connect personal computers directly to the mainframe.

The key difference between these two arrangements is, according to Martin, based on the needs of the users in these organizations. Large, diverse organizations, such as automobile manufacturers, have many functions which do not necessarily share large amounts of data. The users in these organizations will be better served by minicomputers dedicated to specific departmental functions, perhaps connected to terminals, and personal computers with 3270 emulation. Martin also cites the large insurance company as an example of an organization that might connect personal computers directly with a corporate mainframe. Users in this setting might have a primary need for corporate data, such as the records of subscribers, and would be better suited by this arrangement. In both cases it is the needs of the organization's users that are serving as the driver.

Martin cites research that further indicates the logic of Departmental Computing. It is within the department that users are getting much of the information that they use. He states that research indicates that approximately 40% of the data in any given corporation is unique to departments, while 60% is of concern to the organization as a whole. Thus, 40% of the information users are working with on a daily basis has little relevance outside of their departments.

It is important to note that although the terms user and end user are fairly general, it is really the "knowledge worker," the professional that is being targeted by Departmental Computing. Great strides have been made in general areas such as factory automation and word processing; it is the professional who sets the standard for a profitable and innovative organization. Knowledge workers have expanded their use of the personal computer and, for example, spread sheets, but this group continues to consume yellow legal pads and, in turn, the efforts of clerical workers.

Alvin Toffler, in *The Third Wave*, discussed statistics indicating that the average factory worker is supported by $25,000 worth of technology while the average office worker works with $500 to $1000 worth of typewriters and adding machines. According to Toffler, office productivity has climbed only 4% over the past decade, while the cost of computers has actually decreased. With the ever-rising costs of doing business, coupled with stagnating productivity on one hand and technological advances on the other, it is clear that the professional represents a relatively untapped market for automation.

Knowledge workers need to be able to integrate the computer into their work styles, as an aid to thinking. The availability of resources and relevant applications, literally at their fingertips, will encourage the use of these tools by this group.

The Departmental Society

There are many signs that indicate that society in general is moving toward decentralization. The federal government is encouraging more control by state and local governments. Large department stores are competing with more specialized shops. More lifestyle choices are available.

As society becomes less "mass," the role of the organization is also changing, with corporate management having to deal with the issue of diversity both among customers and employees. Jobs are becoming more specialized and less interchangeable as the organization attempts to compete in not only a diverse but a global community. The general rule about decisionmaking in organizations has been based on the 80/20 concept, with 80% of what goes on considered routine, following predictable patterns, while 20% is unique and must be handled by management on an ad hoc basis. In the dynamic environment of the 1980's and 1990's, this is no longer true. There will be many more unique events in responding to specialized market segments.

Diversity creates a need for much more distributed responsibility, with corresponding changes in organizational structure which will facilitate this distribution. Toffler and others predict that more and more organizations will move toward flatter hierarchies, displacing the traditional pyramid. The intermediate level of the management pyramid — middle management — has generally been involved in an information-processing role, filtering information coming from top managment to those on the bottom rung. The computer has made information flow more efficient, diminishing the need for middle management. Concurrently, the role of those at the bottom, the doers, has become more critical with specialization. Doers are increasingly clustering into work groups which in turn become departments. Departments, in turn, are more capable of mobilizing to meet the demands of the marketplace rather than a bureaucratized hierarchy.

The increased flow of information in organizations mirrors the outside world. The average person can turn on a television and watch the news as it is in the process of happening, and those who have been reared on a steady diet of sophisticated media consumption are much less likely to settle for a work environment in which information is withheld by those at the top of the pyramid. Availability of information is not only expected, it is a requirement.

An obstacle to providing information in the organizational setting, human resource considerations aside, has been the lack of technological solutions. With corporate data on a central mainframe there are restrictions on getting this information, particularly when competing with large numbers of users. The personal computer and isolated departmental computers have at least provided a means of storing data, but again, sharing has been another issue. Departmental Computing, with 9370s connected to the central mainframe, as well as to other departments, has the potential of solving this need for information sharing while enhancing the independence of the work group. Departmental Computing facilitates lateral communication — human networking — that is not available in the standard pyramid structure of the organization.

John McCarthy, a senior researcher with Forrester Research in Cambridge, Massachusetts, has been credited with postulating a form of information management which he terms Theory D. Based on the concepts of corporate downsizing and distribution, Theory D information management brings powerful tools to end users. This serves both to decentralize the organization as well as to provide cost savings through reducing overhead and helping users to be more productive. McCarthy's theory is evidenced in the survey of Departmental Computing conducted by INPUT. Fortune 1000 companies, according to INPUT, will increase their departmental software products by 32%

annually for the years 1986 through 1991, from $2 billion in annual expenditures to $7 billion.

It can be concluded from looking at these trends that Departmental Computing, the "chicken or the egg" argument aside, is developing in parallel to some important trends that are occurring in society as a whole, and in organizations. It has the potential of facilitating the decentralization and work group independence being required of dynamic organizations, without compromising the communication necessary for organizational efficiency.

Just Another Wave?

The term Departmental Computing is often used interchangeably, and confused with, other so-called trends in information management, including Distributed Processing, Office Automation, and the Information Center. These trends will be discussed briefly in terms of their relationship to Departmental Computing, as a means of completing the Departmental Computing perspective.

Distributed Processing

There is nothing particularly complicated about the concept of Distributed Processing. It is a term that is loosely applied to the distributed operation of the computer across the hardware components, with networking that allows sharing of information from the central database. The key to Distributed Processing is, as the term implies, that resources are distributed from the central mainframe, and networked to the remote hardware. This can be contrasted to centralized processing, the standard "glass house" concept, and decentralized processing, with departments having ownership of their own hardware and software without being connected to the central mainframe.

Distributed Processing includes functions such as information processing in which data is processed by application programs to produce needed information. It also includes network processing, the control of data and information movement among different locations in the information network. Database processing is a third component of distributed Processing, involving the storage of data so that it is available to users in various locations throughout the information network. These are also critical components of Departmental Computing.

Departmental Computing in many ways is an outgrowth of Distributed Processing. It differs in that it concentrates on work groups, clusters of workers within a common work area, having common business goals and using much of the same information. Distributed Processing has a more general focus, being that of hardware and software distribution. Work groups are not the basis for decisions regarding the distribution of these resources. As a result, Distributed Processing has often been criticized for redundancy, with the same functions spread out over the organization with little regard for where these functions are most needed, or not needed at all.

Departmental Computing is essentially accomplished within a distributed system, with, for example, the central corporate database contained on a centralized mainframe, with departmental applications networked out into the departments in which they are used most. VM is particularly well suited to distributed processing because each user is relatively unaware of where his or her virtual machine is located in the network.

Some of the problems that have interfered with effective Distributed Processing will also interfere with Departmental Computing. Distributed resources are much more difficult to manage than are those centralized in one location. If the remote sites require extensive technical and operations support, or if there is great redundancy of function among departments, then any potential economic savings is lost. Also, poor planning can result in well-served remote sites to the detriment of overall corporate needs, particularly if networking from the central site is not well coordinated.

Departmental Computing assumes a relatively operatorless environment, with the departments able to hold primary responsibility for maintaining these resources. Thus, Distributed Processing is carried a step further, expanded to fit the overall design of the organization.

Office Automation

Office Automation is one of those terms that covers a "multitude of sins." It can apply to anything from a room with a dedicated word processor to a sophisticated, futuristic "paperless office," with document storage and electronic mail.

In the early days of Office Automation, this really was another term for word processing. With advances in technology, it has evolved to the point where, in large organizations, it includes multistation systems which are part of local area networks, storing massive amounts of data, with the capacity to transmit information to remote mainframes via fiber optics, satellites, and microwaves. Office Automation also implies the ability to retrieve parts of the corporate database for reports, with expanded personal computer use by professionals.

A major impetus to the growth of Office Automation is one that has also been an impetus to Departmental Computing — the need to work around corporate MIS to meet the needs of users. Standard office functions have traditionally been viewed by MIS as outside of their realm of concern, if not expertise, and users were left to find their own solutions. And as a result, also similar to early Departmental Computing, Office Automation has been characterized by ad hoc purchases, with departments bringing in a conglomeration of unconnected hardware and software. The positive results from this were temporary; as soon as users decided to share between each other and the corporate mainframe, they were again knocking on the door of central MIS. However, "PC anarchy" had already occurred, and central MIS had no way to connect these diverse machines.

The cost of Office Automation has been a major cause of criticism. Management has expected an expenditure of, say $100,000, to result in a savings of the same amount through a reduction in personnel. Instead, more support staff has often been needed as well as training. Office tools have made the jobs of clerical people easier, but the automation provided by these tools has not replaced personnel. Furthermore, professionals have often ignored these tools, continuing to dictate or draft letters and other documents, and then hand them off to support staff.

Dr. Michael Treacey of MIT, in an address to the Gartner Group Office Systems Conference (February 9–11, 1987), stated that merely improving administrative effectiveness is not enough because this does not lead to organizational effectiveness. Office Automation must be related to the revenue-generating parts of the organization, the areas where improvements can be more quantitatively measured. The effects of automation can be better measured if directed at the departmental level, with automation integrated into the day-to-day activities and goals of all members in the work group, not just those assigned to the clerical functions.

Departmental Computing has the potential of expanding the role of automation past the level of clerical functions, for an integration of automated tools with virtually all activities in the department.

The Information Center

The Information Center developed as a centralized means of meeting the needs of end users, filling a void between the MIS department and individual solutions (or lack of solution). It has been especially effective in helping professionals to make use of applications like the spreadsheet.

In many ways, the Information Center is like a toy store. As users began using Information Center tools more and more, the desire to take them back into their own departments increased. This is especially true for users who have developed a self-sufficiency that precludes the need for the assistance offered by the Information Center, having come to expect software that is so easy to use that they can come up to speed on their own. The Information Center can be at-

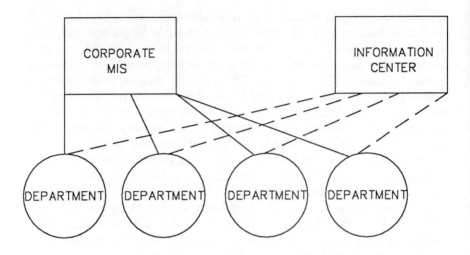

Figure 3-4 The role of the information center in departmental computing

tributed with having placed information resources into the hands of the user. But whether it can continue to support the expanded, specialized needs of the departmental user is another issue. There is a difference of opinion on this topic.

Some industry experts see the Information Center melting away as these resources are folded into the individual departments, the Information Center having served in the function of facilitator of this transition. Others see the Information Center role as continuing in much the same way, serving as a centralized resource where users from any department can continue to go for assistance in developing ad hoc applications. It is seen as an advocate for the end user, and departmental resources notwithstanding, this need will most likely continue in many organizations.

Rick Martin of Sanford C. Bernstein views Departmental Computing as being in many ways a supplement to the Information Center. The consultative abilities of the Information Center will still be needed, as users attempt to interface with central MIS in accessing corporate resources. The Information Center will still be the location of the resources dedicated to the user. Many routine applications specific to the department will run effectively on the department level, but as specialized needs arise, users will need this resource for assistance.

Rather than the role of the Information Center being reduced by Departmental Computing, Martin actually sees it expanding because of the user's need for assistance in obtaining information from the corporate mainframe. "Many of the Information Centers were PC only, so obviously they were an adjunct to MIS. But those PC people are doing some very basic things, like spreadsheets. As Departmental Computing becomes more and more real, even for companies that never really phased up an Information Center, they are going to have to. The user may not know how to get information from the central mainframe, and departments are not going to have programmers on staff to help with this process. So the Information Center function is going to be mandatory. Absolutely mandatory." In many ways the Information Center was a prototype of Departmental Computing, and now these resources are just being spread out more into the hands of the users.

The Information Center is essentially a link between the department and central MIS, serving on an as-needed basis as illustrated by the dotted line in Figure 3-4. Training, specialized assistance, and general hand-holding will still come from this source.

Chapter Summary

The major conclusions made in Chapter 3 include:

- The definition of Departmental Computing is still in flux, but generally implies that specialized applications and data are contained within the departments that use them, rather than shared from a central mainframe.
- For the purposes of this book, departments contain minicomputers attached to a central mainframe, with the ability to communicate with it. These minicomputers may be attached either to terminals, personal computers, or a combination of both.
- Society is becoming more specialized and organizations, in turn, are reflecting this specialization through increased departmentalization and a flattening of traditional hierarchies. Departmental Computing reflects and accommodates this trend while providing a means for organizational control.
- Departmental Computing is in many ways an evolutionary step from other information management trends, including Distributed Processing, Office Automation, and the Information Center.

VM Installation and Maintenance

The process of installing the VM operating system includes the designation of system generation options that in essence tailor the system to the installation. The installation process is discussed in relation to these options. The maintenance procedure and the implications of system modifications are also outlined.

Installing the VM Environment

There are many potential scenarios involved when looking at what goes on when an organization first installs the VM operating system. The basic scenario, however, is one in which a big "box" sits in the middle of a computer room. Most likely, nothing has been loaded on this computer, because the operating system needs to be loaded before anything else. Though there are various VM variations, e.g., VM/SP, VM/IS, VM/HPO, that may be loaded, for the purposes of illustrating the installation procedure, VM/SP will be considered. VM/IS is a preconfigured VM, while VM/SP is not.

VM/IS (VM/Integrated System) is a preconfigured variation of VM that was introduced at the same time as the 9370 Information System. By preconfigured, IBM has basically done the thinking about what the VM environment should look like, and all the customer has to do is lay the system down, with minimal decision making or tailoring. VM/IS includes a VM/SP "starter" system, as well as additional screens and software which enhance ease of use.

VM/SP is not a preconfigured VM, and for the purposes of outlining the significant considerations in defining the VM environment, it will be discussed in more detail. Without a preconfigured system such as VM/IS, the new VM site receives what is essentially a "starter" tape, as with VM/IS. Everything needed to construct a basic VM environment is on this tape; however, some work on the part of a system programmer will be needed. For example, the DASD will have to be formatted and defined to the system. And it will be necessary to take time to decide how everything should fit together.

There are many technical decisions involved in installing a VM environment, such that the IBM documentation must be consulted extensively when undertaking this process. Major issues, including system generation options, have an impact on the subsequent capabilities available to users.

System Generation Options

The system generation options are stored in three CP source "modules." Technically, they are not actual modules but are object code (compiled source code) incorporated within the CP nucleus. However, for the purposes of this discussion, module is a convenient term. The modules contain options that are specified by the system programmer in Assembler macro statements. These modules, which determine the characteristics of the VM environment, are as follows:

- DMKSYS
- DMKRIO
- DMKSNT

The first module, DMKSYS, contains options which are critical to the overall performance and integrity of the VM system. In DMKSYS, several key parameters of the system configuration are determined. The layout of storage sizes and other parameters are indicated, such as which DASD areas are owned by CP. Error reporting, checkpoint areas, and the location of the nucleus are also defined.

Some of the more common macros included in the DMKSYS module are:

- SYSRES — this macro specifies the DASD locations of critical system areas.
- SYSJRL — this macro is used to specify the journaling option, which records resource access (discussed in Chapter 12).
- SYSCOR — main storage parameters are specified in this macro.
- SYSMON — the parameters for the collection of performance monitoring data (discussed in Chapter 6) are defined here.

The specification of options in DMKSYS is somewhat complicated in that specific locations must be defined (e.g., where CP will actually be located). Otherwise, the decisions to be made regarding DMKSYS are relatively clearcut. System programmers generally point to DMKSYS as being the best documented and easiest to define.

The DMKRIO module is used in specifying the I/O device configuration of the VM environment. All the hardware devices on the system are defined to CP through DMKRIO, including Direct Access Storage Devices (DASD), printers, and tape drives. Each of these entries in DMKRIO is used to build control blocks which occupy space in real storage.

Control blocks are associated with all of the hardware on the system. Control blocks can be defined as information that CP needs to know about a hardware device, such as a tape drive. A group of control blocks defines the characteristics of the device, indicating the device type (tape drive, DASD) and the address associated with the device. Control block is a generic term, not specific to VM. It is best to think of a control block simply as a way of maintaining information. When the system is in use, control blocks are kept in real memory and provide a means for fast access of the devices. When a user needs to use a tape drive, for example, the system uses the control blocks to get information about where the tape drives are located and which ones are available.

As new hardware devices are added to the system, these must also be defined in DMKRIO. If not defined properly, the system is not able to make use of them. For example, adding a new tape drive will not enhance the efficiency of the system, because it will be ignored until defined to CP.

The DMKSNT module contains the system name table. This is used to identify the names and locations of core-image code segments that are frequently used by virtual machines. In DMKSNT, the saved systems are defined.

A saved system is simply a more efficient way to maintain programs. Rather than giving each user a copy of a program, CMS included, a copy of each program is stored in a saved system, and this copy serves as a communal copy. A saved system provides two major benefits. The first is that it provides a means of much quicker access than a stand-alone program. The program is already in storage, because it resides in a saved system, so CP always has pointers to it and in turn points each user's virtual machine to it. This is much quicker than accessing a stand-alone program and waiting for CMS to locate it and bring it into real memory. Second, accessing a program through a saved system is more efficient than giving each user's virtual machine a copy of the program, and subsequently having all these copies of the program competing for real memory at the same time. Thus, each individual user's storage area does not have to be large enough to hold a copy of CMS, and the installation avoids the paging that would in turn be necessary to handle multiple copies of the same program. Paging is discussed further in Chapter 6. By being a saved system, the copy of CMS, or a database management system, is write protected. It can be accessed by a user's virtual machine but not modified. Native VM does not check the DMKSNT values for accuracy, so if not carefully entered, the results can be disastrous.

Once the system generation options are stored in DMKSYS, DMKRIO, and DMKSNT, the basis for a starter system is now in place.

The CP Nucleus

The CP nucleus can basically be defined as the core of the VM system. It is the brains of the system, or the code that gives the environment its basic VM attributes. The CP nucleus constitutes the entity referred to as CP.

After the three system generation option modules are ready, the CP nucleus is generated through a program called VMFLOAD. This requires two input parameters, the name of a load list and the name of a control file. The load list specifies the object modules that the organization wants to include — to load — in the CP nucleus. There are options regarding what other VM features, in the form of modules, are included in the CP nucleus. Frequently used modules are placed in the resident nucleus, meaning that these options remain in fixed locations, while less used modules are placed in the "pageable" nucleus. These pageable modules are stored on DASD and brought (paged) into real memory as needed.

The control file defines a hierarchy of file types for the object modules specified in the load list. This allows a site to specify a selection order for an object module when more than one version exists. For example, if the site uses a version of a module with a modification, a selection order can be specified in which the modified version of the module is selected from the load list instead of the IBM-supplied version.

The VMFLOAD process is illustrated in Figure 4-1. The modules, including DMKRIO, DMKSYS, DMKSNT, and many others, are in text format, meaning that they are in the form of code, that includes comment lines and other extraneous content. The VMFLOAD utility takes the modules, stips out the comment lines, and lays the modules end to end (connects them as one unit). These modules are then referred to as a Load Deck (deck being a holdover term from the days when programs were loaded through the use of 80 column cards). A Loader is attached to the Load Deck by VMFLOAD. The loader is a program that ties the Load Deck together and serves to create the CP nucleus. When the Initial Program Load of this Load Deck is performed, the nucleus is loaded into virtual storage, then taken from storage to the DASD location designated for CP to reside (where CP is stored). This DASD area is referred to as SYSRES, and the process is managed by programs that are "kicked off" by the Loader.

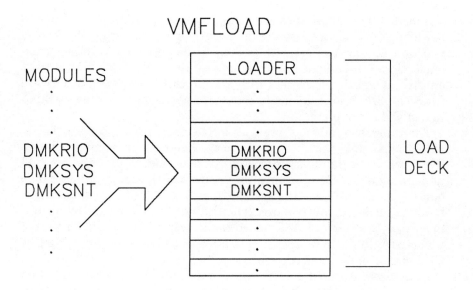

Figure 4-1 The generation of the load deck with VMFLOAD

The Loader really works in conjunction with other programs to transform the Load Deck into a CP nucleus. After the system generation process is completed, and VM has gone through the Initial Program Load (IPL) from the SYSRES, CP exists. The new CP resident nucleus is now loaded in real memory and VM, if the required tasks have been performed correctly, is available for further use. An environment has been set up in which VM can continue in an operable status.

The newly created VM system contains a CP directory, which is basically a list of userids and information about the virtual machines identified by the userids. The basic starter VM system will have a very small number of userids — an operator's userid and a userid from which to perform maintenance. VM/IS will have many more userids because of the large number of application packages and other facilities that are bundled with VM/IS. From here, the directory of users can be further expanded, and software applications added. The building of the directory is discussed in Chapter 5 under security. With standard directory maintenance procedures it is at this point necessary to manually map out the DASD assigned for user storage space and find out where the free space is available. Userids with corresponding minidisks will need to be "laid down" in that space. The directory references the userids of those users who will be using the system.

In addition, other parameters can also be set up at this time. Parameters related to the kinds of error analysis needed for the environment will be set, as well as monitoring parameters. If standard

VM monitoring capabilities are going to be utilized, these will have to be configured to reference the performance requirements of the machine. If a system security package is being added to the environment, this will be added and configured. Security under VM is most effective when tied in closely with the directory, and system software to accomplish this task should come into play soon after the installation of VM is complete.

There are a number of preinstallation steps involved with the installation of VM. Assuming that the system is not preconfigured, and the system programmer has carefully read the documentation, and understands the VM internals, the creation of the actual nucleus may only require a few hours. The postinstallation considerations, however, can be much more complicated. DASD needs to be formatted, or additional DASD added to the system. If the CPU is part of a network, then there are considerations involved in connecting this CPU with others.

In environments where there are multiple CPUs, the installation process may in essence only have to be undertaken once. After that, the CP nucleus from one machine can be placed on tape and transported to another machine, to be brought up with the installation's configuration automatically in place (provided the machines are being "cloned" with the same real device configuration). Once VM has been configured, it can be duplicated to be installed as a preconfigured version on another machine, providing that machines are an exact match, including I/O, memory, and devices. This capability will be a critical element in achieving both time savings and uniformity in a departmental environment. And by taking the time to carefully develop a VM configuration that meets the needs of the organization, central MIS is not faced with a conglomeration of different configurations, with the maintenance and installation problems associated with this lack of coordination.

Maintenance in the VM Environment

Maintaining the VM operating system revolves around VM product releases, which introduce new VM capabilities, and Program Update Tapes, which provide fixes for previous problems. In the early years of VM, there were few product enhancements involved and users could subsequently operate under the same release for long periods of time. Now, VM is being aggressively enhanced, and it is important to keep current with releases, to have access to new capabilities, and to assure that necessary VM support will be available from IBM.

IBM provides guidelines for setting up the VM system, and these guidelines include the use of a single virtual machine from which to perform system maintenance. This virtual machine is traditionally identified by a userid known as MAINT, and it is a centralized maintenance userid that essentially "owns" VM, including CP, CMS, and associated DASD. MAINT is associated with a series of minidisks which are allocated for:

• IBM-supplied CP source code
• IBM-supplied CP source updates
• IBM-supplied CP object modules
• IBM-supplied CMS source
• IBM-supplied CMS source updates
• User-supplied source, object, and update files

Object code is code that is already compiled, which can be loaded into memory and executed. Source code, used by installations that wish to make modifications to VM, is code that has not been compiled. Source code requires more space on DASD; for example, a source code statement in assembler might require 80 bytes, while the same statement, compiled, would require 2 to 6 bytes in object code. Source code includes comment statements, which are not part of the actual program. Generally, modifications to source code are not recommended.

The MAINT minidisks provide a means of keeping the components of VM updated in an efficient manner, protecting, for example, the IBM-supplied modules from those that the VM site has modified. MAINT is associated with a large number of minidisks, and because of this, systems programmers often criticize the single maintenance userid approach as being cumbersome. Most VM installations, however, find MAINT to be sufficient for performing the maintenace tasks of the whole system.

New Releases of VM

The frequency and number of enhancements in new VM releases varies between different variations of VM. With a new release tape, IBM provides EXECs which assist the system programmer with the installation process. These EXECs initiate some functions and present the programmer with questions concerning the characteristics and needs of the individual site.

The new release of VM is often installed and tested on a second level machine. This is a virtual machine within VM that is established for the purpose of serving as a testing environment for the release. It is a guest operating system, acting as a VM within VM. The new release is installed, a CP nucleus created, and the system brought up. At this point, new enhancements can be exercised and current applications tested to determine how the new release will fit into the environment.

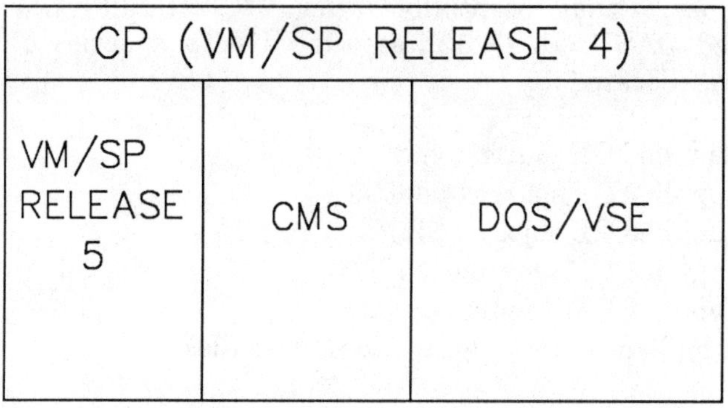

CP (VM/SP RELEASE 4)		
VM/SP RELEASE 5	CMS	DOS/VSE

Figure 4-2 Bringing a new VM release from test to production

Figure 4-2 is an illustration of a CPU with a production environment under VM/SP Release 4, with CMS users, VM/SP Release 5 in a testing mode, and DOS/VSE as a guest operating system. These competing demands on the CPU are all being mediated by CP.

When a new release of VM is received at the VM site, the procedure undertaken in moving up to the new release is critical. Installing a new release of VM is not by definition a difficult or time-consuming process. VM is already an integral aspect of the computing environment, and the new release adds capabilities as well as fixes to any previous problems. The new release may have an effect on application or system software, as well as introduce changes for users, and this may necessitate phasing in the new VM release over a period of time. VM's ability to manage multiple virtual machines facilitates this transition; the new VM release can be running as a guest operating system until the organization is comfortable with it.

With a new release there is always the potential of introducing changes which result in a basic incompatibility between the VM system as it is now running and the new release. Spool space, the holding area for communications between virtual machines, is vulnerable to damage during the installation process. Spool space contains, for example, a note that one user is sending to another. The size and shape of spool file blocks may be changed in a new release. The spool file block is kept in the system's real memory and is used to track where spool files actually exist on DASD. It is used to create the interface between the spool file that is out on DASD and the user, providing a means of locating spool files that users request. If the spool file blocks change, even a small amount, then when the system is shut down, it will be impossible to return through either a warm start or a checkpoint start. The spool file blocks are no longer valid.

The VM system goes live with the new release of VM through a system generation (sysgen), with either a cold start, a warm start, or a checkpoint start. These concepts are based on spool space. When bringing up the new VM release through a cold start, all spool files are lost. Cold starts are sometimes necessary between releases, depending on the needs of the organization, but can cause major disruptions to users if spool files (e.g., notes sent from one user to another through CMS) are not adequately backed up beforehand.

A warm start is how the Data Center generally brings VM up after a normal shutdown. There are two areas included on the DASD on which the VM operating system is stored (the SYSRES) that contain startup data. One of the areas contains data for a warm start, while the other contains checkpoint data. A checkpoint is something that the system does occasionally in which spool file changes in real memory are recorded in the checkpoint area. These are recorded there so that if there is a sudden loss of power — a system crash — the spool information can be reconstructed when the system comes back up. The system does this checkpointing after any significant change takes place in spool space.

When the system is shut down, for the purposes of coming back with the new release, a more involved type of checkpointing is performed. The information stored in the checkpoint area contains all of the spool file blocks and changes, but this information must be reconstructed in memory. This may take some time. The information stored in the warm start area does not have to be reconstructed. It is more or less one for one, so that the spool information can be placed in memory without the need for reconstruction. A warm start may take 3 minutes to get past the point of spool file availability, while a checkpoint start might require 15 to 20 minutes to get to this point. A variation of the checkpoint start is a force start. During a checkpoint start, if there is a problem in sorting through the chains of data to reconstruct the spool area, the process will stop. During a force start, the start process will continue in spite of potentially losing "damaged" spool files.

A warm start can only begin from a normal shutdown, while a checkpoint may be needed after a system crash. The checkpoint is really a safety mechanism, taking an occasional "snapshot" of the system while it is running so that in case of an accident, there is a way to track the spool files. It is recommended that while the new release is installed on a second level virtual machine, spool files be created, and the new release forced to crash, to make sure that the checkpoint is working according to the expectations of the site. Normal shutdowns and warm starts should also be performed. This can all be done within the second level machine without affecting the production environment.

A new release of VM is a tape with a complete copy of the VM operating system, not only the actual changes and enhancements. At the cutover point, when the organization is ready to go "live" with the new release, the virtual machine on which the new release is operating becomes the production, rather than the test, environment. VM sites can continue operating under an old release of VM, but IBM discontinues supporting these old releases after a certain amount of time has passed.

Program Update Tapes

Program Update Tapes, referred to as PUTs, are tapes that contain a collection of fixes for any reported problems on the most current release. IBM customers register Site Profiles with IBM, with the Site Profile being a basic list of software and other information about the organization's unique VM configuration. The PUT that each VM site receives is thus tailored, containing only the fixes that are relevant to the configuration. Fixes are referred to by IBM as Program Temporary Fixes (PTF). A PTF is temporary only in the respect that the fix will be a permanent part of the next release. The PUT also contains PTFs in Error (PE), which are fixes to PTFs.

In addition to fixes, the PUT contains information sections concerning problems to look out for, and procedures for doing maintenance. Generally, the entire PUT tape should be applied to the system, rather than manually going through and choosing certain fixes. In some cases, however, an individual modification from the PUT can instead be applied to a specific problem. If so, it is important that the system programmer retain and file any or all output from the PUT application process; this can later be used to trace any further problems that occurred. Installation of the Program Update Tape is done from the MAINT userid.

IBM may send out many PUTs between releases. Each of these PUT tapes is cumulative, containing all fixes that were sent on any previous PUTs, since the last release, as well as any current fixes. Thus, the tapes gradually contain more and more fixes, until the next release. Each new PUT is identified by a new PUT level and maintenance level, with a one-to-one correspondence between these two levels. If support is needed, the Data Center will not only identify the VM release number under it is operating, but also the PUT level.

The Program Update Tape is not simply loaded "on top" of VM. It is loaded on one of the minidisks associated with the MAINT virtual machine. On the PUT, in addition to the actual fixes, are files which direct the application of fixes contained on the tape. These files are referred to as the auxiliary control files (AUX files), each identified according to the VM module that it updates. Through the use of the CMS update process, the fixes are applied to CMS and CP source files (source code). The CMS update process is a facility which, with the use of the auxillary control file, applies updates to a source program. This saves the system programmer from having to manually go into source code and edit modules to apply the fixes. In effect this update is similar to editing a document, with CMS update actually going in

VMFASM

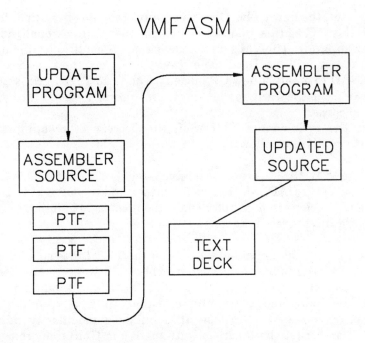

Figure 4-3 Generating updated object code with VMFASM

and doing this program editing for the system programmer. The auxiliary control file points to the fixes that are included on the Program Update Tape. The process of reassembling the files that have been changed follows this sequence:

1. The auxiliary control file points to the fix.
2. The fix is essentially pulled into an assemble file and reassembled.
3. The assembler is run against the updated file.
4. The fix is now part of the object code.

Installing a PUT tape is actually a relatively simple process. The tape includes the updated text, as well as the source code of the PTFs that were used to create the updated text.

When applying PTFs that have been sent by IBM to correct a specific problem, or when applying local system modifications, the process is a bit more complicated. A CMS EXEC called VMFASM must be used. This process is illustrated in Figure 4-3. VMFASM serves the basic function of transforming source code and PTFs into updated object code that is usable for the VMFLOAD process. VMFASM includes two programs which run under CMS — an update program and an assembler program. The update program takes the original source VM source code, and updates this source code to reflect the updates, the new PTFs. Once this source code has been updated to reflect the PTFs, this updated source is then run through an assembler program. The VM source code is then assembled (compiled) to produce a new Text Deck. The Text Deck can then be used in VMFLOAD to create a new CP nucleus. The term Text Deck is also a holdover from the card reader days, and literally means a deck of punched cards.

With the inclusion of VMFASM, the process of creating a CP nucleus would be as follows:

1. Use VMFASM to create text (object code).
2. Use VMFLOAD, which uses the loader and the CP text to create a CP nucleus in a virtual reader (the nucleus load deck).
3. USe IPL to create the new CP nucleus.

IBM includes the updated text files on the PUT tapes so VMFASM should only need to be used under special circumstances. Any needed PTFs are quickly made available on PUT tapes, and should not need to be added individually. Attempting to apply fixes selectively is akin to shooting oneself in the foot. IBM builds a modularity into its products such that the functions within CP and CMS cooperate with each other efficiently. A small fix in one module may affect the functioning of many other modules. However, operating systems are very complex, and when installing a PUT there is always the risk of introducing regressive changes. That is why a subsequent PUT will contain fixes to previous fixes. It is also why system programmers have excellent job security.

System Modification Issues

With the aggressive enhancements that IBM is adding to VM, it is much less common for organizations to make modifications in their VM source code. However, situations arise in which a modification seems the best way to provide a desired function. Some system software vendors also modify VM source code to achieve specific product features.

The ramifications of a source code modification are most likely going to be apparent when a PUT is installed. In most cases local fixes will not be impacted directly because the PUT is only affecting certain sections of code. However, the update works by validating a certain section of the code to see that what is being applied there is actually what it is supposed to be. If it is, the fix is applied. If a section of code was changed in the PUT that causes the local modification to no longer fit, the modification will be rejected during the update process. This is accomplished with sequence numbers in the assemble files and updates.

The updating process with system modifications is performed by VMFASM. As described earlier, VMFASM makes updates to an assembler program and reassembles the updated source code. During the process of updating the source code to reflect fixes, an error will occur when a portion of the code is found that has been locally modified. The utility nevertheless goes on with the assemble. Generally, there is a hierarchy that the utility goes through in reassembling the source code. At the top is IBM source code, followed by any changes from the PUT, followed by any additional PTFs that may have been received since the last PUT. At the bottom of the hierarchy are local modifications. A local modification may survive the reassembling process. But if it affects, or is affected by, a modification that was made in another section of code, it will no longer work. And it may keep another aspect of the system from working properly.

Local system modifications have many implications for the subsequent operation of the VM environment. One concern with modifications is that they must be maintained. As described above, each time that IBM modifies VM through a PUT, then the local modifications may need to be updated to keep up with the changes. When a local modification is not carried forward, the result is that a "bug" is created in VM. This is potentially a major maintenance burden.

A second risk is that if not done correctly, local modifications can introduce bugs into the operating system at the time of creation. These bugs may not be apparent until an application program attempts to perform a critical function and the system fails. It is sometimes difficult to estimate all the potential ramifications of the local modification because of the complexity, yet efficiency of VM's design. One problem may be solved but many others created if the modified section of code is also accessed by other modules.

Timesharing organizations have many horror stories about local VM source code modifications. These groups have been known to make numerous modifications to CP to provide various capabilities for their customer, resulting in modifications that they subsequently could not keep up with. Once a customer, or a group of users, has been given a function it is very difficult to take it away. System modifications are really a way of trading short-term solutions for long-term problems. The cost of developing a modification to VM may seem insignificant. However, maintenance costs can be extensive for debugging, converting to new releases, and dealing with the unpredictable impact that a modification in one module can have on other modules.

Installation and Maintenance in the Departments

The issue of keeping multiple departmental CPUs up to date with the same release of VM is one that must be considered carefully. Maintaining a network of machines is a nightmare if each department is doing something just slightly different from another, and if all of these variations require extensive maintenance assistance from the technical staff.

It is important to maintain organizational standards, and all users need to have access to the same software releases. With the lack of available technical personnel at the department level, it is clear that careful planning, and innovative solutions, must be applied to this problem. Installing constant PUTs on a system with 100 or more midrange CPUs is a potential nightmare, especially if each of these machines has developed its own configuration independently.

The key to streamlining the installation and maintenance of departmental processors is to standardize the software and hardware configurations of these machines, and to carefully plan configurations. If the departmental machine is a 9370, for example, and they are being purchased in bulk, then it is best to choose two or three configurations and then duplicate throughout the organization. Considerations for standardizing the hardware would include choices about the machine size and devices such as printers and disk drives. Software considerations include types of applications, database management systems, and office systems.

Initial planning should begin with the development of prototype systems. In conjunction with user groups, a departmental machine can be brought into the organization and various hardware configurations tested for efficiency and affect on the central site. This seems a time-consuming exercise, and it is. However, the alternative is to throw the machines out into the departments and see what happens. The midrange departmental machine could easily go the way of the personal computer in large organizations, with no coordination of applications or data.

Software must be a careful component of the planning process. Users will have many different software requests, and it is important that central MIS encourage only a limited number of software packages to be loaded on the departmental machines. It is recommended that application programs also be prototyped at the central site, and then a limited number of applications included on the departmental machines. VM/SP lends itself to providing a basis in each department for departmental solutions. Central MIS can develop a few prototype systems, with VM/SP on each one, and various groups of application software packages constituting a software configuration. In a sense this is similar to purchasing a bundled system. Central MIS develops the prototypes and clones them for the departments by loading the prototypes onto tapes and then distributing them.

Prototyping a departmental system is similar to the prototyping that is done in manufacturing. Adjustments are made, with further testing, until the prototype is ready for mass production. Some devices may not work well together. Even under VM some application packages will not work well together. Once the combinations of options are tested to the point that any bugs are worked out, one or more configurations is ready for mass production.

Obviously, system modifications to VM should not even be considered when developing the prototypes. This creates potential problems that are in turn multiplied around the organization. Central site maintenance is much easier when a new release of VM is tested at the central site and then distributed to the departments through either tape or communications.

Each time a new release of VM, or a PUT, is available, it will be necessary to distribute these to the departments. Through the development of prototypes, this process is facilitated. The new release, for example, can be tested on prototype machines in central MIS, or within selected departments. When the release is ready for distribution departmentally, it can be loaded down to a tape, and this tape distributed to each department. With new application software releases, these can also be tested through the expertise of central MIS, and then in turn the tapes sent to the departments that have the specific software application as part of the departmental configuration.

It is possible to use communications lines to download software updates from central MIS to the departmental machines. Currently this can be an involved process, with downloads having to be scheduled around the normal system use, and potentially tying up communication facilities for long periods of time. If scheduled as an overnight job, for example, downloading from the central site may require personnel on hand to manage this process. If there is an error, the time requirements are lengthened even further. Until this process becomes more streamlined, sending out a technician to install a tape in each department will be the method of choice in managing the installation and maintenance procedure.

The best way to manage the installation and maintenance effort at the departmental level is through careful planning, before each department goes off in divergent directions and MIS is left with a conglomeration of unique problems.

Chapter Summary

The following are major issues discussed in Chapter 4:

• The basic characteristics of the VM environment are specified through three modules: DMKSYS, DMKRIO, and DMKSNT. These modules are used by the organization in determining how the operating system will be set up.

- The CP nucleus, created through the system generation procedure, is the core of VM and is the critical element in the installation process.
- New releases of VM introduce new features and enhancements. The new release can cause basic incompatibilities with the way in which the system had been running, and it is recommended that the release be tested before being moved into the production environment. System modifications further complicate the installation of the new release.
- Between each release, Problem Update Tapes (PUTs) are distributed by IBM with fixes to any problems in the code.
- In a departmental situation, it is recommended that a few prototype configurations be developed and distributed to departments. This streamlines the subsequent technical support effort.

5

Security in VM

Data that is contained on a computer is a precious corporate resource, being the "keys to the kingdom" in the form of financial records, customer lists, and other sensitive information. Security is a key to integrity of this data, and as such is a cornerstone of the VM environment. The VM operating system offers some level of system security, based on passwords that are contained in the directory. In Chapter 5, the directory is described in more detail, as a basis for an overall VM security strategy.

VM's Provisions for Security

Data security is generally thought of as prevention of unauthorized access to, or modification of, data. Without data integrity, which refers to the maintenance of data in its correct form, the information system, whether it is a personal computer or a sophisticated distributed environment, is of minimal benefit to users. Threats to data integrity, generally thought of as being maliciously oriented, may also be the result of simple error. It is the job of the security system to protect against any potential threat to data integrity.

There are three major entities in the information processing environment, including users, their data, and the resources that users rely on for storing and maintaining this data. In VM, there are also two types of relationships which govern the access to the data, ownership and access. Physical security, through pass keys and door locks, offers some protection over the hardware resources and, by association, the software contained on the machines. Through VM's system of passwords, users maintain ownership to the data associated with their assigned minidisk, and users may in turn grant access to other users as they see fit. VM, in its vanilla form, has made provisions for a level of protection of the major entities.

The spirit of VM is user control. It is inherently open and accessible to end users, providing a flexible environment for interactive productivity. There are some VM installations that find the security provisions adequate for their needs, particulary those with few if any users. Once there is user access, the security issues become much more complex. To ignore the security issues is to risk one of the most valuable assets of the organization.

The Directory: Who's Who in the User Community

Virtual machine access, even if it is access to a user's own virtual machine, begins in the directory. It is here that userids, passwords, minidisk addresses, and other vital information about the users in the VM environment are stored. As such, the directory is the place where security begins and, too often, ends. The directory was briefly introduced in Chapter 2 in the discussion of CP. CP controls the directory because it is through CP that the user is allowed access to the computer.

The CP directory, also more broadly termed the VM directory, serves as a repository for information including the definitions of users, their CP privileges and classes, and the location of their minidisks (where data is stored by users). A user is identified by a userid which may be up to 8 characters in length. Each userid in the directory also has a password associated with it.

A user may grant access to the data stored on his minidisk to another user. This is also accomplished through the use of a minidisk password which is also stored in the directory. There are two types of data sharing in VM. The first is the directory link, which is used mainly for common applications like CMS. This is automatically executed when a user logs on, and is maintained until the user explicitly detaches this link. Directory links facilitate the process of gaining access to frequently used applications. For example, through a directory link an accounts payable clerk, when logging on, has automatic access to the accounting software package needed to perform this job function.

Users may also share data through user links. A user may explicitly link to share another user's minidisk if the directory contains a link password for that user's minidisk. For example, a user may devise a link password, request that the security manager enter it in the directory, and then give this LINK password to other users so that they can access his data. This is a separate password from the user's logon password, but may ultimately accomplish the same purpose. Also, a password of ALL provides data sharing to any other user, by default.

This is a reserved password, only to be used when granting access to all other users.

Without granting access to a minidisk through a link password, the "default" in VM is not to grant access at all. Passwords are defined in the same directory statement that defines the minidisk. As a result, as the system programmer is setting up a user and defining the minidisk, it is at this same moment that he or she will indicate minidisk link passwords. Thus, without a password, there is no linking to the minidisk.

In VM there are three options that may be specified when designating a password. The three types of passwords:

1. READ. This password permits access to data on a minidisk in a read-only mode. Users may look at the information contained on this minidisk, but cannot modify it. Also, this reading may be accomplished at the same time by multiple users.
2. WRITE. A WRITE password permits users to both read the data on the minidisk as well as modify it. In other words, users with WRITE access may make changes to the data. With this type of password, however, only one user at a time may write to the minidisk; other users may only read the data until the individual user who is writing has completed this task.
3. MULTIWRITE. This type of password has the potential for creating a nightmare, and because of this is seldom granted. As the term implies, it permits access to data on a minidisk in a non-exclusive write-mode. When accessed in a multiwrite mode, data can be modified concurrently with other users. MULTI-WRITE is not supported for CMS use because of the potential for data destruction.

The log on password, which may also be up to 8 characters in length, is required to log on to a userid, thereby gaining access to the system. CP audits these passwords, monitoring the number of invalid passwords issued by a user when in the process of logging on to the system, or attempting to gain access (link) to the data of another users. The installation can specify the maximum number of invalid passwords that will be tolerated, after which CP will prevent the user from further attempts. With each of these invalid attempts, CP generates an accounting record that identifies both that an invalid password was issued and which invalid password was used (actually, as part of the SYSGEN process, the VM site can indicate a threshold count, above which CP starts cutting these records). CP accounting records are discussed in Chapter 12, in the CP accounting section.

The password in effect validates the logon request, ensuring that the person requesting access is really the owner of the userid, and subsequently the one to whom this privilege was given. As will be discussed later, this is a classic area of security failure. Users frequently allow their personal passwords to be known to others, or display them in conspicuous places, and a security breakdown results.

The CP directory itself is stored in plain text format in a file located on a minidisk. The file containing the directory is customarily called USER DIRECT, with USER being the file name and DIRECT being the filetype. This is essentially a "humongous" file that continues for pages and pages with directory entries and any associated comments. There is an entry in the CP directory for every user in the system. The unfortunate systems programmer — generally referred to as the Security Manager — who is responsible for maintaining this directory has a major task in keeping this large file updated. The directory file is stored in plain text format and edited by a standard VM editor, such as XEDIT. With the continuous maintenance of new users, keeping the directory updated using XEDIT can be a very time-consuming process. Access to the directory file is protected by a LINK password that is associated with the minidisk on which the directory file is located.

The following is the first record of a directory entry for an individual user. The first line in the entry identifies the user:

USER GRM 3M; 2M 8M ABG

This information indicates that the userid is GRM, followed by an encrypted version of GRM's password. The user identified by GRM has a 2 megabyte virtual machine, by default, which the user can expand to 8 megabytes if needed. The user has CP privilege classes of A, B, and G.

User GRM also has information in his directory entry which shows the location of his minidisk:

MDISK 191 3375 314 8 VMPK11 MR SHARE

This information indicates the address of GRM's 191 minidisk, with 191 being the identifier, or "virtual address," generally given to the minidisk on which a user's data is stored. According to this statement in the directory entry, also referred to as the MDISK record, GRM's 191 disk is stored on 3375 DASD, with 3375 being a type of DASD. The minidisk begins at cylinder 314, for a total of 8 cylinders. A physical DASD is divided into cylinders, with users being assigned varying amounts of DASD with cylinder being the unit of measure. The volume serial of this DASD is VMPK11 (a means of identifying the DASD). MR signifies the type of link that the user has to the minidisk. The user can write on the minidisk unless another user is currently writing on it, in which case the user could access it in read-only mode. SHARE is a read sharing password. If no password had been indicated at the end of the minidisk definition statement, then sharing would not be allowed.

Defining the minidisk address requires caution. It is necessary for a site to keep a map of minidisks, as a way of tracking where they are located. Some organizations develop a program to help with this task, such as extracting minidisk statements and sorting them. System software products will also assist with this process at varying levels. If the locations of minidisks are not tracked carefully, what can result is two or more users being given minidisks at the same address. This is referred to as overlapping minidisks; it is discussed in the next section.

Privilege class, which was also indicated in user GRM's directory entry, has been an important concept in VM. Privilege class controls at a high level what VM commands individual users can issue. The standard privilege classes are as follows:

- Class A — Primary System Operator. This individual is allowed to control and even terminate the total VM operation.
- Class B — System Resource Operator. At this level, the user is allowed to examine the status of the system-owned units and make allocations to requesting users.
- Class C — System Programmer. A Class C user can examine and modify real storage, including the ability to examine and modify the main storage of other users.
- Class D — Spooling Operator. This individual can alter the characteristics of real spooling devices and queues. This would affect, for example, the queues for printers and other devices.
- Class E — System Analyst. This class allows the examination of real storage, but without the ability to modify it.
- Class F — Engineer/Service Representative. A Class F user is allowed use of extended I/O capabilities, preventing error recording while running. This individual might be involved in making modifications to enhance response time.
- Class G — General User. This class is reserved for most users of the system.

With VM/SP Release 4, installations have the ability to create up to 32 CP privilege classes as well as to dynamically assign capabilities. This illustrates IBM's recognition of the increasing role that VM plays within organizations, and the complexity of user roles within this environment.

A user's directory entry will contain many more lines of information, depending on the kinds of applications and data that the user is able to access in the system. Each user is also given an 8-character account code, which is further discussed in the chapter on accounting.

When the directory is modified, such as when a new user is added, the file is saved. Following this, the source directory is placed online using a command called DIRECT. Running DIRECT is essentially indicating to CP that this is a "new" directory. CP then reads the file in, recompiling the directory and rewriting the machine-readable version out to a designated area on the system-owned minidisk (the system residence volume). With an online directory now in place, users are defined, privilege classes are set, and minidisks are defined.

When the user is officially part of the directory and able to logon, he or she is in charge of a dedicated virtual machine. From his terminal, the user has access to DASD storage, a virtual card reader, a printer, tape drives, and possibly communications lines.

The Password Problem

Users access VM through the terminal, which is either connected directly to the system (local) or, in a Departmental Computing situation, through a network (remote). Because the terminal is the point at which the user enters into the VM environment, it is also at this point that security problems might begin. Two scenarios illustrate the security problems that may occur within VM.

A fairly sly systems programmer, even without the necessary CP privilege class, can gain access to the plain text directory on minidisk storage and can subsequently gain access to the virtual machines of the user population. From here it is possible to accomplish anything, including going into the payroll database and redressing all kinds of grievances, real or imagined.

A user might name his password after his dog, SPOT, and tell another user in the department the story of how he arrived at this password at lunch. If a person at the next table were to hear this information, he could log on after hours as the other user, using the SPOT password, and read or write on the data on that user's minidisk.

Passwords are contained in an easily readable form which can result in passwords, and subsequently data, being subject to unauthorized access. If an unauthorized user is able to obtain the password for the directory minidisk, this individual has access to a large amount of data because of having the passwords to other virtual machines and minidisks, including, for example, the owner of payroll information. He who can access the directory truly has the keys to the kingdom.

No matter how many locks there are on a door, if the keys are easy to steal, there is no security. VM, because it was originally positioned as a testing and time sharing system, may have security "holes" where multiple users are concerned. VM is not strong in password protection. People are human, the potential for security breaches are great. Users give their passwords to other users, or they tape the password to the side of the terminal, or they use easily guessable passwords, such as the names of pets.

Furthermore, the directory can only be maintained by whomever is designated as the system programmer. With many users being maintained this can subject the system to the possibility of human error, either in designating the minidisk address or in indicating the password. If a user's password is also given, either verbally or in writing, to the user's manager, confidentiality is totally lost. At least three people have the key at this point.

The password is the first major loophole in the security of VM. For an installation with few users, perhaps a scientific application, the security provided by VM may be more than adequate. However, the larger the VM population, the greater the opportunity for the potential weaknesses in the use of passwords to become security loopholes.

Sharing Data

Even if logon passwords provide adequate protection, the security issue is further complicated once users start to share data. VM does provide a means of limiting data sharing to a subset of users, through link passwords at the minidisk level. It is important to make a distinction between minidisk and file at this point. Restrictions on data sharing between users go only as far as the minidisk level, so that once a user has given minidisk access to another user, that user can see everything on the minidisk. Users cannot protect individual files on the minidisk.

The link password is the means in VM of protecting the user against unwanted links, allowing the owner of the minidisk to attach a password to it. Again, because this password resides in the directory, the user may or may not have an easy way of setting the link password. It may involve coercing a system programmer into going into the directory file, setting this password, and then recompiling the directory to reflect the change. Getting this accomplished in many organizations is the result of a complex series of work orders.

Assuming that the user is actually able to get a password set on his minidisk, sharing is now possible. In fact, as a means of being ready for any situation, the user may have had three passwords set on his minidisk: ALICE, a read access password, HENRY, the write access password, and FRANK, a multiwrite password. With these three passwords, when another user attempts to link to this user's minidisk, the person will be prompted by CP to enter the appropriate password. The user with these passwords must have provided one of them to the user with whom he wishes to share his data. If the other user cannot name the correct password, the link will not be allowed by CP.

Sharing data, through the LINK command, a CP command, is a three-step process. First the user wanting to access must enter the LINK command, for example:

LINK GRM 191 AS 291

With this command, the user is asking for access to user GRM's 191 minidisk, which is the one on which GRM's data is stored. By specifying a second virtual address (291), the user is essentially asking for his own "copy" of the data in his own virtual machine, which will then be access as if it were the linking user's own minidisk (called 291).

CP will then prompt the user for a READ password, which in this case must be entered for the linking process to continue.

Once the password is validated, the accessing user enters a CMS command called ACCESS:

ACCESS 291 B

The user then has access to GRM's minidisk. In this example, the user has read access, but could have requested either write, read, or multiwrite mode.

ACCESS, a CMS command, results in access to the user's data, through CMS. Unlike CP, the minimal security built into CMS is easily circumvented. Thus, once access has been granted, a "hacker" can accomplish much more than the link-granting user intended to occur. An unauthorized write-access can result in data that is altered or destroyed. This can be particularly fatal if the data is altered so slightly that the loss of integrity is not apparent until a much later time. Even an unauthorized read access can have major implications if sensitive data is involved.

It is also possible to gain access to minidisks owned by others through an implicit link. This type of link can be established between a userid and a software product, so that a user has automatic access to a software application at the time of logging on, without requiring a separate password. Though enhancing ease of use, implicit directory links can also be misused. A system programmer with directory access can grant herself the privilege of sharing another user's data without using passwords. Once data sharing is granted with a directory, data can be accessed without password verification.

Overlapping Minidisks

Getting into the data of others does not take a whole lot of investigative work. With overlapping minidisks, this process becomes even easier because it can be accomplished without the need for a password.

When users are defined in the directory, as discussed earlier, their minidisks are also defined by three parameters: the real DASD volume it resides on, the physical start address, and the length of the minidisk. As discussed previously, if this is not carefully mapped it is easy to assign the same minidisk space to two different users. In fact, if the mapping process is based on manually prepared lists, even if done carefully there is opportunity for human error. There is nothing in native VM to prevent these overlapping minidisks from occurring. Furthermore, because of the ease at which this can be accomplished, it is not uncommon for hackers to gain access to unauthorized data through defining an overlapping minidisk.

The results of an overlapping minidisk can be disastrous. Suppose a user identified by the userid TOM has a minidisk that contains nothing of significance. Another user, identified by SUPRHUSH, has a minidisk that contains confidential information. If TOM has access to the directory he could conceivably change the definition of his minidisk to correspond exactly with the definition of the minidisk belonging to SUPRHUSH. For example, SUPRHUSH might reside on a DASD identified by VMPK51, start at cylinder 281, and continue for three cylinders. All TOM has to do is define a minidisk for himself with the same parameters. TOM would thus gain access to the "crown jewels." Though each user owns a separate virtual machine, and a different logical means of accessing the minidisk, the results are unfortunately the same.

The only situation in which overlapping minidisks are really necessary is for maintenance purposes. It is quite common for system programmers to have deliberately overlapping minidisks for maintaining the system. For example, one of these traditional userids is MAINT, which typically owns a series of minidisks covering full DASDs, from beginning to end. By using MAINT, the system programmer could then go in and perform maintenance on individual user's minidisks so that this space is better utilized. However, this also means that anyone having access to MAINT can subsequently logon and have access to the physical location of all other users.

VM has no native protection against defining these overlapping minidisks. Not only do they offer the same access as that afforded by a link, but use of the link command generates a CP accounting record which could later result in discovery. Without a very time-consuming audit, overlapping minidisks can continue on indefinitely. The most reliable protection against this situation is through system software.

The VM environment allows each user to play operator. This is one of the major strengths of VM and should not be compromised. However, this capability must be managed, with protection that does not restrict the availability of resources.

Making VM Secure

Based on the potential security loopholes in the VM operating system, most installations find that it is necessary to "shore up" this situation above what is offered through native VM. This might include "homegrown" solutions that are developed inhouse, as well as system software. Considerations for enhancing security include password protection and access rules.

Expanding Password Protection

Much of password protection is based on persuading, or coercing, users into being more responsible for their passwords. If users continue to tape passwords onto the side of their terminal, or otherwise ignore the security implications, then of course security is a lost cause no matter what protection mechanisms are put into place. However, there are automated methods which, though not absolving the organization of responsibility in developing security policies, at least assist in getting the users more involved.

The major issues around password management include:

1. Automatic expiration of LOGON passwords.
2. Enforcing installation standards.
3. Providing users with the ability to change passwords.

If passwords stay in effect for months and even years at a time, their integrity will most likely decline with time. For example, if a user has given his password to another, the chances that this password has in turn been given to someone else, and even passed on further, multiplies. But without automatic expiration of passwords, once the password expires, the chain is broken. Password status needs to be constantly reassessed, both by the security manager and by users. To become complacent about passwords is to allow the security cracks to widen.

Automatic password expiration is a means both of forcing attention on the critical importance of password status, and stopping any chains that may have developed through users that have given their passwords to others. For example, a security system can provide the option of having users' passwords expire every 3 months, thus forcing each user to obtain a new password. This is more likely to work if the user is informed a few days ahead of time that the password is about to expire, and then provided with a full screen menu to assist with changing the password, as well as online help in doing this.

Password change can be enforced through preventing further use of the system until the password has been successfully changed. Merely reminding the user that the password should be changed, without backing this up with consequences, will most likely not result in action.

Password expiration implies that there is an overall organizational password policy. This includes not only the intervals at which passwords will expire, but any patterns to which passwords must adhere. For example, the possibility of guessing another user's password is made more difficult if users are required to have at least four characters in their passwords, or if they are not allowed to include various symbols. Through security software, these standards can be enforced automatically without requiring constant monitoring by the security manager.

Depending on the needs of the organization, the password policy can go even a step further, past the issue of access control. Password information can be encrypted in the directory, making this information impossible to read. Thus, if the directory is the object of unauthorized access, the passwords cannot be read. The logon process involves reading the password on the employee's record, and then comparing the password entered to the one on the record before access is allowed. With this policy, it is particularly important that passwords be encrypted, because the password on the employee record would then be visible to others during an online query. Through security software, the password could be encrypted in both places.

Password encryption is generally based on the National Bureau of Standard's Data Encryption Standard (DES). Encryption can be very expensive, resulting in increased system overhead due to the process of encrypting and decoding. Also, data itself can also be encrypted, especially if it is sensitive in nature. This adds even further system overhead. The costs must be weighed against the need.

A key to the success of a password expiration system is that the user needs to be involved both in choosing the password and making the actual change. Randomly generated passwords are difficult to memorize and irrelevant to users. Even if a user chooses the name of her dog as a password, after 90 days she will be forced to think of something else. When users have some level of control over what affects them directly, cooperation is enhanced. They are also more likely to make these changes if they can be accomplished without having to go through a lengthy process of filling out forms and having to get special permission.

In addition, allowing users to change passwords creates a constant awareness of passwords and, by inference, system security. Rather than having an anonymous system with passwords assigned by a central technician, someone the users might now know, this system places accountability for system security more directly on those most responsible for it. Some VM shops do, however, assign passwords from a dictionary rather than allowing users to choose them. It is a matter of organizational policy.

System security can be yet further enhanced through the development of user interfaces which, based on the user's userid, present a screen after successful logon which lists the applications that the individual is qualified to use. This interface is further enhanced if forward and backward scrolling, and selection by PF key or application name are allowed. A caution lies in the listing of applications. Includ-

RULES FACILITY
DATABASE

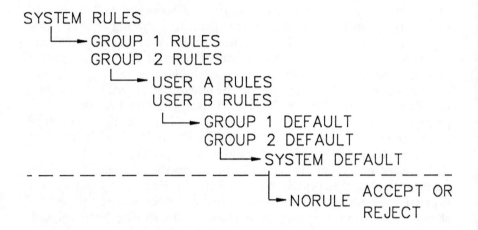

Figure 5-1 The security system hierarchy of rules

ing those for which the user is not qualifed may result in encouraging attempts at penetration.

Access Rules

System security software packages that "hook" directly in CP allow the establishment of access rules which in effect supplant the need for minidisk passwords. Because of the cumbersomeness involved in indicating these passwords for each user's minidisk, as well as the potential security loopholes that these passwords create, the ability to establish rules saves time and enhances security.

The basic concept of rules in security management involves the establishment of rules at various levels, from the overall organizational level down to the user level, which are first evaluated by CP before an access request is granted. Rules allow for the control of access at organizational levels, thus ensuring that access to information reflects both organizational structure as well as the needs of users. The trend in security packages is toward access control by rules rather than password. This is true in part because users are careless about minidisk passwords, and because rules are both easier to use and understand and much more flexible.

System software packages with a rules facility generally allow the system administrator to establish groups of users, perhaps based on departments, and then set up access rights based on users being inside or outside of the group of the owner of the minidisk resource. Users are also allowed to indicate to whom they wish to grant access privileges. This implies a hierarchy, as indicated in Figure 5-1.

At the top of the hierarchy are system level rules, which override the rules at lower levels in the hierarchy, taking precedence over any other access privelege in the system. For example, a product designed to perform system backup would be allowed to link to the minidisk of every user in the system, thus allowing all data to be backed up. This rule would be set at the system level as an overriding rule, to assure that even if a user has refused others to access his data, his minidisk would still be backed up.

Rules based on a hierarchy can then be set all the way down through the organization. For example, users in a specific department might be linked from certain applications. In addition, a user can also allow another user to link over to his minidisk, without having to designate and then divulge a minidisk password. A user might grant access to another user through this rule:

ACCEPT JIM LINK 191 RR

This user has allowed another user, JIM, to access his 191 minidisk (where his data is contained) in read-only mode. This rule would have been entered through the system software package. Referring back to the earlier LINK example, rather than using, for example, a read-sharing password of ALICE and telling only the "right" people of this password, and hoping they don't write it in a conspicuous place, rules allow access to be designated before the fact. There is no password involved, so there is no worry concerning to whom JIM might divulge a password.

Rules, including those written by users, are contained in a database which is maintained by the security system software. With the rules facility in place, CP intercepts certain access-granting CP commands, and passes the command to the system software where the command is evaluated in the rules database to see if there is a rule governing this request. The software then sends a message back to CP to indicate whether the request should be accepted or rejected.

- CP commands to be consideration for rules include the following:
- AUTOLOG — the process by which a user's virtual machine is initiated by someone other than the user
- LINK — a command which allows one user to share another user's minidisk
- LOGON — the process of initiating one's virtual machine

- TAG — instructions on how a spool file is to be handled
- TRANSFER — moving a file from one userid to another, or from one spool type to another
- SPOOL — DASD area for temporary storage of reader, punch, or print files

At the bottom of the rules hierarchy are defaults. If a specific request has been evaluated down through the hierarchy and no rule has been indicated to govern whether or not it should be granted, it is passed down further to see if there is a default for the group level. At the group default level, if there is no rule governing the request, it is then passed on to the system default level to check that there is a system level default. These defaults do not imply an absence of rules, only that if a rule has not been specified at a higher level in the hierarchy, then rules have been specified at these levels to handle the request. Thus, the default can be either to grant or reject the request.

At the lowest level of the rules hierarchy is the system default level which evaluates the request if no rule has been written at any of the previous levels. At this point, the VM system is either open or closed.

An open system is one in which, if no rule has been found, CP is allowed to accept the request. Conversely, a closed security system is one in which if no rule has been found to govern a request, the request is rejected. Organizations often find that it is safest to be a closed system, though in the early stages it may be necessary to be open, until after all the analysis is complete and the trial period over. After all eventualities and possibilities have been thoroughly analyzed, it may at this point in time be feasible to become a closed security system. The implications of being open, particularly with the creativity inherent in experienced users, are legion.

As indicated, the rules facility is provided by system software which hooks in the CP directory. These rules can be established because of standard user exits in VM provided by IBM in 1984, called the Access Control Interface (ACI). The access control facility essentially intercepts eight CP commands, the ones discussed earlier (AUTOLOG, LOGON, LINK, SPOOL, TAG, and TRANSFER).

ACI is essentially a package in which a system service called *RPI communicates with a userid by the Inter-User Communications Vehicle (IUCV). IUCV provides a means for two cooperating virtual machines to talk with each other — not the two humans running these machines, but the programs running on these machines. For example, a program running on one virtual machine can "shoulder tap" a program on another virtual machine, obtain needed information, and then return to what it was doing. IUCV also communicates with CP through system services, such as *RPI.

To make use of this facility, a userid is specifically authorized in the directory to connect to the *RPI system service. Once an authorized userid connects to *RPI, every time one of the included CP commands, such as LINK, is issued by anyone else in the system, CP intercepts it and passes it back to that user's virtual machine. The request is then evaluated based on the rules structure and passed back with a reject/accept decision. CP is not actually aware of what checks are being made or the basis for the decision. A return code is sent back to CP to indicate the decision. ACI was actually developed for a security system software product marketed by IBM, but this facility has also been adapted for use by other software vendors.

Security system software that hooks into CP through the Access Control Interface is able to accomplish command verification without system modifications. There are three modules in native VM which are essentially "dummies" that don't do anything. As supplied, they are such that if accidentally called by a program there is no resulting error message, but nothing happens. These modules — labeled DMKRPI, DMKRPW, and DMKRPD — are replaced by system software offering rules capabilities with three modules of the same names. These modules replace the dummy versions with modules that utilize *RPI and provide the capability to designate rules. Again, without a security product, these modules essentially just sit. Because of the nature of the ACI modules, replacing them with the vendor's versions is not considered an operating system modification. There are no negative consequences to be expected from this additional layer of checking.

The rules facility provided by system software not only provides more comprehensive protection without passwords, but is also much easier to use and manage.

Security System Software

The basic rule of thumb in considering any kind of security solutions for VM, whether developed inhouse or purchased, is that they should protect the system while not discouraging users from subsequently using the system. VM is a user's system, and security should not interfere with the feeling of control and free access to information. By implication, system security functions should be as transparent as possible to the user, so that the security job is performed without interfering with the user's job.

Security software also allows an organization to further refine the access controls needed to make sure that system use is conforming to overall organizational standards. Software allows the ability to prevent users from logging onto the system on the basis of factors such as physical location, time of day, and the nature of the applications generated. In effect, software can enforce the rules and policies of the organization.

Based on the unique environment provided by VM, the major considerations for enhancing the security offered by native VM can be summarized as follows:

* Terminal and userid protection.
* Hacker protection.
* Last logon information.
* No system modifications required.
* Open or closed protection allowed.
* Availability monitored by CP.

Many of these considerations have been outlined within this section, but there are options, particularly surrounding password protection, which can contribute to a more secure VM environment.

Password protection affects not only the overall security of the system from the organizational point of view but also whether users themselves feel comfortable in the environment. Comfort is the result of both ease of use and overall trust. Passwords, assuming they are encrypted in the directory, should only be available to the security administrator, if anyone. Some packages go as far as to limit knowledge of the password to the user himself, with managers and the security administrator denied this knowledge. This reinforces the feeling of control that is important in the VM environment while placing responsibility for maintaining the password on the user.

Passwords can be further protected from hackers through terminating the access environment after a specified number of incorrect attempts at entering the password. Thus, if someone tried to log on as another user by guessing the password, the ability to guess would be terminated after, for example, three password attempts. This frustrates the hacker who may have compiled a repertoire of possible combinations and has been limited only by his or her own patience. This is an important consideration particularly for security at the departmental processor level, where access to facilities is even harder to monitor. Both violations and approved access to protected data need to be documented. These attempts can be recorded and maintained in a special file for later review by the security administrator.

System software with user exits further enhances security by allowing organizations to build in a means of assuring that unique standards and policies are met by users. An example of user exit functions includes the validation of a new account number before it is updated in the directory, or the validation of a password to make sure that it contains a certain number of characters and ends in a certain letter. A user exit is basically a place in the program where it branches out, the information that has been entered is checked, and then the program continues on. For example, when a password is being created, once it has been entered, the software program can branch to a user exit where the password is checked and, if standards are met, the program can continue. If the password does not correctly meet the standards, a message can be sent back telling the user to try again. Thus, user exits serve the dual purpose of both enforcing standards as well as guiding the user in performing the task.

File level security continues to be an issue in security management. Security at the minidisk level offers very good protection. However, if a user gains access to another user's minidisk, he or she has access to all the files contained on the minidisk. With the CMS file system, there is really no way to adequately and totally protect an individual file. With extensive modifications to CMS itself, some security system software vendors advertise this level of security. For a general user, the implications of the CMS modifications aside, this means of providing file level security may work. Experienced users, however, can easily implement a different version of CMS and bypass the system defined protections completely.

Implementing System Security

When changes in the security system are being implemented, or when a system is being introduced, it is important that this be accomplished with as little shock to the users as possible. The system needs to remain operational, with security introduced systematically.

It is recommended that the implementation of security begin with directory maintenance, introducing the system as new users are registered. This process can also be a means of introducing naming standards, which refers to how userids are devised, and standards for account numbers and passwords. After this, the rules facility, with rules that were not available in native VM, can be added.

There is often resistance to the implementation of security. Users are not given enough advance preparation, due to a lack of education, and changes in logon messages are confusing as a result. There is also resistance due to changes in professional roles, as well as the introduction of new roles, and lack of understanding concerning the duties associated with these roles. The changes in the user role, with increased responsibility for password management, has been discussed.

Other roles in the security scheme include the directory manager, who is responsible for defining new userids and deleting old ones. This individual will also manage DASD space that has been configured as being available for CMS minidisks. In other words, the directory manager is responsible for giving a piece of DASD to a particular CMS user in the form of a minidisk, and for moving DASD around from one location to another. The security administrator is responsible for installing and maintaining the security product, if the organization is using one, and making sure that the product conforms to site requirements. The administrator also implements password management and writes system-level rules.

A new role, that of security group manager, may emerge if there is extensive use of the rules facility. A security group manager may, for example, be located in each department. Tasks associated with this function include writing group rules for userids, allowing users to share resources between others in the group. Once a population has been defined on the basis of security groups, the group manager oversees the management of access rules for a specific set of userids on the system.

The role of auditor is critical in the VM environment, particularly with regard to security. The auditor examines security data to see if security policies are being enforced, detecting any attempts at violation of security policies. Generally, again through system software, an automated process is set up to extract audit information. This data is moved to a minidisk to which the auditor has access, allowing reports to be run which are based on specific selection criteria.

System software has been stressed in these pages as being the means of providing the additional functions neccessary for assuring the security of the VM environment. There are other options, one of which is to develop a security management system inhouse. Most organizations have found that developing their own software is very impractical, considering the time involved and the subsequent maintenance expense. With the rapid enhancements being added to VM, keeping up with these changes through the efforts of an in-house development makes this option even more unrealistic.

And of course there is also the possibility of having a trusted person manage the security, and forbidding users to attempt unauthorized access. This, unfortunately, is even more unrealistic, but can be enforced if written into job descriptions. Security is everyone's responsibility.

Security in the Departments

The issue of security in the Departmental Computing environment can be compared with the Trojan Horse. As this story goes, the townspeople spent a lot of time building a fortification around their town, but they did not take time to watch out for the enemy within the walls. With Departmental Computing, it is easy to create boundaries between departments while ignoring the implications that carrying new resources into these departments might have for the security of the organization at large.

Once machines are placed in departments, the potential for security violation multiplies exponentially. For example, though the "glass house" is locked as tightly as Fort Knox, terminals in the departments might be sitting relatively unattended. It is not impossible to imagine that a computer science student moonlighting as an evening maintenance person might come upon a terminal that has been left logged on, and proceed to maneuver around the information resources of the total organization.

Distribution of data among various departmental computers is very difficult to track, making it also difficult to manage and protect data that is sensitive. Keeping this data secure may be the most critical factor in the implementation of Departmental Computing. Thus, with increased organizational decentralization of processing resources, the implementation of controls becomes that much more difficult. This is further complicated by the fact that users are becoming much more sophisticated, and more able to move through the loopholes.

The issues in Departmental Computing security are really much the same as they are in protecting a single system VM environment. The system must provide adequate protection without interfering with the day-to-day computing activities of users. The directory must be the foundation of the system, with users involved in maintaining their own passwords. A rules facility needs to be available to provide quality enhanced protection and auditing. Security system software also facilitates security at the departmental level, checking the legitimacy of each attempt to access the system. Furthermore, the rules facility can monitor subsequent access to other resources, including the central site. The practice of encryption might also be expanded to provide "end-to-end" encryption, assuring that data is protected as it is moved from one location to another.

Chapter Summary

Major points discussed in this chapter include the following:

- The potential security loopholes in native VM begin in the directory, and it is here that the solutions also need to begin.
- VM offers security primarily through the use of passwords, both for logging onto the system and sharing data with other users.
- Security enhancements to VM generally focus on increasing the controls around password management as well as providing a facility for designating access rules which replace the use of minidisk passwords.
- The security issues in Departmental Computing are much the same as with VM security in general, but the potential loopholes are multiplied with the distribution of resources.

6

Monitoring for Performance

Performance monitoring is a task that often seems either superfluous or futile, depending on one's perspective. In the early stages of VM use, it may seem unnecessary, but when the system begins to push to peak capacity and beyond, it may be too late. In this chapter, the aspects of VM which need to be monitored are described, followed by guidelines for accomplishing the monitoring process. Departmental performance monitoring is also discussed.

Defining Performance Monitoring

Performance monitoring refers to the ability to find out what's going on in the system, the time frame being the here and now. For example, if response time is so poor that users can press ENTER, leave the room for a few minutes, come back and see that the terminal is still in RUNNING mode, then there is a performance problem. If users can press ENTER, leave the building for an extended lunch and then return to find the terminal is still in RUNNING mode, then the performance problem is serious. This is an exaggeration but, if performance monitoring is neglected for an extensive period of time, the symptoms can become quite pronounced.

The process of performance monitoring involves the collection of data about what is going on in the system, particularly with regard to two major areas: CPU utilization and input/output (I/O). This is performed by system software that performs this function, including products available from IBM. Monitoring products basically sample what's going on in the system, taking this data and storing it in data files. This information is subsequently displayed in various formats, on the terminal screen or through reports. When there are system bottlenecks, as in the case of response time, performance monitoring provides a means of isolating these bottlenecks. System programmers can then make adjustments accordingly, or, if the performance monitoring system software is "knowledge based," adjustments can be made automatically.

Performance monitoring differs from capacity planning, with which it is often confused, in that it is temporal. Its focus is on "getting the best from what you've got," as opposed to figuring out what you need in the future.

Performance monitoring data is also stored and used as input, with other data such as accounting records, for the capacity planning function. This is described in Chapter 13.

CPU Utilization

In performance monitoring, how the CPU itself is being utilized is generally the first consideration. For example, if users are complaining because of poor response time, the problem may be that the utilization of the machine — the CPU — is astronomical. Perhaps the machine is no longer large enough to accommodate the usage it is getting, or perhaps it is not being used correctly. These questions still have to be answered.

VM consists of program modules that "own and manage" the real resources of the system, such as the CPU itself, and storage and I/O devices. One of the primary jobs of CP is to provide a means of interfacing, or mapping, the virtual resources onto the real resources. For example, each user, or virtual machine, is mapped to a defined region on a real DASD device. This is the minidisk, created through the directory entry discussed in Chapter 5, and it indicates the exact real location. When an I/O request to DASD is made (as when a user retrieves a file from a his minidisk), CP translates the virtual address of the minidisk to the real address location on the actual device.

All mapping of virtual to real devices is not necessarily as "static" as minidisk mapping. A virtual printer or punch is not mapped to another real spooling device; rather it is mapped to an area on real DASD that is used to simulate printers or punch devices. This is a storage buffer, simulated by CP, called the System Spool Space. Spool space is assigned by CP to each user or virtual machine. The user may think of each completed set of printed output as being associated with a particular spool file. Inherent to spool file processing, "dynamic" change to storage is inevitable.

Both real and virtual storage is usually organized in blocks of 4096 bytes. Random Access Storage residing on the processor itself is commonly referred to as "real or primary" storage with a 4096 byte block referred to as a "frame." In contrast, slower "auxiliary storage" usually refers to external DASD storage with its corresponding "page slot."

The whole concept of Virtual Storage is based on the Dynamic Address Translation Tables (DAT) that permit CP to map a virtual storage page slot to a real storage frame.

In order for CP to provide efficient mapping of different storage devices from expensive fast devices to slower and inexpensive devices, CP maintains a strict hierarchy of virtual storage. In spite of this storage hierarchy, a page of virtual storage may appear anywhere within the hierarchy.

A basic characteristic of VM is that there is never enough real storage (i.e., the "fastest") available to handle all the users on a system all the time. Because of this "contention," CP comes in with its own storage management algorithms designed to move pages from real storage frames to auxillary storage slots and back again. The goal is to keep the CPU as active as possible without being overloaded. This process is referred to as paging, and it is important to an understanding of how CP is able to mediate the demands of multiple users and maintain the virtual machine illusion.

CPU Contention

The concept of contention, with users competing for the resources of the CPU, becomes clearer when considering how CP handles virtual processors. In the VM environment, each virtual machine is given a "CPU time slice" whereby each machine gets its fair share of the real processor. This is illustrated in Figure 6-1.

The virtual machine illusion is achieved because CP limits the actual amount of real processor time allotted for any task. The many concurrent tasks requiring real processor time for execution are managed primarily by VM's Scheduler and Dispatcher.

The Scheduler maintains two lists of virtual machines. If a machine is "runnable," then it is either in the "Eligible List" or the "Run List." The Eligible List is a physical state in storage that serves as a temporary holding spot for virtual machines whose projected storage requirements (their working sets) exceed available page frames. The Run List contains those virtual machines whose working sets match the available storage page frames. Virtual machines are selected and moved from the Eligible List to the Run List only when storage conditions permit it.

The Scheduler ensures that if a machine is runnable, then the virtual machine is either in the Run List or the Eligible List. The Scheduler projects the working set that the virtual machine will require based on the data known from previous storage during the time of the terminal session. In other words, the Scheduler looks at the user's activities thus far in the session and estimates the CPU resources that will be needed to meet the request.

CPU TIME SLICES

Figure 6-1 Virtual machines sharing the CPU through time slices

The virtual machines are sorted in both lists according to a value called the Deadline Priority. The lower the deadline priority value, the better the position. The Deadline Priority is based on the current time of day (TOD) and a queue priority value derived by the Scheduler. All transactions start in a category called Q1. A virtual machine that is in the Run List is considered to be "in-queue." Thus, the terms Q1, Q2, and Q3 came about. In order to calculate this queue priority value, the Scheduler considers a number of variables including the virtual machine's priority specified in the VM directory, the average CPU use for that terminal session and an internal paging bias factor.

Virtual machines may appear anywhere on the lists, top, bottom, or in between. The Scheduler scans the eligible list everytime a processor change in state occurs, to determine if the projected storage requirements can be satisfied. If there is not enough storage, then the virtual machine must wait. When storage becomes available, then the virtual machine is moved to the Run List. This process is shown in Figure 6-2. As indicated in the figure, virtual machines are moved from the Eligible Lists to the Run List as an adequate time slice becomes available. First priority is given to interactive users of short duration.

Once a task is requested, the Scheduler initially assumes that the CPU time slice required to complete the task will be of short duration. This is in line with the basic underlying philosophy of VM to give first

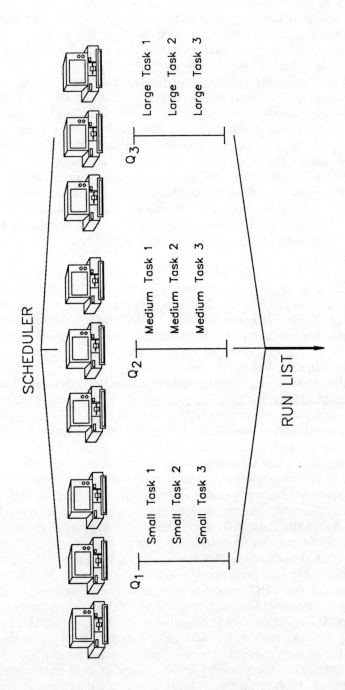

Figure 6-2 Virtual machines are moved from the eligible to the run list by the scheduler

priority to the interactive user. When a virtual machine gets to the top of the Run List, the task is ready for execution. The amount of time that the virtual machine receives from the CPU is called the "time slice," while the actual amount of time in which the task must complete is called the deadline priority.

As a task executes, two consumed amounts of processor time are accumulated: (1) Problem State, which is the amount of CPU time devoted exclusively to executing the user's task, and (2) Supervisor State, which is the amount of time that CP does other work on behalf of the user, such as paging and I/O. The task either completes and finishes before the allotted Q1 CPU time slice runs out or the task does not fully complete. In either case, the virtual machine goes through a process called Queue Drop, during which a new Projected Working Set size is calculated. If the task completes during the allotted amount of time, the user's terminal becomes available to accept a new transaction. Those virtual machines that "ran out of time" enter the Q2 state.

VM usually succeeds in keeping the paging rate of the system at a tolerable level by maintaining separate Eligible Lists for Q1, Q2, and Q3 users. The Q2 Eligible List is a separate list in storage from the Q1 Eligible List. It contains those virtual machines that need more processor time to complete their transactions. CP recognizes that the users in the Q2 Eligibility List will require more time than originally assumed. In fact, VM calculates that the Q2 users will require a CPU time slice that is exactly eight times longer than the CPU time slice allotted to Q1 users. However, in order to maintain concurrent requests and give everyone their "fair share" of the CPU time, the users in Q2 are called for execution only one-eighth as often as the Q1 users.

When a user in Q2 status is called for execution, he or she may or may not finish the transaction during the allocated time slice. The Queue Drop process repeats and if the transaction is completed, the user's terminal becomes available for the next request. If the transaction does not complete, the entire process is repeated for a total of five times before the Scheduler decides that the request requires an even longer CPU time slice from this point on.

If a virtual machine enters the Q3 state, once again it is placed on the Q3 Eligible List until enough storage becomes available. However, in this case, the CPU time slice is eight times as long as the Q2 time slice, or 64 times as long as the Q1 slice. Of course, the converse holds true and the Q3 time slice is allocated only one sixty-fourth as often as the Q1 time slice. Finally, the virtual machine will remain in Q3 status for as long as it takes to complete the transaction.

To summarize, the purpose of the Scheduler is to maximize system throughput yet maintain acceptable user response time by judiciously allocating CPU resources. What makes this task difficult is that these goals of maximum throughput and minimum response time are often at odds with each other.

Paging Revisited

Paging at first glance may seem to be a rather esoteric concept. However, paging is important to gaining an understanding of the function of CP. This section provides further clarification of the paging function.

VM is designed to make efficient use of the CPU, and one way this is accomplished is through "swapping" between virtual memory and real memory. Real memory is what CP actually has to work with to answer the requests of users, while virtual memory is where pieces of work are stored that are not currently needed. The process of swapping between real and virtual memory is called paging, and working set size is the number of pages that will be required to answer the requests of the virtual machine.

It helps to begin thinking about paging just as one might think of the pages of a book. Suppose that one walks into a library and picks up a large novel that consists of an empty cover. The reader opens the cover and the title page appears. He turns the title page, and it is swept away only to be replaced by page 1. After page 1 is read, this is also swept away, and replaced by page 2. This process could continue indefinitely until the book is completed. The job is finished, but the reader never had to be burdened with thumbing through pages that were already completed, or having to manage a heavy book.

By dividing a user's work into pages, and using the working set size, CP is able to keep one page of it at a time in real memory, and then after it is not needed, the page is sent back into virtual memory and replaced by another page. As a result virtual memory is not cluttered with a lot of waste, and CP is able to accommodate, in a limited amount of space, the work of many users. Again, one page of each user's request is handled at a time, yet many users are handled simultaneously.

A computer generally has 4 to 16 megabytes of storage (above this amount is considered extended architecture). This real memory is broken into 4K pieces, and CP uses these 4K pieces as a basis for mapping out how the virtual machines will be accommodated as they compete for space. During the process of paging, as more space is needed to accommodate another user request, CP keeps track of the pages. It brings pages of one user's request into real memory while swapping out pages of another user's request into virtual memory. CP keeps track of which pages in real memory are active and which ones are least active. Through another algorithm, the inactive pages are swapped out to provide, for example, an 8K piece of real memory.

This seems like a very efficient process and it is. There are dangers, however. For example, if CP is being inundated with requests from many online users, the paging process may become so rapid that this is all CP has time to do. If there is not enough real memory available, then CP has to do a lot of going back and forth between real memory and virtual storage to try and accommodate everyone. As discussed previously, there is contention in the CPU. Response time becomes ridiculous because CP is so busy paging that no work is getting done. This is referred to as "thrashing."

Referring back to CP problem state and CP supervisor state, paging is a supervisor state function, while doing the actual work required to answer user requests is problem state. So when the system is thrashing, there is an imbalance between the two states. Supervisor state is far outweighing problem state, and system overhead has gone wild.

Another way to think of paging is that CP promises all users — all virtual machines — that each has control of the whole computer. Thus, CP overextends itself. However, through paging, CP is able to provide the illusion that this promise has been kept by balancing real memory between the users, swapping unneeded portions, or pages, out to virtual memory. This virtual memory is DASD storage that CP has access to for maintaining this process. This is DASD dedicated for CP's use as a paging area that is defined during the SYSGEN process. If too little has been allocated, this will also result in system degradation if CP does not have a large enough area to swap inactive users into.

A good example of paging might be the user who logs on to the system and then goes off for awhile. Suppose the user has logged on, edited a few files, then decides to take a break for a few minutes. If the system is loaded with many active users, this user may be "swapped" out to the area of DASD used by CP as virtual memory. In other words, the user is paged out. But CP remembers where the user was placed. When the user returns and presses the ENTER key to make another request, CP basically goes out to the virtual memory area and brings the user back into real memory so that the request can be met.

If CP is, for example, 170% committed, this is not necessarily a problem. CP has determined the working set size of each of these users, and providing that each does not make a request at the same time, each will be accommodated by CP through the paging process. The users won't even realize that they are sharing a limited resource with many others; that is, unless all these users press ENTER at the same time. The result is that the system is "brought to its knees."

One of the tuning knobs available as a a result of performance monitoring is the ability to set the maximum working set size of each user's virtual machine. This keeps each user from making too large a request at one time, and eases paging activity.

Tuning the VM CPU

Tuning the CPU in the VM environment is a challenge for a number of reasons. In systems that may be reaching maximum capacity, the paging and memory subsystems need to be closely monitored. In line with the basic philosophy of VM, the Scheduler is biased in favor of short interactive transactions over long CPU-intensive transactions. The Scheduler attempts to avoid "thrashing," the loading and unloading of pages for long transactions, by estimating the required working sets ahead of time to improve the throughput of longer transactions.

As discussed earlier, various adjustments are made to the Run List and priority. The net effect is giving virtual machines that require longer CPU time slices ("compute bound" virtual machines) control of the CPU after the I/O bound machines have started their I/O and are waiting to complete. Once a particular virtual machine has been identified as a "CPU hog," the Scheduler moves the machine to a lower position in the Run List in order to improve throughput for the more interactive transactions.

The Scheduler is responsible for ensuring that all virtual machines receive their fair share of the CPU, which is greatly influenced by the virtual machine's priority set in the VM directory. A priority of 64, with a range of zero to 99, is considered normal. The VM operating system provides the system programmer with a number of special CP commands, such as CP SET PRIORITY, that serve as tuning knobs in manipulating the CPU time slice algorithm.

Practical Tuning Considerations

The tuning process needs to begin with adequate measurement. There are a number of software and hardware tools available on the market to assist in monitoring internal operating system statistics. However, it should not be overlooked that the relationship between the virtual system and the real system will influence these numbers and will be different for each installation and configuration. The user population is different in every organization, as are the demands made on the VM environment. Thus, performance analysis and tuning must be continually evaluated based on considerations including:

- Is the response time and service provided to the users satisfactory?
- If not, can the problem be attributed to resource contention?
- What components of the system are preventing resource delivery?
- What can be done to the system to improve the situation?

In order to effectively answer these questions, measures and data must be available that indicate and describe how virtual systems and CP manage the load, the utilization, and the contention, all of these observable due to the interaction of real and virtual resources. These terms must first be defined in relation to the types of measurements needed.

"Work" may be considered a transaction, or a request for a particular resource to perform a certain function. A "load" may be defined in terms of the rate at which work arrives at a system resource. Load is dependent on a number of variables such as the speed at which a resource can perform its work. Consequently, data must be adjusted site by site to be valid. If a system were truly balanced, the load that any resource could handle would be strictly proportional to the speed of the device. In real world applications, this is rarely the case. Systems are never truly "balanced" and there are usually resources that cannot deliver service as fact as requests for work are received.

"Contention" occurs because work requests are waiting for a resource to become available. Measures of contention are reflected by data that indicate "best" service relative to "actual" service or, in the worst case, system degradation. It is the objective of performance monitoring to determine which resource is responsible for the actual contention and to relate that to the expense of increasing the capacity of that resource.

"Utilization" is usually expressed in terms of a percentage that represents the amount of time that a particular resource is busy relative to the actual elapsed time. Often the data reflecting utilization is expressed in terms of "thresholds" that are assumed in the absence of contention.

Any assessment of load, contention, and utilization must be dependent upon the installation's objectives, configuration, and capacity of the system. For example, if a user experiences a 3 to 5 second response time at the terminal, a measure of whether this was "good" or "bad" is really dependent on the application. A 3 or 5 second response time for an exhaustive database search might be fantastic. On the other hand, if all the user is doing is waiting for a simple edit function to occur in a word processing application, the situation might be considered intolerable.

Most measures of CPU utilization concentrate on the percent of time that the processor is "busy." However, this can be misleading. The CPU can be busy performing the Supervisor functions normally thought of as "overhead" (managing main storage and other system resources) or busy running a virtual machine (consuming processor time) in Problem State. Therefore, CPU utilization is the resulting value of both the amount of time that the processor is busy in Supervisor state as compared with the amount of time that the processor spends running in Problem state.

It is common mistake to attribute too much value to CPU utilization statistics alone. For example, you can't predict "demand" from total CPU utilization. As the Supervisor state approaches its upper limits for the particular processor, a degradation in Problem state will start to occur, reflecting the possibility of thrashing. The objective in tuning the CPU is to maximize the use of running in Problem state, not approaching the limit of total CPU utilization. Problem state is influenced by the job mix, the type of task requested and the priority assigned to the virtual machine. If tuning efforts result in more time spent in Problem state, the efforts are a success. CPU utilization measures become meaningful only when comparing total CPU utilization relative to the percent of time spent in CP Supervisor state (CPS) and the percent of time spent in pure Problem state (CP).

The rate at which tasks arrive at the CPU within a specified amount of time reflects the CPU load. For example, this might be the number of tasks per second. The dispatchable task count or, more properly, the number of virtual machines added to the dispatch list may also serve as an indication of the CPU load. Contention, on the other hand, is represented by the number of virtual machines that are competing for concurrent access to the CPU. One indication of contention is to take into consideration the number of runnable users. However, such a measurement should also take into consideration CPU Wait state, especially when the amount of CPU wait for long running tasks is excessive compared with the amount of processor execution time.

Primary storage is difficult to measure in strict terms of utilization, load, and contention because this resource has the highest replication factor in the entire system. Storage load may be expressed as the amount of frames that are required at any one time, while storage utilization compares the amount of primary storage required with the amount of storage available. Again, any absolute values are misleading and should be analyzed as relative measures. Yet, "magic" numbers or "rules of thumb" suggest that for most single processor configurations a value of no more than 70% should be obtained for the ratio of the sum of the working sets (SUMWSS) over the sum of available frames (APAGES).

CPU and main storage have been analyzed in terms of the relative importance of examining system wide utilization, load, and contention. It is beyond the scope of this book to relate these concepts to other important aspects of the system such as I/O and DASD analysis. The need for the examination of any aspect of performance must be based on the fundamental objective of improving service and delivery of the VM system to users.

Input/Output Control

The area of input/output control is another key area for performance monitoring in the VM environment. I/O is most simply the process of putting information into the machine and taking it out, and involves the use of devices that include tape drives, printers, and especially, DASD (Direct Access Storage Devices). Input and output can be a very smooth process until too many users attempt to access a limited number of devices. Then, the same kinds of contention, and

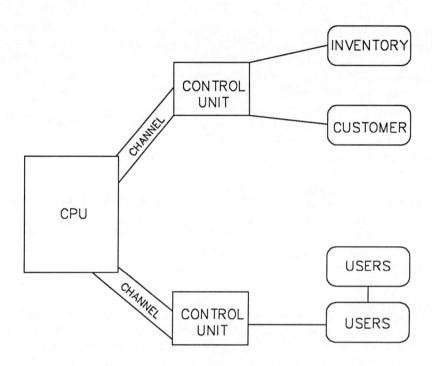

Figure 6-3 The CPU and DASD I/O device connection

poor response time, can result just as when there are problems in CPU utilization.

Accessing I/O Devices

The major consideration in I/O control is storage, or DASD. Though the mechanics of DASD are discussed more fully in the DASD management chapter, DASD will also be used as the point of departure for discussing how CP manages the input/output process. When there is a problem in I/O, it is often DASD-related. Perhaps users cannot get to the information that they want quickly enough, or they cannot store information quickly enough. The natural conclusion is that there is not enough storage space. However, the problem may not be one of quantity, but of how the DASD is distributed.

A DASD is a mechanism that stores information. As discussed in Chapter 5 on security, users are assigned space on a DASD in the form of sections, called minidisks. Other corporate information that is shared by users is also stored through minidisks on DASD to which users have access. Also, CP utilizes its own DASD for various purposes. Depending on the needs of the organization, a large number of DASD may be connected to the CPU. A DASD is a real device just like a printer; it performs a specific function and is accessed as needed, under the control of CP.

Figure 6-3 is a diagram of a CPU, illustrating the connections between the CPU and the DASD I/O devices.

Much of the I/O process is a function of 370 architecture, and under VM this is managed by CP. 370 architecture features an I/O subsystem which, though very complex, handles the function of inputting or outputting information in a three step process. The following is a very basic description of the I/O process.

1. The I/O process begins with a "start I/O." This is issued after the program running has issued a series of commands for one of the I/O devices to begin the series. For example, if a user has entered a command to query a database, the program which accomplishes this would issue a command to access the appropriate database for the user. CP would intercept the command and issue the start I/O to access the DASD on which this database is located.

2. The start I/O command would then be sent to an I/O channel. As illustrated in the diagram above, various channels are connected to the CPU, and CP would route this command to the channel that leads to the information that the user wishes to access. The channel passes the command to the I/O control unit, which directly controls the use of the I/O device. In this case the control unit would take the information from DASD and send it back to the channel.

3. When the operation is complete, the information goes from the channel to real memory (the "active" memory of the CPU) to be sent to the user's virtual machine. The I/O channel causes an I/O interrupt, with status bits stored into real memory. The data would then appear on the user's terminal. This causes the user also to be informed that the I/O is complete.

The start I/O is important in that when it is issued, the channel actually takes over, accessing the control units, and freeing up CP to continue with other user requests. In effect, the channel offloads the CPU. Because each I/O device can perform only one operation at a time, the channel's role is critical in sending the requests to the control unit, which can manage the actual devices as each device performs one task at a time. In this respect, the control units are like "little computers" for the CPU, managing the devices so that the CPU can continue with other work. Without the channels, the CPU would be backed up with requests, waiting for devices to free up, and other work would not get done.

Each channel operates independently of the other channels, in terms of software, so they can all operate simultaneously. The channels really act as pipes, taking data from the CPU to the control unit, and then back. A CPU can handle many channels, and the control unit attached to each channel can support multiple tape drives or disk drives, also with the capability of positioning each one of these devices simultaneously.

The control unit, also called the controller, manages DASD or other devices. Once the control unit receives data from the channel, it decides what to do with it. With DASD, for example, a user may have requested a file that is currently being read from a DASD unit. The control unit will hold a command, wait until the file being read is completed, then send that file back to the channel to be handed back to real memory where it is in turn intercepted by CP and provided for the user. In the meantime, once the DASD is no longer being accessed, the next command that the control unit is holding will be executed. Thus the control unit is able to act as traffic manager, taking information from the devices, such as DASD, and passing it to the channel, as well as giving work to the devices.

At any rate, with time spans of milliseconds, a lot of work can get done at a very fast rate.

Sources of I/O Problems

Because of the critical role that the channel plays in offloading the CPU, it is important, with many users accessing a variety of devices, that an adequate number of channels be available to handle the I/O demands of the environment. And it is easy to see how many organizations assume that a new CPU upgrade is indicated when the problem is really one of channel contention.

Channel contention is basically the result of too many requests being sent back and forth through the same channel. By adding channels and spreading out these user requests for device access over more available channels, this may solve the problem. However, the issue can also be one in which there is an adequate number of channels, but a poor arrangement of DASD. As discussed, information that is shared by users is also stored on DASD. If the DASD containing widely used data is all contained on the same set of DASD, while another set of DASD contains information that is seldom used, then there is an imbalance that will result in an overloaded channel and an underused channel.

For example, the organization's inventory control information and customer information might be contained on the same DASD string, while less often accessed data owned by individual users is contained on another string. (A string is a term that generally refers to eight DASD devices connected to the same control unit). This arrangement may be a source of contention if inventory control and customer information are both frequently accessed. The result of contention in the channels is poor response time. Users will have to wait just to have their request get through the channel. By spreading users and data out among available channels, no one channel is inundated too heavily with requests. If a channel is busy more than 35% of the time, response time is at risk. By balancing the load of the channels, their efficiency is maximized. Thus, the inventory control information might be stored on DASD located on a different channel, to balance channel load.

Overall load balancing is an important consideration in keeping I/O in check. Some work requires an inordinate amount of I/O, major database searches, for example, and these tasks must be spread out over the course of the day. If the system is being used 24 hours, this work can be spread out even further. Job mix depends on what the system is being used for — for purely interactive, production, or batch work, or database applications. During the day in particular, if work is not distributed evenly, the I/O throughput will be dramatically reduced. Workload balancing is discussed in Chapter 7.

The DASD itself can also be a source of contention. Advances in technology have increased the speed at which data stored on a DASD can be accessed, but where data is located on a DASD can affect the overall speed. In addition, DASD that is cluttered with old, unused files, can also lengthen access time. These issues are discussed further under DASD Management in Chapter 8.

Monitoring in VM

Performance monitoring involves the collection and measurement of data about system performance, analyzing workload characteristics and actual equipment use. This data provides input into decisions regarding the optimization of equipment, as well as user-related issues such as response time. VM provides some built-in capabilities for performance monitoring, and system software products are also available for this purpose. Performance monitoring can be interactive, with a window into current system performance, and it can provide after-the-fact information in the form of reports. These reports generally include a look at what has happened in the system, and possibly include reasons why certain factors are occurring and what can be done to improve performance.

VM/SP has a built-in monitoring capability, in the form of a CP monitor that produces records containing sampling information collected periodically about various events. In and of themselves, these records aren't directly useful. However, in conjunction with system software products, they can provide useful information. The CP monitor is activated with the CP command CP MON ON, through the SYSMON macro in the DMKSYS module in CP. This monitoring facility collects data that is available in CP, and then sends it to a virtual reader. Once this data is collected, it can subsequently be interpreted.

IBM has available two products that make use of the data provided by the CP monitor. One takes the system measurements from CP and turns this data into reports that are more usable than the raw data. This information includes the Resource Availability Index, which provides averages taking into account various IBM statistics factors such as the priority in the execution of tasks. Another product is interactive, taking a snapshot of the current state of affairs in the system, identifying the sources of bottlenecks.

With system software, the potential performance monitoring capabilities are increased greatly. To illustrate these benefits, the VM environment can be compared to a gas station with many pumps, with dials on each of the pumps. These dials could be indicators of various functions, providing performance statistics. Suppose that an attendant sets these dials to zero, just as a system programmer might do when initializing the system.

In a VM system, by starting at zero, it would then be possible to ascertain an optimal performance level that could then be used as a baseline, based on factors including CPU utilization and paging, as well as I/O. With this baseline data, performance monitoring system software can actually freeze data as reference points. Then, if in the future this data exceeds these baseline thresholds, the software can either take an action to correct the situation and bring performance back in line with the baseline, or send a message to the system programming staff to notify them of the problem.

These thresholds may be based on different kinds of statistics. Once the baseline values are known, if a problem occurs during the course of a day, a message can be sent which will direct the technical staff to correct the problem, or the system software can actually make the adjustment. An example of a corrective adjustment might be to adjust the CPU algorithm, perhaps limiting working set size, until response time is back on track. A serious problem, such as channel contention, might require programmer intervention to make I/O adjustments, such as shifting minidisks to less accessed DASD to balance channel load.

To accomplish these tasks, some monitoring system software products hook directly into CP, ignoring the monitor data generated by CP. This results in the products collecting information directly, generating it into CMS files to be presented to the user. This has, potentially, a substantial overhead savings.

An example of the use of performance monitoring system software is in solving the problem of idle users. When there are a large number of users logged on, even when many of them are not actively using the system, there is an increase in supervisor state. CP must still keep these users active. This is a small amount of overhead, but can add up with large numbers of users. A monitor product might have a threshold of, for example, 1 hour for inactive users. Once this threshold is passed the inactive user would be logged off automatically.

From Monitoring to Tuning

Performance tuning in VM has traditionally been very subjective, and a direct result of the expertise available at the installation. As problems such as poor response time became apparent, it has not been uncommon for organizations to simply "throw hardware" at the problem. An upgraded CPU or more CPU has often been a unfortunate alternative to taking the time to correct the problems. Monitoring provides a means of preventive maintenance, pinpointing the actual problems, rather than merely the symptoms, as a basis for taking corrective action.

The performance baseline is really an organization-specific ideal. Tuning is a means of keeping system performance as close to that ideal as possible, even if it means going in and "fixing" the system to bring it back in line with the baseline. Symptoms of performance problems that can potentially be solved with tuning include I/O contention, channel contention, tasks that aren't getting done or are taking to long, and complaints from users. Tuning implies the here-and-now, going in and making adjustments that will show immediate results.

The goal of system tuning is really to optimize the computer resources of the organization, taking the baseline and ironing out the peaks in the workload of the computer to match this baseline, on a 24 hour basis, as closely as possible. This might involve determining current computing load, and when peak usage occurs, and then working with algorithms such as working set size to keep the CPU utilized as effectively as possible. It might also involve monitoring the I/O and physically balancing DASD to keep the channels from becoming overloaded.

The here-and-now orientation of tuning also demonstrates the dual side of data center management. The technical support staff can tune system parameters to derive certain desired benefits, but management must decide what these benefits will be. This implies a willingness of the technical staff to work within directives set by management, with an ability to look at the "business case" side to a decision. The directives must go beyond the technical perspective in solving organizational problems based on an understanding that the computer resources must meet the needs of users.

Performance monitoring is also a management consideration. This also implies that management understands the constraints involved in tuning. Good tuning can prolong the hardware by keeping it running at its maximum as long as possible. However, there comes a time when hardware resources simply must be expanded. Management can assist in solving performance problems by encouraging users to use the off-peak hours, perhaps through building in a rate structure (described in chapter 11 on system accountinga.

The use of the term MIPS is an example of the expectations that management can place on the technical staff. MIPS, an abbreviation for millions of instructions per second, represents the ideal level of performance that a given machine should be able to provide. This is an average, often provided by a sales rep, which may very well be valid for the average organization. However, few organizations fall into this category. In fact, many refer to this term as being an abbreviation for "misleading information about processor speeds." As an ideal for I/O performance, it is fine. But installations have their own unique characteristics which make this average an unrealistic expectation.

Tuning remains very much a labor-intensive process, requiring high level systems programmer expertise. System software products certainly aid in this process, particularly those that analyze not only the present state but provide a perspective on the past as well as the future. This kind of information provides a basis for more educated decision making. Monitoring system software is moving in the direction of both correcting performance problems to keep the system operating close to the baseline and notifying the systems staff when there is a problem that cannot be corrected.

As performance monitoring system software evolves technologically, it will be a key to the achievement of the "operatorless environment" necessary for optimal Departmental Computing.

Performance Monitoring in the Departments

The proponents of Departmental Computing often talk about this concept in terms of the operatorless environment. This implies that the departmental processors, particularly the minicomputer, will operate without the need for extensive system support, including both technical and operator support. For example, an operator would not be needed to "babysit" for the machine, loading tapes, etc. And a technical staff would not be required to perform services such as trouble shooting and software maintenance. Directory management, for example, could be accomplished from the central site, or through a non technical manager.

Performance monitoring is an important issue for the departments. The basic performance monitoring considerations are much the same, except that a high level of automation of performance monitoring at the departmental level is needed, as well as connectivity with the central site. Machines must be able to essentially monitor themselves, with the ability to make decisions and carry these decisions out. Through system software, the organization essentially establishes

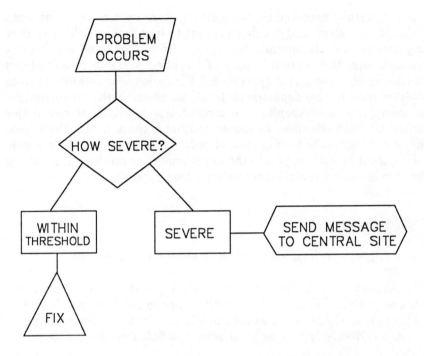

Figure 6-4 The departmental system monitor decision process

rules of thumb and sets system defaults, while the software basically carries these decisions out. For example, if excessive paging occurs during peak times, the monitor product might reduce working set size, or log off inactive users after a shorter period of inactivity, until the peak has passed.

Because the central site in a departmental situation will be responsible for any required maintenance of the departmental machines, the monitor installed on the departmental must be able to measure the importance of decisions. For example, any adjustments made by the monitor over a 24-hour period should be communicated, through a report, to the central site. The individual responsible for maintenance should be able to come into work in the morning, and look through a report that lists any adjustments that were made to each departmental machine over the recent 24 hours, with the adjustment sorted in descending order by priority. With the number 10 signifying a major problem and 1 being minor, the list could begin with the tens. This list can then be used as a basis for making any needed manual adjustments. In addition, some problems in performance might be so critical as to require immediate attention from a systems programmer, and in these cases the monitor would need to notify the central site of severe problems. Thus, the departmental system monitor would go through a decision process as illustrated in Figure 6-4.

It is generally accepted that 370 architecture requires a fair amount of support, with a "body" being present to handle any difficulty that might come up. Historically finding qualified personnel has been a problem, and the current supply of qualified systems programmers has dwindled. Monitoring systems software allows for this expertise to be leveraged at the department level, automating the more routine considerations and keeping the central site apprised of any major problems. With advances in communications, there is also the potential of subsequently tuning on a remote basis, from the central site, rather than having to go into the departments to do this, thus taking the idea of the operatorless environment a step further.

Chapter Summary

The following is a summary of the discussion of Chapter 6.

- Performance monitoring involves analyzing system performance in the here and now, particularly with regard to CPU utilization and I/O control. The user orientation of VM requires that resources be used as effectively as possible to accommodate multiple online users.
- Effective CPU utilization involves a balance between Supervisor state, which is system overhead, and Problem state, the processing of user requests.
- Problems in controlling the flow of I/O can be a result of inadequate DASD, but can also be a result of inadequate load balancing or lack of available channels.
- VM provides the basis for monitoring, but this must be supplemented through the use of monitoring system software.
- Departmental Computing by definition implies minimal availability of technical personnel in the departments, and this creates special challenges for VM monitoring.

7

Balancing the Workload

During peak hours of system activity, when multiple online users simultaneously make demands on the limited resources of the system, the result can be excessive paging by CP, and poor system response time. In non peak hours, on the other hand, the same system may be underutilized. Through workload balancing, CPU resources can be better managed through scheduling and batch operations, and peaks and valleys in the system load can be leveled.

The Overloaded CPU

The major issue in workload balancing is trying to get the most out of the information resources, 24 hours per day. It is not uncommon for an organization to utilize its information resources only when employees are on site. The work of a 24-hour period is "scrunched" into an 8-hour shift, and the computer sits idle during the other 16 hours of the day. Figure 7-1 illustrates the workload situation in almost any VM installation.

This is often referred to as a "double hump" level of CPU utilization. There is a peak at 10 a.m., when users are hitting their morning stride, and then another peak at 2 p.m. after lunch. From 8 p.m. until 8 a.m. the next morning, there is very little use.

To meet the demands of peak performance periods, at 10 a.m. and again at 2 p.m., an organization may seek to purchase a CPU that is more powerful than the one currently in use. This, however, is a realistic option only if the CPU is in peak use around the clock. Most likely, an upgrade is not needed. The organization already has additional computing resources available, namely, the resources that are untapped during non peak hours.

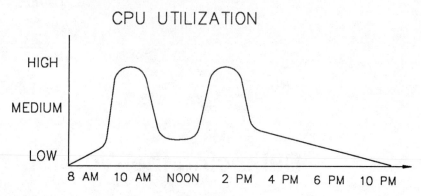

Figure 7-1 The daily CPU utilization cycle

Computing power is very much like electricity in that it cannot be "stored up." If it is not used when it is available, it is gone. An organization whose computing resources are untapped during non peak periods is wasting these resources and, hence, wasting money. When a CPU upgrade is made solely on the basis of current peak demand, what is purchased in addition to this capability is, potentially, additional capacity that will remain largely unused. Thus, even more money is wasted. If a large organization already has the CPU with the most capacity, then users will have to be divided among multiple machines. This creates a whole new set of problems.

A better solution is to level out the double humps over the 24 hours of the day, to supplement the computing power of the peak periods with the underutilized computing power of the non-peak periods. This is the job of workload balancing. At the departmental levels, workload balancing may also be a means of spreading work out among departmental machines for even more effective utilization. By optimizing the current use of the machine, effective workload balancing can delay a hardware upgrade or even reduce the hardware requirements of an organization.

Obstacles to Workload Balancing

Lack of excessive controls over users is both the beauty and curse of VM, the negative side being that one user has the potential of "taking over" the system. Native VM does not really offer much in the way of workload balancing because, again, VM was not originally designed for a heavy production environment. In fact, VM is not really very fail-safe in terms of preventing a user from "nailing" the system.

The potential problems that users requiring large amounts of real memory can cause for other users was outlined in Chapter 6. There are many subtle ways in which a single user can dominate the system.

A user with a memory-intensive application can cause the system to page heavily. This paging can increase to the point that other users on the system will not be able to run their tasks. And so the other users sit. A heavily looped program, depending on the scheduling algorithm generated for the machine, has the potential of taking over the machine.

One user's need to complete a task may very well be at the expense of another user. Thus, the freedom from control available to users in the VM environment, coupled with the potentially excessive demands generated during times of peak usage, can result in VM being "brought to its knees." Then everybody loses.

Options for Workload Balancing

The Performance Monitoring discussion in Chapter 6 included Workload Balancing solutions revolving around tuning options, including the manipulation of working set size. The focus in this chapter is on scheduling and batch options for managing the workload of the CPU. As opposed to going into the system and making complex adjustments in algorithms, balancing workload through job scheduling is basically a function of system software. Batch operations can be performed either through VM system software or a guest operating system.

Scheduling

VM does not offer much in the area of scheduling for multiple online users. Once users are logged on, VM has excellent facilities for handling the sharing of the CPU among these users. What native VM does not offer is a user-friendly facility for doing work on a user's behalf while that user is still logged on, or for doing repetitive work. For example, a user cannot initiate a lengthy database search, send it off to be completed and then continue on with another task. His virtual machine is "tied up" until the database search is completed.

It is for this reason that native VM is considered rather limited when it comes to being a production environment. An example of standard production environment tasks might be a financial report that must be produced weekly, or the biweekly running of the corporate payroll. These tasks can be accomplished under native VM, but only if an individual physically logs on to the system and initiates the job on a virtual machine. These tasks will not run automatically on a continual basis unless manually initiated each time they are needed.

Currently, repetitive work such as that described above must be handled manually. Even if standard tasks are built into a CMS EXEC, which is a series of commands grouped together and used like a macro (a group of command statements grouped together and identified by a name), the user still must log on and invoke the EXEC in order to perform the task. This is a workable solution until the person responsible for this task misses a day of work, or forgets to invoke the EXEC that initiates the task. The result is that the job does not get done.

In addition to these standard repetitive tasks there is a large amount of work that is done during standard working hours that does not necessarily have to be completed during that time, the large database search being an example. Work that is not needed until the next day can be put off, through scheduling capability, to the second or third shifts when in most cases the machines are sitting idle. The work can be completed during this time, and will be waiting for the users when they arrive at work the next morning.

Once an installation has the job stream up and running, scheduling is generally an area that is often ignored. The reasons for ignoring the potential of scheduling can be summarized as a desire to leave well enough alone:

• The applications are running adequately.
• There is a lack of expertise on how to redesign the system flow.
• Users are comfortable with the flow, even with poor response time.

The result of this avoidance is the type of CPU utilization illustrated at the beginning of the chapter, with variations of extremes between overutilization and underutilization.

System software that performs the scheduling function accomplishes this through automatically logging on the user's virtual machine through the CP AUTOLOG command, and then executing the request that the user scheduled. Thus, the work is being done through the user's virtual machine, but without the user having to be present while this occurs. Figure 7-2 illustrates how this scheduling occurs with the use of a service virtual machine.

The request is scheduled through the system software product, and sent to a service virtual machine. This is a virtual machine that is under the control of the system software product. The request is stored in a log file and executed at the appropriate time, by a process in which the service machine autologs the user's virtual machine and initiates the request for the user.

Scheduling capability, offered through scheduling utilities from IBM, as well as system software through third party vendors, offers various options. Some of these options include being able to indicate the date and time at which the request should be initiated, and depending on the product offering, options for the automatic rescheduling of the request, on a biweekly basis, for example.

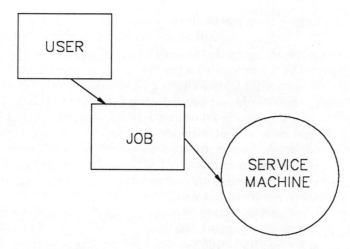

Figure 7-2 Passing a request to a service machine for off-hours processing

The monthly payroll run would be an example of an application for a scheduling product. Parameters are entered which specify the request, the time that the request is to be run, and when the request should be rescheduled for execution. This task would normally be scheduled for a time during which the requesting user is not logged on, 3 a.m., for example.

A drawback to scheduling is that the task may not be performed if the user is currently logged on, because it is the user's virtual machine that is autologged for the performance of the task. If the user in the above example were to work a late night to complete an emergency job, causing him to still be logged on at 3 a.m. on the night of the standard payroll run, then this task would not be completed. The task would also not be completed if the user disconnects instead of logging off at the end of the day, which leaves the virtual machine in essentially an inactive status without being fully logged off. Also if the user forgets to log off at the end of the day, the virtual machine would still be technically under his control, and the task would not be initiated.

Some software products solve this problem by indicating to the user that a request is about to be initiated, if the user is logged on (which the user may cancel), or continue attempts to initiate the request until it is feasible. Also, some installations create virtual machines that are used for one task only, with a userid called PAYROLL, for example. This virtual machine is then autologged by the scheduler.

With scheduling capabilities these resource-consuming functions are offloaded to the times when demand is lowest on the CPU. The double humps are leveled.

Batch Processing Under VM

With the interactive capabilities of VM supplemented by the ability to schedule tasks for nonpeak hours, the need for some type of batch capability is inhibited. But it does not go away. Batch implies not only the ability to schedule major tasks during the off hours, but also the ability of a user to perform these major tasks while still being logged on to his or her own virtual machine, continuing the performance of interactive work. A user may need to complete a major database search or task involving multiple calculations by the end of the day, while also being able to continue with other work. Scheduling work for the off hours will not meet this need.

Some installations solve this problem through system software that offers batch capability, while others use a guest operating system for this purpose. Both options will be considered in this section.

An example of a need for batch capabilities that can be solved by the use of system software would be a construction company that is involved in bidding on jobs. Proposals could be developed and then sent off for batch processing, to perform any needed calculations and printing. While that is occurring, other proposals could be developed online, and sent off for batch processing. Thus, what could be a cumbersome process, waiting for each proposal to be processed before another one is started, or using a scheduler and waiting until the next day, is performed in much less time. The batch system software is as much a production tool as a utility.

System software that offers batch capabilities performs this function through the use of its own worker machines. Rather than scheduling the task on the user's virtual machine, it actually performs the task so that the user can go on with other interactive work. Figure 7-3 illustrates the flow between the user and the batch worker machine.

The batch worker machine does not offer the sophisticated scheduling options offered by scheduling system software. It works more like a traditional batch operating system. The user sends the task off to a service virtual machine, where it is placed in a queue to wait for the worker machine. The worker machine performs the tasks in a predefined order, based on installation-defined priorities. The service machine maintains a log file which records what was sent to it as well as an option file that stores information about priority. Batch system software generally does not allow users to schedule when and how often the task should be run; this is a scheduling function.

Batch system software offerings differ in how the batch function is performed. Some require extensive Job Control Language which is basically unused in the VM world. This causes the batch function to be very difficult for end users. Others offer functions such as full-screen support, multiple CPU support which is important for a

JOB SUBMISSION/EXECUTION

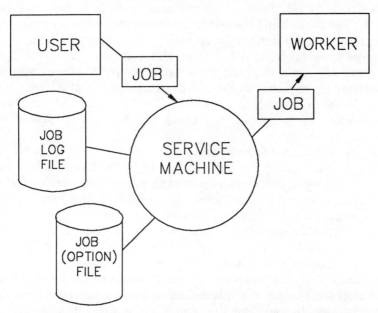

Figure 7-3 The submission and execution process for batch processing

departmental arrangement, and other functions that enhance useability, such as user fluency levels.

Parallel and Serial Processing

Batch processing under VM provides two options for increasing productivity: parallel and serial processing. Though not necessarily mutually exclusive, these options differ in terms of how the batch processing arrangement must be structured, as well as overall impact on the system.

As discussed, batch processing makes it possible to take a large task, send it off to a batch worker machine for batch processing, and free up the virtual machine for other tasks. Parallel processing implies taking this large task, and dividing it into smaller tasks that do not depend on each other for completion, and then submitting these smaller tasks off to multiple worker machines. Thus, instead of a large task being gradually processed by one machine, parallel processing allows the overall task to be processed faster because the pieces of the large task are processed simultaneously — parallel to each other.

An example of a large task would be a major statistical analysis, with forecasting based on various significance levels. Rather than develop one task that would provide results, for example, at five different levels of significance, this analysis could be divided into five smaller tasks. Each different significance could be a separate task. Then the five tasks could be sent to batch worker machines and potentially processed simultaneously, requiring one-fifth of the time.

A large task might still be divided into smaller tasks for serial processing. However, the number of batch worker machines would be limited, and these pieces might still be processed one at a time — in a series. Serial processing implies that there is a limited number of batch worker machines, so that tasks still have to be placed in a queue for processing.

With the virtual machine concept it is easy for users to forget that they really are sharing the CPU with many other users. A benefit of serial processing is that it can be used to reduce the workload of the CPU through limiting user access to certain applications. For example, access to a database management system could be limited to batch use only, with one batch worker machine designated to handle these requests. As a result, two or three users involved in major database searches would not be allowed to cause massive system degradation. Each of these user's requests would go the batch worker, with the tasks placed in a queue and processed one at a time. The work gets done, but without the requests of a small number of users bringing the rest of the system to its knees.

Serial processing solves many problems. Potentially major tasks can be designated as "batch-only" so that the rights of other users are thus protected. During nonpeak hours, the number of batch worker machines dedicated to the potentially CPU-intensive software applications could be increased. This would allow for parallel processing when the system is under less demand.

Essentially, the reasoning behind these two options is the prevention of system degradation. Parallel processing certainly optimizes user productivity, but multiple batch worker machines, in addition to multiple online users, can place a potential drain on system resources. Serial processing controls the demand on the system, limiting the amount of batch processing that can occur, and thus throttles back demand as a means of keeping interactive users a priority. Figure 7-4 illustrates the difference between parallel and serial processing.

The potential drain caused by parallel processing is further compounded by the presence of online users who are also competing for CPU resources. Serial processing places these tasks in a queue so that the drain on CPU resources caused by batch processing never gets out of hand.

Subdividing large tasks into smaller, noninterdependent tasks provides a means for the organization to alternate between parallel and serial processing. For example, during the peak hours, three batch workers can be available for batch processing. Tasks will be sent to these machines and be queued. During the nonpeak hours, the number of batch machines can be expanded to 10. This keeps the peak

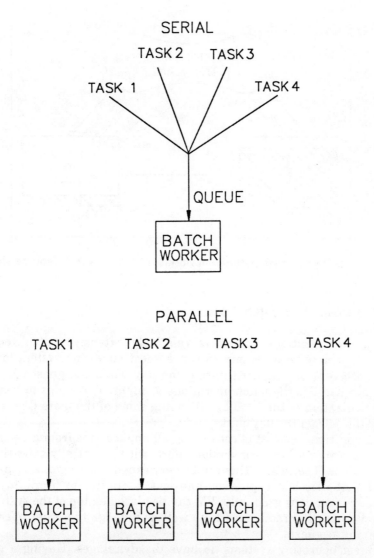

Figure 7-4 Serial vs. parallel batch processing

hours uncongested for interactive use. A further option is provided through the use of site-defined job classes. For example, CPU-intensive tasks can be assigned a job class of B, while less CPU-intensive tasks are assigned a job class of S. Based on the different system demands made by these job classes, 10 batch worker machines could be made available for less demanding Class S tasks, while 2 batch worker machines are made available for the larger Class B tasks. The number of Class B machines could increase during the nonpeak hours. This assures even more efficient system use by a level of parallel processing for small tasks while processing larger tasks in a serial mode to prevent them from dominating the CPU.

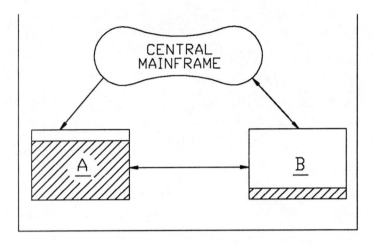

Figure 7-5 Balancing departmental workload through CPU-resource sharing

Using a Guest for Batch Work

For organizations who have relatively extensive batch requirements, it may be necessary to run a guest operating system for this purpose. VM can be used during the day while the guest operating system handles the batch operations at night. This helps to level out the utilization of the CPU by offloading some of the more CPU-intensive tasks from the day shift.

In addition, the cost of converting all applications from a batch system to VM is a large conversion effort, with potentially extensive replacement of software. This can be very expensive. Organizations may find that it is less expensive, and less disruptive to users, to make these conversions gradually. VM can be placed on top of the system, to handle both interactive work as well as manage the other operating systems as guests.

Guest operating systems do have disadvantages. Having a guest, such as MVS, means the addition of another license fee. Also there is increased system overhead as VM manages both users and the operating system. A further drawback is that there are added personnel costs involved in keeping added system programmer staff to install and maintain the guest operating system.

Balancing Departmental Workloads

Departmental Computing, rather than being a workload balancing problem, actually offers the opportunity for increased workload balancing for the entire organization. The 9370 in the department provides true power at the department level, providing the horsepower for departments to get their work done. In addition, with an interconnected system, resource utilization can be enhanced by in effect distributing workloads throughout the network. A primary use of the 9370 will be to provide good interactive response time, and offloading workload will assure that this happens. Figure 7-5 illustrates a departmental situation which could be solved by workload balancing. With a number of processors (9370s, for example) on the system, Processor A is very busy while a processor in another department, Processor B, is not being used at all. With connectivity, these processors could be located in the departments at the same site, or across the country. Processor B is being wasted because of excess capacity while tasks on Processor A are being delayed because there is not enough horsepower to support them.

With interconnected processors the CPU that is underutilized can essentially go out and solicit work from other nodes (processors) in the system. Processor B can solicit Processor A, for example, for large tasks. Processor A can then tag certain uncompleted tasks, the tag being a means of keeping track of them, and then send them on to Processor B for processing. When the processing is completed, the results can be sent back to Processor A. This system can be set up such that soliciting is done by job class, so that only work based on certain factors, such as large tasks, or high priority tasks, or less sensitive tasks, are sent outside of the department.

This scenario assumes both interconnectivity between the machines, as well as system software which provides peer-to-peer sharing among multiple CPUs. Large tasks could also be sent up to the central mainframe in a similar scenario. Workload balancing through interconnected CPUs could minimize the impact of power outages. When one machine breaks down, work can be routed to another. By the same token, preventive maintenance for a given machine could be done as work is routed to another machine.

Multiple CPU support allows the option of distributing software packages to specific machines without having to have these packages loaded on each departmental machine. This saves on overhead for the departmental CPUs as well as potentially saving on licensing costs. For example, those departments with extensive database applications might have a copy of a database management system loaded on them. Departments with less extensive database needs would not have a resident database management system. These departments would instead route database tasks to other departments for processing, with the results being routed back afterwards. This is utilizing the same principle as described in the above example, only this routing would occur automatically for database applications.

In addition to the potential savings in software licensing costs, sharing departmental applications assures more optimal use of the packages that are installed.

Routing of work between multiple CPUs can be done either manually or automatically. In the database situation above, for example, a manual routing might not only specify the task to be done but also specify where it should go to be completed. This can also be accomplished automatically, which is more in keeping with the needs of users. Transparency is important in Departmental Computing, and the less the user has to be involved in decisions such as this, or even be aware of them, the better.

There are drawbacks to distributed workload balancing. For one thing, a multisite setup is very complicated, especially if providing the level of transparency in which the user does not even know where her task was ultimately routed for processing. In fact, even if a user has assumed that a task has gone to a specific department for processing, this may have been altered by the system if that machine was also occupied. The task may have been solicited by yet another CPU and sent off to another location. Tasks being sent off are tagged at the local machine, but this does not necessarily guard against any eventuality. If, for example, the machine to which work was routed goes down in the middle of the processing the task, it may take some time before the situation is discovered and the task placed back on track.

In the standard Departmental Computing scenario, there will not be a departmental operator who can undertake the search for routed tasks that may have been lost in the system. Even if there would be an operator, he would most likely only be able to control his own machine. This situation is potentially very complex and may require a global operator at the central site who can perform this function for all departments.

The interpersonal issues should also not be ignored in considering the balancing of workloads at the department level. These issues can become much more complicated. In the traditional organizational situation in which a large CPU is shared among many users, sharing the CPU is anonymous. Users may be aware that someone on the system is dragging it down, but most likely not be aware of who that individual is. At the departmental level, users are not only aware of the heavy resource users, they are working face to face with them. This may lead to more direct conflicts over how the departmental CPU is used, and it might also encourage members of the work group to be more cooperative.

Some education will be required to help users understand both the limitations of the departmental processor, and how to optimize these resources through various kinds of workload balancing. The departmental environment is essentially a production environment, and it is important that users learn to take an active role.

Chapter Summary

These major points were discussed in Chapter 7.

* The workload levels of the VM environment are subject to the whims of users, with peak utilization occurring during the day shift, especially at 10 a.m. and 2 p.m.
* Workload balancing can be accomplished through scheduling heavy resource-consuming tasks for the evening and night hours, through autologging the user's virtual machine.
* Batch operations may also be needed to free up a user's virtual machine to allow him or her to continue with interactive processing while a large task is completed, and this can be achieved either through system software of a guest operating system.
* The departmental environment provides opportunities for increased organizational workload balancing, through distributing both software packages and workloads among departmental processors.

8

Managing DASD

The issue of DASD is critical in the VM environment, with user demand for this resource growing by leaps and bounds as they integrate the computer into their daily tasks. Accompanying increased use is a need for more and more storage space. The function of the Direct Access Storage Device is discussed, with a perspective on the issue of DASD management.

The Hungry Beast

A common perception about the VM operating system is that it requires large amounts of DASD. CP does require DASD, but the major DASD consumers are users. Interactive processing implies that data is readily available to be accessed, not off on a tape somewhere. This availability requires DASD. As users have become more comfortable with storing information online, the result has been increased demand for DASD.

The cost of DASD is declining with new technology, thus reducing the cost per megabyte of online storage. But that only means that users will grab even more of it. With new technology, DASD is also becoming more reliable. But this means that organizations will gradually rely on tape less and keep more information on DASD. As it becomes cheaper in relation to other storage mediums, it becomes more popular. Consequently, the demand is growing.

DASD is still not free. Supply is limited, with one user's demand potentially impacting how much DASD is available to another user. In addition, there are transaction costs involved with DASD use as minidisks are created, changed, and deleted. Thus, DASD use has implications for both organizational power, with some departments, and some

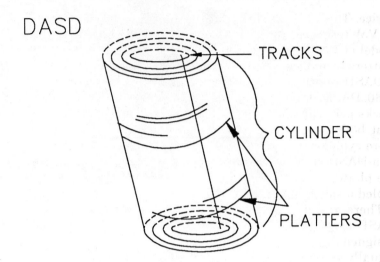

Figure 8-1 The structure of a DASD device

users, being entitled to more DASD than others, and it is an economic issue. Of course, there are those who contend that power is economics.

As with any resource, the ultimate issue is one of supply and demand. The issue in DASD management is to understand how DASD is used, how it is being allocated, and what can be done to use this resource as economically as possible.

Defining DASD

DASD, the Direct Access Storage Device, is often assumed to be a mythical entity that sits inside of the computer somewhere, holding on to information. The minidisk concept promotes this because with each user having a portion of storage associated with his virtual machine, the location of the storage becomes abstract, and even appears limitless. To understand how to manage this resource it is important to view DASD as a real device, just as tape drives and printers are real devices.

In most operating system environments, DASD is defined in cylinders and tracks. Figure 8-1 illustrates the shape of a DASD and shows where the cylinders and tracks are located. DASD is cylindrical in shape, and is divided into what appears like platters. Thus, it looks like a stack of records. The data is stored on these platters; there is a tiny bit of space between each of them that is read and writted on by a device that looks like the arm of a record player. Each platter is divided into tracks, again like a record, and a cylinder is that track taken all the way down through the platters. Under VM, a user is allocated a contiguous physical block of the DASD, which is a real device. This is a minidisk. So a user with four cylinders of DASD (or in VM terms, a minidisk of four cylinders) has, depending on the model of DASD, a certain number of tracks taken down through the platters to make up the four cylinders.

DASD comes in different sizes, identified by model numbers. The 3380 DASD, for example, has approximately 500 cylinders with 12 tracks per cylinder. Certain DASD models are dual density, meaning that both sides of the platters can be read, and this provides even more cylinders for storage. A DASD is referred to as a DASD volume or a DASD pack. DASDs are now being built as sealed units, so both the platters and the rotating arm that reads and writes on them are sealed inside the unit.

There are also two types of DASD. Type CKD (Count Key Data) DASD uses the cylinder as the unit of measure, so that each user is assigned a specific number of cylinders of DASD. The amount of space actually associated with a cylinder is different on each model of DASD of the type CKD, so that a cylinder of, for example, 3380 DASD would contain a different amount of actual space than would a cylinder of 3350 DASD. Type FBA (Fixed Block Architecture) DASD uses a block as the unit of measure, with users assigned blocks of space. In contrast to CKD DASD, the actual amount of space associated with a block is the same on all models of FBA DASD. At the time of introduction, IBM's 9370 was designed to use FBA DASD. VM is capable of using either FBA or CKD DASD, while MVS uses only type CKD.

With advances in technology, the definition of a DASD volume is becoming more complicated. With the advent of dual density and now triple density DASD, IBM gives installations the options of supporting these DASD as "logical" devices. Model 3380 DASD, for example, is treated as four volumes of DASD by the operating system even though it is physically one device.

Users are assigned sections of a DASD — minidisks — by address. An address, as was illustrated in the sample of the minidisk statement in the directory entry in Chapter 5, consists of the start location, where the minidisk begins on the DASD, and the amount of cylinders assigned. In VM, the minidisk which stores a user's data is generally identified as the virtual 191 disk, though users will also have data on other minidisks as well. Because this is a section of DASD that belongs to the user alone, the 191 appears to the user, as well as to the operating system, as if it were a whole DASD. Thus, the 191 is a virtual device, rather than being a real device. In general system use, the user is not aware of sharing with other users. The user shares the device but not the space allocated. This can create VM DASD management problems.

Using 191 as a generic term might appear to be confusing with everyone else in the system also having a data disk identified by 191, but this minidisk is unique to each user's virtual machine. Actually, 191 is a virtual address, simulating a real DASD volume. Each of these 191 minidisks is stored on a DASD, but at different addresses as identified in the directory. Thus, in VM each user's virtual machine basically "thinks" that the 191 is a complete DASD volume, and the only one in existence. The minidisk, though a portion of a real device (the DASD volume) is in itself a "make believe" DASD volume. It is a piece of DASD that the virtual machine "thinks" is a complete DASD volume.

As discussed in Chapter 5, it is possible to accidentally give two minidisks the same address, so that the two minidisks overlap. One user might then have the ability to write on the data of the other users. Without an effective DASD mapping utility, which assists the system programmer in locating available DASD to assign to users as minidisk space, the system programmer must manually find places to fit in new minidisks as the user base expands, or move minidisks around on a DASD to find a space large enough. CP itself does not perform verification to make sure that minidisks are being assigned to free space. When adding several minidisks, identifying unique passwords, and setting up appropriate passwords, the chance for error increases.

It is not only users who require DASD. CP has an extensive need for DASD. The CP nucleus which is built during the generation of CP is built in an area of DASD which is loaded into an area of main storage during CP initialization. Checkpoint space is DASD that is used to recover spool files in case of a system crash, and is used during CP initialization. EREP, the Error Recording Program, uses an area of DASD to record hardware errors. The actual recording code of EREP is part of CP while the formatting part of EREP is kept on the DASD. As discussed in Performance Monitoring, an area of DASD is used during paging, to save or restore copies of memory pages that have to be paged out during heavy CPU use.

Additionally, CMS formatted disk space, other software packages, and shared data, such as that stored on databases, also require DASD.

DASD is not a strictly VM issue. The main difference between DASD on VM and DASD in an MVS or DOS environment is that in VM one allocates chunks of space. The space is preallocated to the user. In MVS, when a job is run and the name of an output file is defined, the user specifies how much space will be needed so that the whole cylinder will not be wasted. If the space allocated is exceeded, there are options for gaining more. However, the system controls where the file goes, on which volume. The result is that a user might have data literally spread throughout the system. VM requires that each minidisk have contiguous space. If a user has 20 files they are all located on his minidisk. In MVS, the locations of these 20 files would be controlled by MVS. Space is unassigned, with users essentially taking what they need within allocation limits. However, MVS does provide a means of mapping the locations of all user files in the system.

In any operating system, the need for DASD can grow at a rapid rate. Of course, if the owner of the DASD is a service bureau, this can be positive. But for an in-house Data Center this is not an attractive situation — DASD is a cost, not a revenue. In VM once a user understands the limitations of his 191 minidisk, he can take an active role in managing his own space utilization.

The DASD Allocation Process

All I/O devices under VM are controlled by CP, and this includes the DASD. DASD for users is generally allocated through the CP directory. The DASD devices are divided into minidisks through a statement in the user's directory entry. This statement, referred to as the MDISK directory control statement, was described in Chapter 5. Once the minidisk is defined for the user through the MDISK statement, the owner has free reign over what is contained in the space. Here is another example of the minidisk (MDISK) statement:

MDISK 191 3380 320 8 VMPK11

The number 191 identifies the virtual address of the user's minidisk. The DASD type, or model, is identified by the number 3380, while the starting cylinder for the use's minidisk is 320. This user's minidisk has been assigned 8 cylinders. The DASD is identified by the volume serial (VOLSER) of VMPK11. The actual formatting of the minidisk is accomplished through the CMS FORMAT command.

The DASD space that is reserved for the use of CP, including the CP nucleus, hardware error reporting (EREP), and spool checkpoint, are specified in another way. Assembler macro statements are included in the three CP modules DMKSYS, DMKRIO, and DMKSNT (discussed in Chapter 4).

A third way of allocating DASD space is through a program called CP FORMAT/ALLOCATE. THis is a stand alone program. When, for example, the FORMAT option of the program is selected, a range of cylinders is selected. This is then formatted into page-size records.

On most DASD devices, CP allocations are indicated through groups of cylinders. Cylinder 0 on each DASD contains the allocation record for the device. This is used during the I/O process to find where minidisks are located on the DASD, and the use that has been assigned to each. The allocation record is either 1024 or 2048 bytes long, with each byte representing one cylinder on the volume. The use for which the minidisk has been allocated — paging, spooling, dump space, etc., is indicated by a code. The allocation record does not indicate what is actually contained on each minidisk — it does not include a list of the files that each user has on his minidisk.

Under MVS, each DASD volume contains a Volume Table of Contents (VTOC) which lists essentially every dataset (similar to a file in VM terms) on the device. By consulting the VTOC, it is possible to see exactly how space is being used. To get this same information, it is necessary to look at each minidisk on the pack, then add the information manually to figure out the space utilization. Again, the virtual machine concept in VM makes a minidisk conceptually equivalent to a whole DASD volume in MVS. So this level of recording is accomplished at the minidisk level.

Adding the actual DASD to the system, before allocation, is really a three-step process. First, the storage medium (DASD) is physically connected to the machine. This is followed by indicating to the operating system that the physical device is now available — the real device address must be specified in the CP system generation through macros in the DMKRIO program module. The third step involves dividing the DASD into minidisks and assigning them to users.

DASD Allocation Issues

The need for DASD is not a function of the size of the computer site. As a function of the demand for interactive processing, as well as human nature, disks will fill up. It is important that installations stay of top of the DASD situation as much as possible and attempt to keep users accountable for their DASD use. Growth in DASD use can be dynamic, but only if it makes economic sense. There are many factors involved in effectively managing DASD; one major factor is DASD allocation.

In native VM there are really no tools available to automate and control changes in the directory. By inference, there is no effective way to manage the allocation of CMS DASD (for user storage space). Allocating permanent storage to a user involves piecing together the information on existing directory statements to identify the space on a DASD that has not yet been allocated. Once an adequate block of space has been identified, the MDISK statement in the user's directory entry is written, allocating the free space to the new user. A problem that often occurs is that there are small pieces of unused DASD between each assigned minidisk. This is illustrated in Figure 8-2.

A system programmer can list the MDISK (minidisk) statements from the directory entries of users on a specific minidisk, and by manually mapping out the DASD assignments, can find where these small pieces of unused DASD are located. For example, carefully mapping the DASD on which these user's minidisks are located would reveal a gap between the minidisk of User A and that of User B. The

MINIDISK ALLOCATION

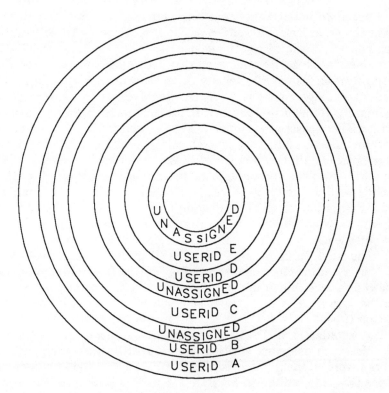

Figure 8-2 An inefficiently allocated DASD

system programmer could then perform what is called manual compression. This involves moving the minidisks around on the device, as a means of reclaiming the wasted space. New users could then be allocated space that was previously sitting idle.

When compression has been performed, and/or a new user added, the entire directory file is recompiled for use by CP. Again, the source directory is stored in one flat file. It can be updated using the standard CMS editor, XEDIT. For a site with a few users, this is manageable. For a site with many users, i.e., more than 50, this can become very cumbersome, particularly with constant user demand for increased space, resulting in numerous directory changes.

Often a user complains about lack of DASD and not having the budget to add any more, came in over a weekend and a system programmer must perform a manual compression of all of the minidisk space in the system. After compression, the system programmer may find that the situation has not changed; there is still no available DASD. The programmer in this situation will most likely realize later that she had created the space, but had not recompiled the directory to indicate this to CP.

Because DASD is a limited resource, its use must be carefully allocated based on policy that takes into account both the economics as well as the organizational concerns. The cost of adding DASD involves much more than the cost of the device itself. For example, the 3380 is a popular DASD device that comes in both single density and dual density format. The single density drive contains 885 cylinders while the dual density contains 1770. A single density 3380 costs approximately $65,000 in 1987 prices, which comes to around $15 per cylinder. These costs are compounded by associated requirements that might include an additional control unit, operations staff, backup requirements, installation, and support and maintenance costs.

In addition to the economic costs, there is also a potential drain on the CPU with the addition of DASD. This was illustrated in Chapter 6 in the discussion of CPU utilization. If the system is loaded with DASD, the potential for channel contention is greater as the control unit must wade through file after file of data to find the one that has been requested. In addition, adding DASD to the system involves the risk of overloading channels with strings of DASD. Channel balancing somewhat solves this problem, but sooner or later the size of the CPU must be upgraded or users must be resolved to contending with poor response time.

With organizational DASD management decisions comes the need to decide which users are entitled to more DASD than others, and the factors involved, including organizational status and job function. On the positive side, unlike in MVS, a VM user is limited to the size of the minidisk, or multiple minidisks. Once an allocation has been made, a user cannot exceed this allocation without going through whatever organizational channels have been instituted to make decisions about DASD. Thus, with an effective DASD allocation control system in place, users are forced to stay within defined limits, and to request more DASD when needed.

There is really no single means of allocating DASD. Because under the architecture the minidisk is something that is owned by the user, and the user is limited by the size of the minidisk, it is important that allocation be based on an understanding of the individual needs of each user. With organizational decentralization, particulary on a departmental and business value basis, DASD pooling is one solution to the allocation issue.

DASD pooling really involves grouping available DASD based on basic need categories, including production, database, workspace, development, users, and the operating system. Each of these functions is allocated a specific amount of DASD, and the devices for each category may be grouped together, in strings (eight connected DASD devices). From a system performance viewpoint, this helps to isolate channel contention within certain categories so that overall system performance is not affected.

For users, DASD pooling might involve allocating a specific amount of DASD to a department, with space allocated to users in each department based on the amount that is available to to a work group. This helps to assure that available DASD for specific categories of activity adequately reflects the priorities both of the organization as well as the work group. Rather than subjecting all departments to stringent, or loose, global standards, this assues better overal performance through giving larger pools to departments that require more storage space than others. Department managers, who understand the individual job functions of the individual group members, can then in turn allocate the DASD to users. This system can be used either in situations when everyone is sharing a central mainframe as well as in departmental situations in which a departmental processor is equipped with a limited amount of DASD.

A benefit of DASD pooling is that users can deal directly with a manager when requesting DASD, rather than having to make a request of a system programmer who really does not understand their specific needs. In turn the system programming staff is freed from evaluating individual user requests. Furthermore, DASD pooling helps to make conservation a work group issue. Users face off with the others in their group rather than an anonymous entity at the central support location.

Minidisk costing is a means of reinforcing the economic issues surrounding DASD use at the time of allocation. Costs can be assigned to individuals, projects or to departments. It is not necessary to perform actual billing. Rather, a "funny money" approach is sufficient. Providing users with reports listing the costs of DASD, based on whatever unit of measure the organization decides upon, creates an awareness of the costs involved with being allocated a minidisk. Users may be asked to justify their DASD use, similar to the justification that would be necessary if, for example, a business traveler stayed in a $400 hotel suite when one costing $100 was available. This costing can serve as input to a program which gets users involved with managing their own minidisk.

DASD allocation is an economic issue. The subsequent need for costing varies among organizations. For an organinization using VM for very specialized tasks only, such as a scientific application, with few users, allocation may not be a problem. It depends on the role of this resource in the organization. In a sense, storage space on the computer can be considered an overhead cost, like electricity, the telephone, and other office supplies. Employees are not necessarily charged by the organization for the use of these services, though they are often encouraged to be conservative in their use of them. Providing costing information for DASD at the time it is allocated is a means of encouraging conservatism in the same way. If costing information is provided, it is important that the unit of measure be consistent, and that users understand how these costs are incurred.

DASD allocation is the cornerstone of any effective program for managing DASD. Those responsible for making decisions about DASD must understand the organzational issues.

Managing the Hungry Beast

A generally agreed upon statistic is that DASD growth is doubling every 2 years. Much of this can be attributed to the growth of the Information Center with trends toward online rather than batch processing with, consequently, growing storage requirements for databases and other end user computing needs. DASD, in fact, is the fastest growing and most costly component of many Data Centers.

Too often, DASD that has been previously allocated is not recovered. Projects are completed, employees leave the company, applications become obsolete. Often this space is not recovered.

Allocation is the beginning of the management considerations that are associated with DASD. It is not uncommon to supplement the capabilities of native VM with software that provides added controls for the management of DASD, either through solutions developed in-house or system software packages. With user demands, potentially compounded with departmental processors, savings in personnel expenses alone can justify the cost of software to control this resource.

There are many areas to take into consideration when looking at the issue of DASD management. DASD compression, the process of reclaiming the unused portions of space that sits between the minidisks assigned on a DASD is one area that can be automated with added software. These small amounts can add up to significant savings when reclaimed without involving a significant drain on system programmer time. Automating this effort lessens the risk of human error, and this process is so tedious that it really does not justify this expertise. Large organizations often have no idea how much DASD is lost through small unused pieces between minidisks because the process of manual location, and then reassignment, is more expensive than purchasing more DASD, to the extent that even when employees leave the company their minidisks are not reclaimed. This reassignment, referred to as migration, is most likely only feasible with software management.

System software packages that handle DASD management include a means of performing automatic DASD compression and migration, as well as other capabilities such as management reporting. Usage of minidisks needs to be periodically monitored to make sure they are being used efficiently, with areas to monitor including minidisks that have not been updated in a specified number of days or that are underutilized. In both cases minidisks that meet these specifications could either be made smaller or eliminated completely.

Software can also be used to manage the pool function, aiding the manager in assigning space to the users in a work group and preventing minidisk overlapping from occurring during the allocation processs. This can also be a security function.

Getting Users Involved

End users are the primary consumers of DASD in most VM environments. Though system software will assist with the process of managing DASD, this really needs to be an ongoing and active process. The reporting and other capabilities should supplement the active role that the users take in managing their own space. With the limitations of DASD on departmental computers, user involvement will also be important.

Gaining control over the use of DASD, and then getting users involved in controlling this resource is basically a three phase process, beginning with compressing DASD, educating users on how DASD can be conserved, and then turning this process over to users on an ongoing basis.

The first phase begins with what is essentially a clean-up similar in concept to cleaning a refrigerator. Through the use of management reports or a concentrated manual effort, it is necessary to first see how DASD is being used throughout the organization, both CP and CMS. Once this is mapped, the unused space can be reclaimed by compressing the gaps between minidisks, freeing up much larger pieces of usable space. This unused space might be not only the result of gaps, but also outdated projects, departed employees, and other wasted space. Because of the complications involved in undertaking the process of reclaiming this resource, as much automation as possible, through system software, will facilitate it. The process of compression is also referred to as defragmentation.

Space that has been reclaimed will be quickly used, and followed by another potential crisis, if users are not educated concerning the importance of active space maintenance. This is where the education of the second phase of establishing control over DASD comes into play.

Common statistics indicate that up to 50% of all the files stored on minidisks are unknown in content or have not been accessed in over 6 months. Thus, there is much available DASD that is simply sitting on this device, containing outdated information that is not being actively used in meeting the goals of the organization; yet it is seemingly too precious to delete. This wasted information is a weak justification for a request for even more DASD. For example, a user may be requesting more DASD, while his minidisk contains many files that are no longer being actively used. In fact at close examination, the minidisk may contain documents that have not been edited or even read for months and even years, including recipes that have been passed around the office. Because of the ownership that users have over their minidisks, these old files are under user control and do not automatically expire with disuse.

Users cannot be held accountable for DASD if they do not understand how it is being wasted, and without an understanding of cost these statistics have little meaning. Providing users with cost figures was discussed with DASD Allocation. Providing this costing information can continue through providing users with figures that show the cost of wasted and unused space to the organization. This is especially effective if this cost is provided both in understandable terms, and is associated with each individual. Organizations often make the mistake of assuming that users not only do not care, but are also incapable of understanding the concepts associated with the use of computer resources such as DASD. When presented in dollars and cents, the basis for motivation is provided.

At the department level, the manager needs to be provided with the same information as individual users. This provides an added incentive through encouraging the person at the top to become more active in overseeing the process of making positive changes in DASD use. Whether this DASD is shared or located on the departmental CPU, it will not be an infinite resource.

The third phase of regaining control over DASD is a culmination of the first two phases. As space is reclaimed and users learn more about the importance of conservation, responsibilities can then be distributed for active user involvement. Users need to be taught not only to delete files that are actively used, but also how to archive — to save offline — those files that may be needed at a later time. System software with user interfaces can aid in this process, otherwise, the education process may be much longer.

The third phase also involves continual monitoring of DASD use, with management reporting and continual tuning to balance I/O load. Management reports, particularly those that are prescriptive in nature, can indicate users, or departments, where DASD is not being effectively managed, as well as areas where further compression is needed.

With user involvement and constant monitoring of DASD, this process becomes cyclical, as illustrated in Figure 8-3. Through constant monitoring, most likely through management reporting, unused space can be reclaimed through compression. The cost of DASD is then passed on to users, and their involvement is encouraged, through actively managing their own minidisks. This provides more unused space, and the cycle continues.

DASD MANAGEMENT CYCLE

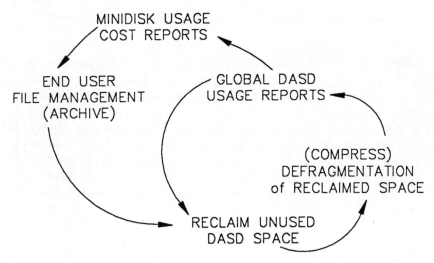

MINIDISK USAGE
COST REPORTS

END USER
FILE MANAGEMENT
(ARCHIVE)

GLOBAL DASD
USAGE REPORTS

(COMPRESS)
DEFRAGMENTATION
of RECLAIMED SPACE

RECLAIM UNUSED
DASD SPACE

Figure 8-3 The ongoing DASD management cycle with user responsibility

DASD Management in the Departments

The issues of DASD management do not change appreciably with Departmental Computing. Even if each department contains its own minicomputer with its own DASD devices, this resource will not be unlimited. If anything the competition may become more intense. Users will be competing directly with their own coworkers for this limited resource rather than with anonymous faces in other departments. The result could be enhanced cooperation, based on an understanding on the needs associated with the various roles in the departments.

Whoever is involved with administering DASD should also be responsible for assuring that it is managed. If the department manager is responsible for allocating the pool of DASD within the department, than this individual should also be responsible for making sure that users understand the nature of this resource and are actively involved in conserving it through whatever means are available.

Departmental Computing implies a reduced need for system staff at this level. As a result, user friendliness in both allocating and managing DASD will be critical to the success of this element. Some organizations may choose to manage DASD at the central site, with the allocation process and management tools administered through the network. Others, depending on the availability of system software with adequate user interfaces, will make this the responsibility of the department manager.

Chapter Summary

The major issues discussed in Chapter 8 include the following:

- DASD is one of the major cost items in the Data Center, and because of increasing levels of online storage, this cost is increasing.
- Users are assigned DASD in the form of minidisks, sections on a real DASD, which appears to each user's virtual machine as a whole device.
- In VM, DASD is allocated in the directory, with each user assigned minidisk space as part of his directory entry.
- DASD must be carefully managed to keep the growth of this resource from negatively affecting both CPU utilization as well as the bottom line. This should include extensive user involvement.

9

VM Applications

The VM operating system serves as a foundation for users and their applications. However, CMS provides many capabilities which perform application-oriented functions. The use of CMS is discussed, with examples of practical features for the user environment. Major VM applications trends are also outlined.

Using CMS

Operating systems, including VM, provide a foundation for the information resources of the organization — applications, database management systems, and other software that support daily tasks. CMS, the Conversational Monitor System, is essentially a user-oriented operating system within the VM operating system. The functions and design of CP and CMS were discussed in Chapter 2. While CP manages the system hardware resources, CMS provides interactivity, and many easy-to-use functions that facilitate the daily activities of both users and system programmers.

While providing a basis for applications, native VM/CMS capabilities, in and of themselves, do offer many practical application functions. Examples of CMS capabilities include the creation and editing of files, a means for various types of communications between users, as well as means creating ad hoc "programs" within CMS which perform a variety of functions.

Creating CMS Files

CMS includes a command language that allows users to work with data files of various types. A file is the basic unit of data in CMS. It can contain data, such as a document, a list, even a recipe for a favorite dish (lamentably, uses such as this create unnecessary demands on corporate resources). Though CMS files do not offer the sophisticated services of a database management system, they provide a means for users to store and manipulate information collected for their own personal needs. A CMS file can also contain a program that a programmer creates and modifies, and then compiles for later use.

The CMS command language includes a command called XEDIT. This command allows you to use the System Product Editor to create files, and to modify them at a later time. CMS files are stored on DASD which, as discussed previously, is assigned to users in the form of DASD areas called minidisks.

A CMS file is created with the XEDIT command, followed by information which identifies the file itself:

XEDIT filename filetype filemode

The filename is a name which the user gives to the file to help him in identifying it at a later time. The filename may be one to eight characters in length, composed of a combination of alphabetic characters, numbers or certain symbols. Generally, filenames have no special meaning to CMS; they are for the convenience of the user.

The filetype is a bit more complicated in that there are many reserved filetypes in CMS. For example, a filetype of NOTEBOOK contains notes sent to, or received from, other users, so files of this type are automatically stored in the user's NOTEBOOK file. Otherwise, unless the file is to serve a specific purpose, user's also have flexibility in naming the filetype.

The filemode helps to identify the virtual disk (minidisk) on which the file will be stored. Generally, users have only one minidisk, the minidisk with an address of 191. For simplicity, this is usually accessed as the A-disk. Thus, the standard filemode is A and, if the user does not indicate the filemode, XEDIT provides a default value of A.

A user wishing to create a file containing an article for a newsletter, might create a file with the following command:

XEDIT PARTY NEWS A

The XEDIT command creates the file PARTY, which will contain the news article. The user has perhaps created other articles as well, all of which are identified by a filetype of NEWS. This data is stored on the user's A-disk.

Once this command has been entered, the user can then begin to write the article, and after it is completed, file it away on his minidisk. To accomplish this, the user simply types FILE on the command line at the top of the screen, and presses the enter key. The file is now stored on DASD, on the user's own minidisk, and the user can either go on with another task, or retrieve this file for continued editing.

Managing CMS Files

Each user can display the names of the files contained on his accessed minidisk(s), as well as other information about the files. This is accomplished with the FILELIST command. When issued this command displays a list of the user's files, with information including the filetype and filemode, as well as the date and time that it was edited. The FILELIST command can be followed by a modifier, such as a filetype, which causes only files with a specific filetype to be displayed. Thus, with the FILELIST command, a user has a quick reference to the contents of his minidisk.

Following is an example of CMS file information that might be displayed after a user issues the FILELIST command:

PARTY NEWS A
MEETING NEWS A
BOSS MEMO A

Having issued the FILELIST command and received the display of existing files, the user can then issue other commands to manipulate the files in the list. For example, an X entered in the command space which follows the name of the file will allow the user to XEDIT — make changes to — the file. Entering ERASE, an XEDIT subcommand, will cause the file to be erased from the user's minidisk. Many functions, including editing or simply reviewing the file, can be designated with the use of PF Keys.

ERASE is an important command for users to understand and make use of, particularly in combination with the ability to archive files, as outlined in the discussion of DASD management. Files that are no longer needed by the user should either be archived, to be transferred to tape storage for use at a later time, or simply erased. These concepts are essential to DASD management. A user who has integrated the "housekeeping" of his minidisk into his ongoing CMS usage will make fewer demands for increased DASD space. He will periodically list his files, review those that have not been used recently, such as letters or memos that he sent, and erase them from his minidisk to make room for future files.

Other CMS file management commands include:

- COMPARE — compares the contents of two files to ascertain if they are identical, and displays the lines that are not identical.
- COPYFILE — creates a second copy of a file.
- RENAME — changes the name of a file to another name, designated by the user.

Editing Files

The System Product Editor, through the XEDIT command, is used to create and edit CMS files that are on disk. CMS allows users to make changes interactively, instructing CMS to make a change, and then continuing on with other changes in files.

When a file is edited, the changes are made in the contents of the file (e.g., a document, program, list, etc.), and then the file is "re-written" onto the minidisk. In other words, the contents of the edited file is written over the previous version of the file. As discussed, when the user is finished editing a file with XEDIT, he simply enters the FILE command, and the edited file replaces the old one. At this point, the user is out of XEDIT mode and back in CMS.

Suppose that the user wishes to make changes to a news article, previously created and stored in a CMS file. If the file currently exists on the user's minidisk, he enters this command:

XEDIT PARTY NEWS

The existing file will appear on the user's terminal screen, and the user may now make changes in the contents as needed. This command was also used to create the file, except that the filemode of A was included at the end of the command. Once the file has been created, the filemode in the XEDIT command has a default value of A.

The user may continue on through a file making numerous changes in content. In fact, the file may be altered such that the new version does not even resemble the previous version. However, these changes are not automatically made to the copy of the file that is being stored. Interactive file changes occur as a result of the FILE command. For example, a sudden power outage will not necessarily cause the user to lose original file contents, but any changes currently being made, previous to a file command, will be lost.

Within XEDIT, there are subcommands to preclude the loss of file changes in case of system problems. The SAVE subcommand can be periodically issued, which takes the current contents of the file and writes over the previous version. This is similar to entering the FILE subcommand, except that the user remains in XEDIT mode after issuing SAVE. Another option is the SET AUTOSAVE subcommand. This subcommand is entered at the beginning (or during) the edit session, and is followed by a number. For example:

SET AUTOSAVE 5

After entering this subcommand, every fifth change, or addition to the file, would cause the file to be saved on disk. The editor issues an automatic save request which causes the current version of the file to be written over the old version.

Within XEDIT, there are numerous file creation options. Blank lines, for adding information to the file, can be added at the beginning, end, or within the file. Lines can also be deleted, regardless of whether they are blank. Lines of text can also be copied, as well as moved from one location within the file to another. In addition, the CHANGE command provides a means of changing one word within the file to another. This might be used, for example, to change all occurrences of the word boy, within the file, to girl.

The CMS file managment capabilities are such that, with the functions of XEDIT, each user can effectively store and manipulate his own personal data, performing many of the functions associated with word-processing and other software (though with limitations). Nevertheless, these capabilities are provided through native VM/CMS.

User Communication Through CMS

In native VM, there are numerous ways in which users may communicate with others. User communication is mainly accomplished through the Remote Spooling Communications Subsystem (RSCS) network, which was briefly described in Chapter 2. Through RSCS, users can communicate through messages and notes, as well as send files to each other.

Sending and Receiving Messages

A user can send a message to another logged on user with the use of the TELL command. The format for this command is simply:

TELL userid message

An example of sending a message would be one user sending a greeting to another logged on user. The message, from userid MIKE to userid GARY, would be (uppercase or lowercase characters are acceptable):

TELL GARY Good Morning

The user identified by GARY would then see the following message on his screen:

MSG FROM MIKE : Good Morning

If the user to whom the message is being sent is not currently logged on, the sends will receive a message indicating so:

GARY NOT LOGGED ON

If a user does not want to receive messages from other users, he may prevent this by entering the command SET MESSAGE OFF. This will prevent message both from other users as well as standard system messages. The command is reversed with SET MESSAGE ON.

The use of the TELL command, as well as other CMS communications commands, makes use of the user's NAMES file. This is a personal directory that the user sets up, using the NAMES command. The NAMES command displays a full screen that is used to enter descriptive information for each other user with whom he wishes to communicate. The entry in the names file includes userid, nickname, the node at which the user is located, and standard address information. The user is responsible for keeping his NAMES file updated.

In the absence of a NAMES file, CMS communications commands make use of the CP directory, so that individual users can communicate without having actually set up NAMES files. The major limitation in not having set up a NAMES file is that the user to whom the message is being sent can be addressed by userid only, and not by a nickname. Also, groups of userids can be set up through the NAMES command, so that a group, e.g., a department, could be messaged through the use of a single command.

The CP MESSAGE command may also be used in sending messages to other users. This command uses the same syntax as the TELL command, however only userids, and not nicknames, may be used in identifying the recipient of a message. The CP directory rather than the NAMES file is used in locating users. An example of the above message, using the CP MESSAGE command, is as follows:

MESSAGE GARY Good Morning

MESSAGE may also be abbreviated as either MSG or simply M. The message that the other receives appears the same as a message sent through the TELL command.

Sending Notes

Notes are similar to messages in purpose. However, notes tend to be longer in length than a message, and the recipient of a note does not have to currently be logged on in order to receive it. CMS notes are sent through the use of the NOTE command.

To initiate the sending of a note to another user, the NOTE command is entered on the CMS command line, followed by the userid that identifies the user to whom the note is being sent. If userid MIKE is sending a note to userid GARY, the command would be as follows:

NOTE GARY

CMS displays a screen on which the sender can type the desired note. The NOTE command places the user in XEDIT mode, so standard XEDIT capabilities can be used in composing the note.

The date and time, as well as the from and to information, is displayed by CMS. The user need only type the message, and then press the PF5 key, or use the command SEND, to send the file to the other user.

A copy of each note is kept in a file called ALL NOTEBOOK, where ALL is the filename and NOTEBOOK is the filetype. This file, which contains all notes sent, as well as those received from other users, can be edited through XEDIT.

Sending Files

Files may be sent from one user to another through the SENDFILE command. An example of the use of this command might be a situation in which a user has created a CMS file which contains a document, like a report. He could then send this file to another user who could in turn read and edit the document online. Passing files in this manner creates a "paperless" vehicle for sharing documents. The SENDFILE command also makes use of the NAMES file, or the CP directory.

The SENDFILE command has the following format:

SENDFILE filename filetype filemode to userid

The essential CMS file identification must be indicated about the file being sent. This is followed by the userid which identifies the user to whom the file is being sent. If userid MIKE were sending a file containing a news article, PARTY, to userid GARY, the command would be as follows:

SENDFILE PARTY NEWS A TO GARY

The command may be typed in upper or lower case characters. SENDFILE may be abbreviated as SF, the filemode is not necessary providing that it is A, and the word TO is also not required. Regardless of whether userid GARY is currently logged on, he would receive this file.

Receiving Notes and Files

During the discussion of sending notes and files, the actual means of receiving these communications was not described. Notes and files are both delivered to the user's virtual reader. Readers are part of spool space, which serves as a holding area until the recipient of the note or file decides what to do with it.

Users are notified that they have a file (a note is also considered to be a file) in their reader through a message that appears at logon, indicating how many files currently exist in the reader. To see the names of the files, the RDRLIST command is used (abbreviated RL). This command causes a list of the files in the reader to be displayed and, similar to the use of the FILELIST command, the user enter commands on this list, or uses PF keys, to manipulate the files.

The following are examples of entries on the reader list. The first entry on the list is a note, while the second is a file.

GARY NOTE A
PARTY NEWS A

Commands that are used with reader files include the following:

- PEEK — The PEEK command causes the contents of a file to be displayed. The user can then look at the contents of the file without having to actually read it into his minidisk area. Thus, once he has read the file, particularly in the case of notes, he can simply discard the file.
- DISCARD — The DISCARD command, as its name implies, serves to rid the reader of a particular file. When DISCARD is entered next to the name of a file on the reader list, it disappears. It is not read into the user's minidisk area, and it is no longer available.
- RECEIVE — The RECEIVE command actually causes the note or file to be read into the user's minidisk area. Thus, if a user is sent a file which contains a document that he wishes to further edit, he can receive the file and it becomes his own, similar to the files that currently exist on his minidisk.

These commands are important to the user's manipulation of the communications that are sent to him. It is also vital to the overall state of the system that users understand how to use their virtual readers. Spool space, similar to the DASD assigned to users, is an area that can become overutilized if not efficiently maintained. If files are allowed to sit in spool space, and accumulate, the DASD allocated to this function will fill up and jeopardize the availability of spool for the whole system. "Housekeeping" of spool space, as with DASD, is a user responsibility.

"Programming" Within CMS

CMS users can write procedures called EXECs which, similar to standard computer programs, are a sequence of commands and statements that perform specific functions. EXECs can be written by the technical staff to make the use of VM much easier for end users, while also providing a means of automating many more time-consuming tasks.

An EXEC is developed through building a CMS file that contains a sequence of commands and statements. The file is given a user-defined filename and, generally, a filetype of EXEC with a filemode of A (depending on where it is stored). An EXEC called FORMAT would be referred to as follows:

FORMAT EXEC A

After the EXEC is built and tested, the function performed by the series of statements and commands within the EXEC can then be performed by simply invoking the filename alone of the EXEC. Thus, rather than the user having to enter a series of CMS or CP commands, he could use the name of the EXEC to perform the function. This not only saves time, but makes the system even easier for users while eliminating a potential source of human error.

EXECs can contain not only CP and CMS commands, but also statements that perform conditional branching and the testing of variables. Similar to other CMS files, XEDIT, the System Product Editor, is used to create EXECs. The design of EXECs can be relatively sophisticated, and include statements that look for certain conditions and either issue error messages, or request input from the user. EXECs are stored on DASD, and may be shared among users through the use of the SENDFILE command, as a user sends an EXEC to another user just as he would send a CMS file. An EXEC can also be shared by linking to the minidisk on which it is located. Because an EXEC is executed by issuing its filename, it is essentially a CMS command in and of itself.

Writing EXECs

CMS EXECs can be written using EXEC, EXEC2, or the REXX language (Restructured Extended Executor). There are many differences between these three means of writing EXECs which are best understood through reading IBM documentation. Fundamentally, however, there are three EXEC processors available within VM/SP.

CMS EXEC is handled by the CMS EXEC processor, while EXEC2 is processed by the EXEC2 processor. CMS EXEC and EXEC2 are very similar to each other, though EXEC2 is much more sophisticated, with multiplication and division functions, extended debugging facilities, and support for user-defined subroutines and functions.

EXECs written with REXX are processed through the System Product Interpreter. It uses a different language and syntax than the CMS EXEC or EXEC 2 processors. Programs being processed by the System Product Interpreter must begin with a comment which begins and ends with an */, as the REXX example below indicates. REXX is a very high level language, and statements in REXX can perform functions that include assigning values to variables, executing conditional loops, comparing values, and performing If-Then-Else conditional execution. REXX is easy to learn and use, designed to be used by users at various levels of technical expertise.

The following are examples of specific applications of EXEC 2 and REXX EXECs which illustrate logic and format.

EXEC 2 Examples

The following is an EXEC written in EXEC 2, which a user would execute to query a printer. For example, the user may have created a CMS file which contains a document, and then sent it off to a centralized printer. Since other users also send their files to the same printer, the file is placed in a queue to wait its turn. The EXEC below makes it easy for the user to see where his file is in the printer queue; rather than entering the commands he merely invokes the name of the EXEC, just as he would a CMS command.

The EXEC, which queries a printer labeled 667A, is named Q667A. The numbers which precede each line of the EXEC are not actually part of the EXEC. They are included to facilitate the explanation that follows it.

```
1.  &TRACE
2.  CP SMSG RSCS Q 667A ACTIVE
3.  CP SMSG RSCS Q 667A QUEUED
4.  &EXIT
```

Q667A is described in the following narrative:

1. Files with a filetype of EXEC, written in EXEC 2, begin with &TRACE. This causes CMS to "call" the EXEC 2 processor to handle it, thus "kicking off" the action of the EXEC.
2. A CP command is issued, SMSG, which queries the printer to see what is currently active on the printer.
3. A second SMSG is issued to see what is in line on the printer.
4. The sequence of the EXEC is now completed.

The results of the EXEC would be displayed on the user's terminal screen, showing what is currently being printed as well as what other tasks are in the queue. The user could then locate his own task in the display.

A second EXEC written in EXEC 2 is provided below. This EXEC, called PROG, is one which would be used by a programmer using AS-SEMBLER language. Several steps are required in "assembling" and running an ASSEMBLER program, and these steps are written into this EXEC. Thus, a programmer who needs to assemble a list of programs could execute PROG, rather than having to perform each step manually.

Again, the numbers which precede each line of the EXEC are to facilitate the explanation that follows it. The PROG EXEC is as follows:

```
 1. &TRACE
 2. *
 3. * THIS EXEC ASSEMBLES AND RUNS PROGRAMS
 4. *
 5. * DEFINE NAME OF PROGRAM TO BE RUN
 6. *
 7. &PROG = PRG3
 8. *
 9. GLOBAL MACLIB CMSLIB OSMACRO
10. &TYPE ASSEMBLING &PROG
11. ASSEMBLE &PROG
12. &IF &RC ≠ 0 THEN GOTO -EXIT
13. &TYPE
14. &TYPE RUNNING &PROG
15. &TYPE
16. FILEDEF SYSIPT DISK FILE SYSIPT A (BLKSIZE 80 LRECL 80 DSORG PS)
17. FILEDEF SYSLST PRINTER (BLKSIZE 81 RECFM FBA LRECL 81)
18. LOAD &PROG
19. &IF &RC ≠ 0 &GOTO -EXIT
20. START *
21. &IF &RC ≠ 0 &GOTO -EXIT
22. &TYPE 'PROGRAM RUN SUCCESSFUL'
```

23. &GOTO -EXIT
24. -EXIT
25. &EXIT &RC

The actions performed by the statments and commands within PROG are as follows:

1. &TRACE indicates that it is written in EXEC 2.
2. An * indicates a comment line, that is not executed as part of the EXEC. This comment line is blank.
3. This comment line provides an at-a-glance narrative of the actions being performed by the EXEC.
4. Another blank comment line, for the purpose of clearer formatting.
5. The description of the EXEC is completed.
6. Another blank comment line.
7. &PROG is a general way of referring to the name of the AS-SEMBLER program that is being assembled and run through the actions of this EXEC. In this execution, the ASSEMBLER program being executed is called PRG3.
8. This is another blank comment line, for the purpose of clearer format.
9. This command indicates the location of macros which may possibly be called by the program (in this case, PRG3).
10. The message "ASSEMBLING PRG3" will appear on the user's screen.
11. PRG3 will actually be assembled at this point.
12. If no errors are encountered in the assemble process, the EXEC will continue. Otherwise, if an error is encountered (the return code is not 0), the processes of the EXEC will not be continued and the user will be exited.
13. &TYPE followed by blanks causes a blank line to be displayed on the user's screen (following the message displayed in line 10).
14. The message "RUNNING PROG3" will appear on the user's screen.
15. Another blank line will follow this message.
16. The actual data input to the program can be defined to the EXEC, as is done in this line. The data is in a file called SYSIPT, on the user's A disk, in DASD. The format is also defined.
17. The output from the ASSEMBLER program should be sent to a printer. Information about how the output should be printed, e.g., an 81 character file, is also included.
18. PRG3 is ready for loading, and this is accomplished with the LOAD command.
19. If an error is encountered in the loading process, the EXEC will terminate and the user will be exited.

20. The START command initiates the running of PRG3.
21. If an error is encountered in the execution of PRG3, the user will be exited.
22. After the completion of the program, the next step is to display the message "PROGRAM RUN SUCCESSFUL."
23. The program having successfully run, the EXEC is now completed also.
24. EXIT is a label for the end of the program, and is followed by the last step of the program.
25. The user is exited, with a return code displayed.

A user with many ASSEMBLER programs to assemble and run would find this EXEC to be very helpful, as it "automatically" initiates each step of a very lengthy process. Again, an EXEC is a capability within native VM/CMS with applicability that is limited only by the creativity of the user.

REXX Example

The EXEC below, written in REXX, was written as an aid for the system programming staff to communicate with users. When a "public disk" — a minidisk containing information that is shared by multiple users — is updated, users must re-accessed it to make sure that they are getting the most current information, including the changes. Each user linked to a shared minidisk has his own copy of the minidisk's directory; thus re-accessing assures that the user's copy of the directory matches the one that is on the minidisk. Notifying users that a change has been made can be a time-comsuming and error-prone process, particularly if many users are linked to it.

The EXEC below, called NOTIFY, automates this procedure by checking to see who is linked to the disk, and subsequently notifying them. As before, the numbers preceding each line of the EXEC are not part of the EXEC itself.

1. /* Notify: Inform users with links to re-ACCESS */
2. PARSE UPPER ARG VADDR.
3. IF VADDR = ' ' THEN CALL EXITRC 101 'VIRTUAL ADDRESS MISSING'
4. IF ≠DATATYPE(VADDR 'X') THEN CALL EXITRC 102 , "VIRTUAL ADDRESS '"VADDR"' IS INVALID"
5. MESSAGE ="CP MSG USER 'YOUR' UVADDR "DISK HAS BEEN UPDATED," "; RE-ACCESS TO PICK UP THE CHANGES.'"
6. LINKS=TRANSLATE(DIAG(8, 'QUERY LINKS' VADDR), ' ',"'!!'15'X)
7. ADDRESS 'COMMAND'

```
 8. DO UNTIL LINKS='‘
 9. PARSE VALUE LINKS WITH USER UVADDR . LINKS
10. INTERPRET MESSAGE
11. END
12. EXIT
13. EXITRC : PROCEDURE
    PARSE ARG CODE MESSAGE
    SAY 'NOTIFY' CODE MESSAGE
    EXIT CODE
```

The actions being performed in the NOTIFY EXEC are as follows:

1. EXECs written in REXX begin with /*, which invokes the System Product Interpreter program. The comment following /* describes the purpose of the EXEC.
2. This command causes the Interpreter to see if sufficient information was entered for the EXEC to run.
3. The virtual address of the public disk must be entered. If this value has not been entered, a return code of 101, followed by the message, "VIRTUAL ADDRESS INVALID," will be displayed to the user (the system programmer). 101 is an error return code that has been built into this EXEC.
4. The virtual address of the public disk must also be a valid address, a valid hexadecimal number. If not, the user receives a return code of 102, followed by the message "VIRTUAL ADDRESS (the address the user entered) IS INVALID."
5. Providing that errors are not encountered, this message will be displayed to the users who are linked to the public disk: "CP MSG (the user's userid) YOUR (the virtual address of the disk) DISK HAS BEEN UPDATED; RE-ACCESS TO PICK UP THE CHANGES."
6. A variable is defined in this statement, with the variable essentially being each user that is linked to the public disk. This statement builds a table that contains the userids of all linked users.
7. A loop begins at this point, going down through each value on the table.
8. This loop will continue until the last entry in the table is a null value.
9. Values are pulled down from the table.
10. The message is sent to each userid in the table.
11. This is the end of the loop.
12. After the purpose of the EXEC is completed, the user (again, the system programmer in this case) is exited from it.
13. EXITRC is a subroutine which indicates how the return code messages should be indicated to each user. This subroutine was referred to in lines 3 and 4 of the EXEC.

REXX is a very high level language with extensive capabilities. In the example, it provided a means of defining specific return codes with IF-THEN logic, went through a looping procedure, and executed subroutines. As discussed previously, it is also flexible enough that users at various levels of technical expertise can take advantage of REXX capabilites.

Major VM Application Trends

VM is an infinitely flexible operating system, and as such lends itself to serving as the basis for a variety of applications. As the "youngest" of IBM's mainframe operating systems, VM has lagged behind DOS and MVS in terms of the number of application packages available for VM sites. This is changing rapidly, particularly with the opportunities in the applications development market presented by IBM's 9370 midrange machine.

There are some specific applications areas with which VM's capabilities have proven to be especially compatible; VM has enabled their growth and they in turn have contributed to the growth of VM. A few of these applications areas, which further illustrate facets of VM capabilities, are discussed below.

The Information Center

The Information Center concept has been discussed extensively in the trade press and other literature, as well as within the pages of this book. However, the relationship between the Information Center (IC for brevity) and the VM operating system bears emphasis.

A typical IC scenario, if there is a typical scenario, is one in which a user comes to the area designated as the IC seeking assistance in using information resources. Perhaps the user wants to develop his own database for storing the names and address of the vendors with who he associates on a regular basis. Staff members are available to assist the user in, if this were a mainframe application, using the fourth generation language interface. Classes are also offered to encourage users to be independent.

The IC is most basically a place where those defined as end users, with little or no technical expertise, have been able to receive assistance and training in using hardware and software resources. The IC is often associated with the personal computer, and it has certainly been a major component of the IC. Spreadsheet, database and word-processing software for the personal computer has been taught to users in an IC setting. However, end users have also been introduced to mainframe applications in the IC.

Mainframe requirements for end users include both ease-of-use as well as the ability to "play" without adversely affecting the activities of other users. With interactivity and the virtual machine concept, VM was quickly recognized as the operating system that met the needs of this group. VM accommodates large numbers of users, providing each with a measure of independence, as well as mediating the demands of both users and multiple application software packages. Users can quickly grasp the basics of CMS and, perhaps through interfaces, begin accessing corporate data for database applications.

The interactivity provided by CMS means that end users can get answers quickly without having to go through the steps of designing a batch job that is processed at a later time. With the added benefit of EXECs which further simplify CMS functions, as well as CMS communication capabilities, the ease-of-use of VM is further enhanced.

A goal of the IC staff has been to assist with the activities of end users, to train them, as opposed to doing work for them. VM capabilities have facilitated this process at the mainframe level by enabling users, rather than adding more barriers.

Computer-Integrated Manufacturing

The manufacturing industry has recently been extremely receptive to new information management technologies, particularly as a means of staving off the threat of foreign competition. Computer-Integrated Manufacturing (CIM) is not so much a technology as it is a way of managing technology. It is an umbrella term, covering components that include robots, "just-in-time" philosophy, integrated flows and Computer-Aider Design/Computer-Aided Manufacturing (CAD/CAM). When combined and managed together, these technologies constitute an efficient manufacturing environment. This is the goal of CIM.

A user in a "classical" CIM environment would use the computer as a tool in virtually all aspects of his job. Changes to the product line would be designed on a terminal screen, with prototypes represented in detail through state-of-the-art computer graphics. Production in CIM is scheduled to reflect customer orders, the orders entered through an order-entry system that interfaces to a production scheduler. The schedule would thus be dynamic, changing to make the best use of resources in meeting demand. Workers on the production line would be either supplemented, or replaced, by robots that are moniotored through software designed for this purpose.

Many of these capabilities have been implemented with great success. However, they have been used individually, and their overall impact on the organization has been limited. For example, CAD/CAM has reduced the cost of making design changes in products. But if other factors in the environment have not also been updated technologically, such as shop-floor control and accounting, the effect of

CAD/CAM is limited to specific functions. CIM is a way of looking at the total environment.

There are many implications associated with making CIM work in an organization, including those of a political nature as the organization adjusts to technological changes affecting product development, quality control and inventory. One necessary ingredient for CIM to work is the coordination by MIS in providing required tools. CIM is similar to any other information technology in that it requires planning and coordination with the other information resources within the organization. For example, the isolated CAD/CAM system, sitting off by itself on a non-networked departmental machine, will be limited in impact if not brought into the fold of the total systems manmagement strategy.

With MIS having a coordinating role in CIM, the role of the central site will be critical in making sure that diverse applications and hardware are networked and standards are enforced. Thus, the operating system on the central mainframe will need to manage multiple users and software, and most likely will be networked with departmental machines. The VM operating system meets the requirements of CIM for many reasons. CIM requires interactivity, with applications that make analyses and provide data that must be acted upon immediately. Shop floor control is an example of an interactive application, with the flow of product components being constantly adjusted to meet just-in-time inventory demands. VM's virtual machine flexibility allows each user to maximize his system use, without placing the total environment in jeopardy if an error occurs. And, because VM serves as an umbrella environment for guest operating systems, it is adaptable to the organization's overall approach to CIM.

Artificial Intelligence

Artificial Intelligence is a very broad term which most basically refers to the ability of the computer to "think" like a human. Expert systems are the most widely used and understood examples of Artificial Intelligence (AI) technology. Expert systems are programs that include the knowledge of many human experts, in a codified form, that is subsequently available in programs that make the kinds of decisions that these human experts would make. In a sense, an expert system leverages the efforts of expert personnel, analyzing factors and making decisions in their absence.

AI has been applied in many areas, including CIM. Robots on assembly lines, for example, can be monitored and maintained through expert systems which react to performance problems, either indicating solutions to humans or actually making standard adjustments. Human intervention is thus leveraged through the assistance of the intelligent software in its role of troubleshooter, or replaced altogether if the robot's performance is also corrected automatically. Banks are beginning to user expert software for the loan process, seeking software which can automate the process of decision-making for smaller bank loans. AI capabilities do not necessarily replace the judgement and thinking process of humans, but they do supplement human thinking, particularly in more standardized kinds of decisions.

VM is adaptable for AI applications because it provides a means of rapid, real-time decision making. A key element in AI is the ability to draw upon data from a variety of sources, from various databases, process this information and then recommend courses of action. VM provides a basis for this process, while also mediating the demands of other applications.

The Development Center

The Development Center is a separate area in an organization in which applications are developed, tested, and debugged before being transferred to users (the production environment). The Development Center serves an important function in the organization, as a place in which new technology can be evaluated for its usefulness within the organization, and needed standards built in. In a sense the Development Center is similar to the Information Center, except that it serves the needs of the MIS professional rather than the user.

Within the Development Center, new software can be tested and configured to assure that it will work with other software packages and fit within the standards of the organization. When new enhancements to currently existing software packages are released, these can also be tested within the Development Center. For example, a new release of VM might be tested here before going "live" in the user environment. If a new application is being developed in-house, this also takes place within the Development Center where necessary work can be accomplished without disrupting, and in turn being disrupted by, the day-to-day activities of users. Similar to the IC, the activities and staffing of the Development Center are flexible, depending on current need. Also, there is an extensive amount of training that occurs, particularly related to quality assurance and maintenance tasks.

VM's capabilities have historically been invaluable in the process of developing and testing software applications. Developers are more efficient when working in an interactive environment, and by using VM's editing function, programs can be compiled, loaded and tested in a matter of minutes. Because each program being tested is in its own virtual machine, other applications and users are not affected if a problem occurs. Once programs are ready for the production environment, VM also lends itself as the conversion tool, serving as an umbrella operating system. For example, the application currently being used and the new application can be run simultaneously, each

Table 9-1 Applications and recommended VM variations

Application	1st Choice	2nd Choice	3rd Choice	4th Choice
Application Development	VM/IS	VM/HPO	VM/SP	VM/PC
Information Center	VM/HPO	VM/IS	VM/SP	
Development Center	VM/IS	VM/HPO	VM/SP	VM/PC
Artificial Intelligence	VM/IS	VM/HPO	VM/SP	VM/PC
CAD/CAM	VM/IS	VM/HPO	VM/SP	VM/PC
Graphics	VM/HPO	VM/IS	VM/SP	VM/PC
Office Automation	VM/HPO	VM/IS	VM/SP	VM/PC
Vector Processor	VM/HPO	VM/XA/SF		
Scientific Applications	VM/HPO	VM/IS	VM/PC	VM/SP
Conversion	VM/HPO	VM/XA/SF	VM/SP	
Departmental	VM/IS	VM/SP	VM/HPO	

within its own virtual machine, until the application being tested is ready for daily use. At this point, use of the old application ceases and the new one takes over, with minimal impact on users.

Which VM Variation?

The variations of VM were discussed in Chapter 2. Because of the different levels of demand that applications create for the operating system, some VM variations may be better suited than others for certain applications. The above chart is a sampling of applications, with suggested VM variations (from "Which VM is Right for You?," VM Software, Inc., 1986).

VM Application Issues

With limited software, VM sites have been forced either to build their own software applications or to purchase solutions that were perhaps not optimal for their needs.

VM is associated with an environment that is oriented towards the needs of users. Many vendors have capitalized upon this orientation by offering application software that requires minimal installation and maintenance support as well as "integrated" packages that provide a variety of solutions. Application software with these features can potentially have many benefits, but the actual impact on the VM environment can vary among vendors.

Integration is in many ways a double-edged sword, depending upon the definition of integration. A package that ostensibly meets a variety of needs may be nothing more than a group of dissimilar products that are bundled together for a reduced price. The purchaser ends up with products that work, but not with each other. Maintenance and installation are streamlined no more than if the individual components had been purchased from many vendors.

Software can also be over-integrated. Some components of a product may be more useful than another, or the site may wish to phase in features over a period of time rather than disrupting users with extensive changes all at once. Application packages that have too much integration do not allow for a phased-in approach, and interfere both with the flexibility of the user environment to adapt to changing needs as well as the flexibility of VM.

Another common problem in the VM environment is applications software, as well as system software and database management systems, that were originally developed for use under another operating system, such as MVS, and have been modified for use under VM. Throughout this book, the unique qualities of VM are being described. Software that works well in a batch environment, and has been modified to work within VM, will not generally take full advantage of VM's many capabilities. Worse yet, operating system modifications may be required that subsequently impact other applications.

The best option when choosing software for the VM environment is to seek flexible integration, with solutions that are comprehensive, yet allow for a phasing in of features so that the impact on users can be controlled. Products, or components of products, need to interface with each other, yet the organization needs the ability to choose which aspects of the product to implement first, and which ones to phase in later. In addition, products must have been developed exclusively to work in the VM environment.

Chapter Summary

The following points were discussed in Chapter 9:

- Though operating systems provide the basis for applications, rather than being applications themselves, VM/CMS has capabilities that allow users to perform many practical tasks.
- Users may create and edit their own CMS files, containing lists, documents and other data, through the use of the XEDIT facility.
- Communication within CMS is accomplished with the MESSAGE, NOTE, and SENDFILE commands.

- EXECS, written in CMS EXEC, EXEC 2, or REXX, are essentially "programs" within VM that facilitate both ease of use for users and the technical staff, and lessen the potential for human error.
- Major applications areas, for which VM serves as the operating system foundation, include the Information Center, Computer-Integrated Manufacturing, Artificial Intelligence, and the Development Center.
- It is important that software products in the VM environment be designed exclusively to work under VM, and that product implementation be flexible enough to meet the demands of the organization.

10

Disaster Recovery

The issue of Disaster Recovery is critical in the VM environment, with multiple users storing valuable information on DASD. The need for system backup is further complicated with departmental use. The system backup options in native VM are described, with guidelines for managing the disaster recovery function.

Defining Disaster Recovery

The need for a disaster recovery plan, in the context of organizational computing, is generally understood in terms of natural disasters. The term tends to conjure up images of fires, floods, and, beyond the realm of Mother Nature, nuclear holocaust. Disaster recovery is really a rather nebulous term, and is probably about as close to having a universal definition as "user friendly." The definition depends on one's perspective, with a developer looking at the problem much differently than a user.

It does not take an especially lengthy amount of experience in the VM environment, particularly where there are many users involved, to develop a broad view of disaster recovery. Mother Nature becomes a very mild threat when compared to the disaster potentials of inexperienced users, combined with a technical staff that is also inexperienced in providing the safeguards needed to protect users from hurting themselves. Increasingly the function of disaster recovery is not so much a concern for the event of a hardware problem as it is a protection against user error. If a user erases a file inadvertently, or deletes a large portion of a database, there must be a means of bringing this back with minimal disruption. Disaster recovery might be better described as end-user disaster recovery.

The terms related to disaster recovery, except in the most extreme cases, are very site-dependent. An extreme example of a disaster is one in which the Data Center has been bombed. Whether the site is large or small, this qualifies as a disaster. The grey areas are situations in which a string of DASD is lost. At a large installation, this string may not contain "critical" information and may be a nuisance to the users involved, but not a disaster for the organization. At a smaller installation, or in a department, where that string might constitute all of the DASD on the system, the loss of that string is a disaster.

The means of protecting the organization against the event of disaster, however this is defined, is through system backup. System backup can be defined as an installation-driven transfer of data to a different medium, from DASD to tape, for example. Backup is designed to provide the installation with complete coverage in the event of a disaster, such as a hardware failure, with a schedule for performing backups determined by the organization. In addition, backup implies protection for the entire organization, rather than one user backing up his own data. At the same time backup also protects each individual user, insuring that if data is lost there is a means of restoring it. A provision for backup is a consideration among all operating systems, not only VM, though operating systems vary in terms of their provisions for this need. System backup basically implies making a copy of everything that is on the system, so that if there is a loss of data, the copy is available for restoration. VM has a built-in facility for system backup which, depending on the complexities of the environment, may or may not be adequate.

System backup has generally been thought of as a tape management issue, with DASD being backed up to tape and then placed in storage. While this has not disappeared, backup to DASD is also becoming more common for many reasons. With advances in technology, DASD is becoming much less subject to disaster and thus much more reliable as a storage medium. DASD is also becoming less expensive, and does not require the extensive manual intervention and physical storage associated with handling massive numbers of tapes. Of course, DASD cannot be stored offsite, and in the case of a "smoke and rubble" disaster, transporting DASD may not be possible or desirable. Backup to DASD is discussed later in this chapter, as well as in Chapter 11.

The disaster recovery plan can be a very complex plan, involving the storage of twin tapes, backup to DASD, and an alternate site in case of a major disaster. Or, it can simply involve a periodic backup to tape, using the capabilities of native VM. The basic question involved in making this decision is based on how important the data is to the organization as a whole. If corporate financials are stored under VM, or other information that is critical to the operation of the organization, or of the department, than the potential cost of losing this data will outweigh the costs involved in protecting it.

"It Will Never Happen To Me"

Disasters, natural or otherwise, occur when they are least expected. Yet, the person in the organization responsible for making decisions about this preparing for the possibility of disaster all too often does perform this function with an "It won't happen to me" attitude. Finding the time and resources, particularly for organizations with competing user demands and a two year backlog of applications, this does not seem as critical as getting through an average week. The short-term demands often receive the attention even when faced with a future probability; people don't generally take the time to buy their own gravesites either.

With the increasing number of organizations moving towards computerization of all vital information, preparing for a disaster has never been more important. Disaster recovery is a necessary business expense; in many industries the organization is responsible for information lost during a service outage, banks being an example. Insurance companies, realizing the importance of recovering lost information management capabilities as soon as possible, may give premium reductions to organizations that can prove that they have a workable disaster recovery plan. Disaster recovery has moved from being a means of "getting the auditors off our backs" to a key issue for the entire corporation.

There are two primary means of performing system backup in native VM, TAPE DUMP and DASD Dump Restore (DDR).

TAPE DUMP was the first actual backup capability that IBM provided for VM users. It is a CMS command of which many technical people have been particularly fond. Using this means of backup basically involves sending a message from the user's terminal to the operator's console, requesting that a tape be mounted. The TAPE DUMP results in all of the contents of the user's minidisk being transferred — dumped — to tape (or, recorded on tape). Individual files can also be transfered to tape with TAPE DUMP. All of the contents of the minidisk is recorded on the tape.

Generally, once the data is transferred to tape, the tape is either placed in storage or the user retrieves the tape and subsequently places it in a desk drawer or on a bookshelf (or in a pile on the floor). Even with a reliable backup system, many users want to do their own backups. Either they do not have confidence in the system or they want this added level of control. The result is users who TAPE DUMP at will, and fill up available space in their offices with tapes. And the potential security breach is obvious, as tapes are often labeled with their contents and left in unlocked areas. Also, because these tapes are made on an ad hoc basis, unless they are carefully labeled, it may subsequently be very difficult to find a needed tape, especially six months after the fact. Technical people have often used TAPE DUMP to backup various versions of a program so that if something is lost it can be restored. If the organization performs a backup on a weekly basis, programmers have often backed up their own programs in between these backups. TAPE DUMP allows users to backup files on any minidisk that is accessed by CMS.

DDR, or DASD Dump Restore is a program that provides a full system backup. It provides the organization with the ability to backup everything in the system — everything on DASD — from a central standpoint. Generally, users will use TAPE DUMP, while the system is backed up with DDR. The full system backup procedure is initiated by the operator. Tapes are manually selected, hopefully based on a carefully designed labeling system. After the procedure is completed, the operator manually logs and labels each tape. These tapes might be reused weekly, or stored for a certain period of time. One minidisk can require two or more tapes to record all of the information that is stored on it, and the process is very time-consuming.

Restoration of a minidisk, using a tape produced through DDR, involves providing the actual cylinder or block information (indicating the area on the DASD on which the user's information is stored) to restore the minidisk on top of the original area. This can be a very error-prone procedure in finding the exact place for the restoration and very tedious. To restore a specific file, the operator must get a temporary minidisk, restore the minidisk to it using the actual cylinder or block information, and then transfer the selected file from that minidisk to the user. Meeting file requests from users is a time-consuming procedure and requires extensive human intervention. There is a strong potential for accidentally reusing tapes, thus destroying the data that is already recorded on them, as well as making errors in coding physical cylinder or block information.

VM does not catalog each tape that is used for backup. This is the responsibility of the operator, who must be careful to record the identification number of the tape on which information is stored. Without this, restoration may not be possible.

DDR does not allow for incremental capabilities, so that when it is used a full backup must be performed. An incremental backup is one which only backs up changes that have occurred since a certain date, without having to backup data that has not changed since the last backup. With a small shop, this may not be a problem. For a larger shop with a high end machine and 80 or 90 DASD volumes, the backup procedure can take hours, or a whole weekend. Users are forced off the system while this is occurring. It is possible to get around the incremental limitation in DDR by running the backup procedure on a disk-by-disk basis, backing up some volumes more often than others, depending on what is stored on them. This also staggers the time involved in this procedure over the average week.

In an end-user computing environment, it is not uncommon for users to "trash" their files. Even in a program development department where users are more experienced there is still the possiblility of human error. Applications developers often experiment with different versions of the same program, trying one program, making a modification, and then trying that. After a few days, it may be necessary to return to the first version of the code. If this data is not backed up every night, this capability is lost. Two or three critical versions of the program may have been lost since the last backup. As an example, an installation performs a backup every Friday. However, if today is Thursday, and the user needs to restore a file as of Tuesday, this cannot be done.

DDR is actually a utility which, in general, is available to any user. It runs standalone (directly on the hardware and not requiring an operating system) as well as under CMS. Most users use DDR under CMS. DDR does provide physical validation of the data. If an I/O error is encountered, the error will be reported. But DDR does not provide logical validation: it does not make a distinction between CMS disk, and disks from other operating systems, thus errors in logic will not be reported. Also, DDR is making a physical copy of a real disk. DASD comes in various types. Data transferred to tape through DDR must be restore to the same type of device from which it came.

The issue of offsite storage, with both DDR and TAPE DUMP, must be solved by making duplicate tapes of the backup data obtained through these procedures. Once DDR is run, for example, the tape must subsequently be copied again if it is to be sent offsite to be stored in case of a disaster.

Disaster Recovery Planning

Planning for a disaster seems like an unnecessary academic exercise until considered, not so much in relation to the possibility of hardware problems caused by a natural disaster, but instead the probability of users committing errors such as erasing an important file. Events such as this must also be planned for, with adequate data recovery available. Recovery implies the need for system backup, an important element of the disaster recovery plan. System backup can be a nuisance, and it is easy to forget. But it is an element that is a crucial piece in providing comprehensive protection for the VM environment.

Achieving adequate disaster recovery preparation begins with a plan that is designed based on both the needs of the organization as well as the capabilities of VM. As discussed, native VM offers capabilities that allow data to be backed up by both users and technical personnel (TAPE DUMP and DDR), and this may be adequate. However, the needs of the organization, particularly if the information management strategy involves Departmental Computing, may be such that these means of backup will have to be supplemented by system software.

Development of the disaster recovery plan can be thought of as a five-phase process, beginning with an assessment of the organization's needs through the test of the plan after implementation. These phases are described below.

Phase One: Identify the Issues

The first phase in the disaster recovery plan can be summarized with the following considerations:

- Identify all systems
- Define the terms
- Know the exposures

Protecting the VM environment against the event of disaster must begin with a consideration of which systems must be protected, questioning end users as to which systems are critical. Essentially an inventory of all of the systems that the users are currently using must be performed, and may in fact be the only time that a comprehensive overview of all organizational capabilities has occurred. This is necessary to narrow the user's focus, to limit them to perhaps a choice of three out of five systems. These systems might include groups of specific applications or a database management system. It is only human nature to assume that every system is critical if given the opportunity to make this choice. Obviously, there must be a provision for backup for all systems, but in the event of a true disaster, some systems are more critical than others. In addition, depending on departmental function, some departments are also more critical than others.

In the process of performing an inventory of all organizational systems, this research commonly leads to a need to also perform some type of documentation. It is not uncommon to discover that much of the day-to-day functioning of an application, for example, is based on the knowledge and understanding of one or two key individuals. What should be documented so that recovery of the function is assured is instead stored mentally, with procedures operating in the status quo until there is a breakdown. To adequately protect the functions performed by an application it may be necessary to develop written procedures which can then be stored offsite, in case a key individual is unavailable at the time of recovery.

A second result of taking a comprehensive look at systems may be finding that as many as 75% of the applications currently being used are not really critical to the survival of the organization during a disaster recover period. Though relied upon by users, heavily used applications may still be placed on the "back burner" until the most necessary concerns are met. Alternatives may be available which can be used until the system is ready to support less critical applications, even if this means developing manual procedures. In the event of a severe disaster that involves extensive damage to the corporate data, it may be necessary to temporarily hire added clerical help for a month or more until the system is ready to bear the burden of meeting all demands of the corporation. This interim processing procedure can be an important outcome of the overall systems inventory. This interim procedure does not need to be a detailed document, but rather a set of guidelines.

The initial disaster recovery planning needs to be task-oriented, outlining what is involved in recovering the major functions of the organization as soon as possible. The technical aspects of the VM system need to be a specific focus of this initial planning, looking at what must be done to get the system up and running and the critical data available. The other benefits of this phase of planning, including guidelines for manual procedures, are secondary to the focus on tasks involved in recovering the most critical VM capabilities.

In any case, the disaster recovery plan needs to begin with a definition of what constitutes a disaster for the organization. This may lead to the development of hierarchies of disaster and system levels. Examples of disaster levels might include:

* Code 1 — The machine room is leveled
* Code 3 — The nationwide network is down, but operating locally
* Code 10 — A user has destroyed a departmental database

Associated with these disaster levels are groups of procedures based on the severity of the disaster, as well as how important the specific lost functions are to the organization. For example, a lost database in the finance department might be more immediately disastrous than a lost mailing list. Because of this, system priorities should also be associated with each system in the organization, based on the initial inventory. Examples of system priorities are:

* Priority 1 — Requires immediate and full recovery
* Priority 3 — Requires full recovery, but may be deferred over a 30-day period with the assistance of temporary clerical help

The key to making disaster recovery levels and system priorities work is to keep them as simple as possible. For example, defining 40 disaster levels and 60 system priorities, and identifying them with complex codes will introduce complexity such that any potential benefits will most likely be obscured.

Potential exposures need to also be defined in Phase 1 of the planning process. It is important to get a feel for where the major exposures are located; e.g., which areas are most critical and must therefore receive the most protection. If the corporate financial system is a top priority, then this will be an area that will have to be backed up often. If this information is located on a departmental system, than this department will need to institute extensive backup procedures. Those systems that present the most exposure will also need to have guidelines for alternative procedures associated with them to assure that in the event that the system is damaged, the function will continue to be performed. If the system in the finance department experiences difficulty, caused by users or nature, employees will still need to receive paychecks.

Phase Two — Hardware Requirements

The focus of Phase Two in the VM disaster recovery plan is on hardware requirements, and these considerations are summarized as follows:

- Choose a professional alternate site or a buddy system
- Examine device type dependencies

Hardware considerations are the foundations of most disaster recovery plans, the reason being that a natural disaster, causing a power outage, will affect the hardware first. Once the most critical systems are defined in Phase One, it is important that a means of restoring these systems as quickly as possible be developed. The alternate site is a widely used means of accomplishing this.

The alternate site, also called a hotsite, is a fully equipped computing facility that provides organizations with the capability of taking what is essentially a copy of their VM system, and dropping it in. The alternate site is then ready to begin processing the essential functions if for some reason the organization experiences a loss of computing power. There are many companies offering alternate sites, with some more equipped than others. Also, some timesharing companies offer this service on the side. With a well-organized backup system, so that the alternate site is kept up to date with the essential data, the alternate site can potentially be a means of achieving very fast recovery in case of a major disaster. It is important to consider the location of the alternate site when choosing one. If it is located in the same geographical area as the organization contracting its services, and thus experiences the same disaster, it may be in as much trouble as its customers and therefore unable to come to their rescue. Also, if many organizations in a geographical area contract with the same alternate site, and each of these organizations experiences the same disaster, there is also the question of which of these groups receives priority during the recovery process. It is also important that the alternate site have provisions for stringent security, as most likely very sensitive data is being stored. Adequate testing of the recovery procedure, also a consideration, is discussed in Phase Five.

An alternative to the hotsite is a cold site. A cold site is a facility that provides an environment suitable for the installation of a computer and associated hardware. This environment generally includes a raised floor, air conditioning, and power supplies. The subscriber is then responsible for contacting the hardware vendor for acquisition and installation of needed hardware to resume processing activities.

A severe disaster might also result in a loss of documentation. This must also be stored at the alternate site. On a daily basis, only a few pages of a technical manual might be used with any regularity. But these few pages may be crucial, and in the event of disaster, attempting to construct them from memory will be impossible.

In addition to the alternate site, the buddy system is an option for the disaster recovery plan. This involves signing a reciprocal site agreement with an organization who has a similar configuration. Each group agrees to be a "buddy" to the other, providing alternate processing in the event that one of them experiences a disaster. This can be an inexpensive and viable option providing that both organizations are compatible, and agree to be available to the degree necessary. Organizations with departmental processors in remote locations have the added option of designing an intra-organization buddy system, with a processor in one part of the company prepared to serve as a backup to a processor in another location. This achieves the same level of protection as a buddy system, with added commitment and security. Departmental disaster recovery is discussed later in this chapter.

There is also the "I am my own best buddy" system for disaster protection. This is a complete redundancy system. Some installations are so specialized or large that commercial recovery sites are of no use. Therefore, they have their own disaster recovery centers. This is expensive but may be necessary.

As implied, without adequate backup, the alternate site or buddy is really nothing more than a collection of blinking lights. If data is not backed up on a regular basis, and checked to make sure that the backed up data is actually usable, then the disaster recovery plan truly is an academic exercise. Generating twin backup tapes, either through the use of system software that accomplishes this simultaneously, or by manually copying tapes, is a means of offering an added level of protection. One copy of the backup tape can be stored within the walls of the organization, to assure restoration of information in case of user error, while the other can be stored at the alternate site. It is important not to neglect the onsite backup requirements while focusing on the alternate site. If all backup tapes are sent offsite, timely restoration may be dependent on how quickly tapes can be expressed from the alternate site.

In choosing either an alternate or a buddy site, device dependencies should not be ignored. For example, hardware compatibility, including not only the CPU but other devices such as tape drives and DASD, is critical. The alternate site, for example, must support the same density of tape drives, or provisions must have been made to have tapes recopied to the correct density before sending them to the alternate site. The alternate or buddy site does not necessarily need to be a mirror image of the organizations contracting for disaster recovery assistance. Again, if the essential systems have been designated as having first priority, than the alternate site need not have as large a CPU as the organization it is backing up. In fact, rarely is an exact mirror image even possible. What is most important is that the operating system and performance requirements can be met by the backup site if disaster occurs.

Personal computer requirements should not be ignored in disaster recovery considerations. When the personal computer wave started, organizations purchased many of these machines without regard to compatibility. Because of extensive use in end-user computing, personal computers will also need to be available, and important data backed up periodically and possibly sent offsite. Actually, the average personal computer user is most likely much more aware of the need for backup than is the average mainframe user because they are much more involved with the processes of the machine. The ideal situation for the inclusion of the personal computer is to connect these machines to minicomputers, upload the data and then backup it up from the host. Corporate standards for backup will facilitate this process.

Phase Three — Software Requirements

The software considerations included in the VM disaster recovery plan include the following:

- System synchronization
- System backups
- Technical support

Coordination of release levels are an important element in planning for the use of a backup system, whether this backup is a processor located in another department or remote location of the same organization, or whether it is at an alternate site. Software products have maintenance levels such that older releases are no longer supported. Applications running under a new release may not be useable, or restorable, under an older release. For example, database systems can be very sensitive to differences among releases. Data loaded under a new release, with applications designed around the enhancements of the most recent release, may not be useable if restored under an older release. In the case of logical databases scattered around over various departmental processors, if the database management systems loaded on these processors are not of an identical release level, data moved from one machine to another may not be restorable.

System synchronization is another important planning consideration. This concerns systems or applications that have multiple components that must be backed up as of the same point in time. Database management systems are also a good example of this need. A relational database management system may have data that is stored on five minidisks. If a backup is performed while the database system is actually running, with users causing the data to change, then the five minidisks may as a result be backed up at different points in time. The first minidisk, for example, may be backed up as of 11:30 a.m., while the second minidisk is backed up as of 11:40, and so on. If a personnel record was being updated at 11:35, it may actually span two minidisks, and thus not "completely" exist. When restoring these five minidisks, the database management system might not run, or it might fail when encountering the personnel record being updated at 11:35. User applications that involve multiple files may have the same synchronization problems.

The system of backing up should be organized around the needs of the organization. Some data does not need to be backed up often, and it may be adequate to back it up every few days. In the departmental environment, backups can be performed on a departmental schedule, with some departments backing up more often than others. The key considerations that underlie whatever schedule is chosen need to be based on the goal of achieving the recovery of whatever the organization has decided is a minimal configuration of VM in the event of a disaster. The needs of individual user groups and departments are really secondary to this consideration. Whatever the most critical systems were deemed to be during Phase One, these need to be the first considerations in the backup plan. If this information can change daily, then it must be backed up as often if the ongoing efficiency of the organization is dependent on this timeliness.

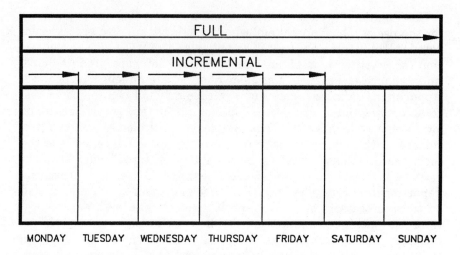

MONDAY   TUESDAY   WEDNESDAY   THURSDAY   FRIDAY   SATURDAY   SUNDAY

Figure 10-1 Full vs. incremental system backup

The issue of full versus incremental backups becomes a major consideration when deciding how organizational data must be backed up. The larger the organization, the greater the impact of this decision. A full backup, or "dump," backs up everything in the system. This can be a very time-consuming procedure as well as requiring large amounts of physical storage space for tapes. An incremental backup, on the other hand, backs up everything that has changed since the last backup. Data is backed up in increments, based on either the last system backup, or the last incremental backup.

The concepts of full and incremental backups are illustrated above. System software is necessary to facilitate this level of specification, particularly if the incremental backups are to be based on dates. An incremental backup requires less time and resources than a full backup, because only what has changed is being backed up. However, incremental backups lengthen the recovery prosess because data is spread over more tapes. Also, performing more tape mounts increases the potential of operator error.

An effective ongoing backup procedure will most likely require a combination of both full and incremental backups. A smaller installation may find a nightly full backup sufficient, but a larger system may not be able or find it necessary to do a ten to twelve hour backup nightly, so this procedure might occur one or two times per month. During the intervening time, only what has changed since the system backup can be captured through a nightly incremental backup.

Organizations relying on native VM for system backup, without the aid of system software, can develop a system of both incremental and full backup. This would most likely involve the use of CMS EXECs, in combination with TAPE DUMP and DDR.

The window of time available for full dumps at the average VM installation is most likely diminishing. VM is probably accommodating many users and applications, with large and growing amounts of DASD. It is unlikely that there is time available on a regular basis to shut the system down for a long period. Incremental backups certainly help in this process, but these must also be scheduled prudently. Incremental backups still require more tapes, and more tape mounts. Thus there are personnel requirements, storage requirements, and by implication, the possibility of human error in tape handling and labeling. Careful record-keeping in tape storage helps with this process, but there are other issues. It may be necessary to reconstruct a minidisk as of a certain date, or a user may wish to restore a specific file, but not everything on a minidisk. Human error is also introduced in these processes.

As concerns the definition of the critical systems for the organization, at the core of these systems, and therefore the most important data to be backed up, is an "IPL'able" VM system (a basic VM system that may be brought up through the Initial Program Load). A disaster dump tape must always be available that contains enough portions of the system to make VM available once that portion of the system is restored. These areas, which were defined in Chapter Four, include the following:

• System residence volume
• CP nucleus
• Directory areas
• CMS

This will provide a minimal configuration of VM, which will in turn be a basis for restoring the critical applications.

Phase Four — Personnel Requirements

The fourth phase of the disaster recovery plan involves personnel considerations, including:

• Administrative logisitics
• Technical coordination

Administrative responsibilities for the disaster recovery plan are really site-dependent. They include issues that may easily slip through the cracks in planning, and include considerations such as transportation of backup tapes to the alternate site, and coordination of staffing requirements locally. It is not uncommon for the organization to be in a panic when a disaster hits, and attention to administrative details before the fact can assure that the necessary details and responsibilities are carried out. It may be helpful to categorize responsibilities locally, in transit, and at the remote site. The same attention to administrative detail must also be dedicated to considerations to less catastrophic disasters, for example, who is responsible for restoring data that a user has inadvertently lost.

Technical coordination implies the mobilization of personnel who have been trained in the procedures necessary for carrying out the disaster recovery plan, and assuring that the minimal configuration of VM is available as soon as possible. Individuals involved in technical coordination should have the expertise to recover all hardware and software aspects of the systems designated as being priority. Technical persons involved in operating systems may not understand what is involved in restoring a database, or a network. A "guru" in operating systems may not be helpful with other aspects of recovery.

To facilitate this coordination, a single disaster recovery coordinator may be appointed, with team leaders reporting to this person in case of a disaster. This person might be located at the central site, with each department having a designated team leader. People are the key element in whether disaster recovery is a success or a failure, and selection of this team, whatever the basis for its composition, is important. Responsibilities for each team member need to be clearly defined. At many installations a single team member may have a variety of responsibilities, while at a large site the team may be made up of individuals with very specific functions. Also, responsibilities continue after the disaster, notifying vendors that the disaster has occurred, and placing customer service teams on alert to assure that customers experience a minimal reduction in service.

What is critical in designating responsibilities is that recovery occurs as soon as possible without excessive concern for standard organizational chains of command.

Phase Five — Testing the Plan

During the last phase of the disaster recovery plan, the plan is tested with goals that include the following:

• Evaluate overall effectiveness
• Adjust to changing requirements and personnel

Phase Five is really an ongoing process, because provisions for disaster recovery, particularly as regards disasters, must be tested regularly. Testing is most effective if it is unannounced. This is not to say that overzealousness, pulling the plug on the total system, is in order. In a network situation, with remote sites, this would truly be a disaster. It is better to choose one system, prepare ahead, and test it in such a way that the whole organization is not crippled. An alternative to a shutdown is a structured walk-through, in which key individuals get together in a room and walk through the scenario and their respective responsibilities. This is similar to a role play, and runs the risk of being no more than a well-conducted meeting.

Scheduling the disaster recovery test, quarterly or semi-annually for example, provides a means of testing reliability. A disaster recovery team can be sent to the alternate site to conduct the test at the same level, based on system priorities. This indicates not only how the internal staff is prepared, but the alternate site as well.

The disaster plan, and backup schedules in general, should be reevaluated on a regular basis. Applications and system configurations change often, and so do organizational priorities. If a new system becomes a priority, such as a new financial application, it needs to be backed up as often as necessary and built into the recovery plan. New releases of critical software need to be installed on the backup sites.

A disaster recovery plan can take from six months to two years to develop, yet at the end of the development period, much of it may be outdated. Software, for example, changes so rapidly that it may be virtually unrecognizable after two years. Data centers also change drastically over a two year period, with requirements and personnel evolving rapidly. Flexibility to handle these changes should be built into any plan for anticipating disaster, however it is defined in the organization.

Disaster Recovery in the Departments

Departmental Computing provides the opportunity for extensive flexibility in designing a procedure for system backup that meets the unique needs of the organization. In a departmental environment, each department may have its own schedule for backup. Some departments will only need to back up data every few days, with data that is two or three days old being adequate for recovery, while others will need to back up data on a daily basis.

A major issue in backup at the departmental level is technical expertise, or lack thereof. Most likely, departments and remote sites do not have the system programming and operations personnel. This talent is not generally available in large enough quantities to meet these needs, and it is not economically feasible to spend, for example, on the average of fifty thousand dollars annually to pay each system programmer for "babysitting" a minicomputer. As regards the 9370, these machines are designed to operate in environments where this expertise is not available. Yet, system backup must not be ignored.

A rather extreme, though not unrealistic, situation has often occurred in organizations which have adopted their own departmental solutions independent of the other departments in the organization. For example, an accounting department might have its own multi-user minicomputer system. An accounts payable clerk, accidentally destroying a large file, might go to the designated system administrator to ask that the file be restored from backup data. This individual, who might also be the head of the word-processing group, could respond with, "What's a backup?" It is situations like this that have brought central MIS and the departments back together. However, in spite of connectivity, the dangers of lack of coordination continue to threaten the success of computing in the departments. With sites spread out around the country, each with their own processsors, the potential for allowing these critical activities to slip through the cracks is even greater.

One solution to the backup problem is to have a system programmer act as a traveling backup coordinator, going from department to department to perform necessary system backups and other general maintenance activities. Other more realistic solutions are based on the ability of departmental processors to network with each other as well as with a central mainframe.

Connectivity with the host site offers many advantages to the department. Commands can be issued by the technical staff at the host site, central MIS, to the departments which result in data being backed up. Each department can be on its own schedule, depending on frequency of need, with the host being responsible for making sure that backup is occurring. System software at the department level could also take care of backup, with the software on the departmental processor issuing the command to the host mainframe. Thus the department could actually trigger the need for backup, and communicate this upwards, with the central mainframe actually doing the backup.

The most economical means of coordinating system backup where departments are involved is most likely through the central mainframe, with initiation being the responsibility of either the central site or the department. Scheduling of backups can be performed manually, or through the use of system software. Scheduling was discussed in Chapter 7. It is important to consider the overall workload of the central mainframe. Even a large host is limited, and cannot backup the data of one hundred sites, for example, simultaneously. Departmental backup schedules will need to be organized around this limitation.

Through backup at the host site, the department has automatic off-site — alternate site — protection. In case of a loss of service in the department or at a remote site, the means of restoration is located within the organization. At least at the departmental level, arranging for offsite storage of backup tapes and the administrative headaches associated with this, are eliminated. The ideal situation is to take data from the remote site and back it up to media that is owned by the host, and to do this automatically. The host then holds all of the backup data, on whatever medium, in one place. For purposes of disaster recovery, the backup tapes for the total organization are then sent off for alternate storage, without requiring that the departments be involved with this. At most, this process might require a command to be issued from the department, and system software could initiate this command. The fact that backup is occurring is not necessarily hidden from the user, but nevertheless intervention is minimal.

Technically, moving data from the departmental processor to the central mainframe is not yet a simple process. Data can be "pumped" down a datalink to the central mainframe, but transmission speeds at this point in time are not fast. With a central mainframe the size of IBM's 30XX series, the processing power is available to accomplish centralized backup. The communication capabilities to accomplish this in an efficient manner are rapidly being developed. Creating backup tapes at the departmental level, even if the tape commands are issued at the central site, will be a popular means of backing up data for the foreseeable future. These tapes can then be stored physically, or on DASD, or through a combined use of both media, at the central site.

Having multiple processors that are connected with each other also creates the potential of peer-to-peer backup. A scheme can be developed in which departmental processors serve as backups to each other, not only for system backup but for alternate processing in case of a disaster. This can be referred to as a ring configuration, and further expands the potential for processors within the same organization acting as alternate sites for each other. Also, this expands the usefulness of the departmental processors. Smaller departmental systems, with a few remote processors, will especially benefit from peer-to-peer backup. For example, System A can backup to System B and vice versa without creating a need for offsite transport. Again, this assumes communications capabilities between the two machines such that data transfer is feasible.

If a department is performing backup on a frequent, e.g. nightly, basis, most likely this will be an incremental backup. In most cases, this will best be accomplished through the use of DASD. Managing a tape system is costly because of storage and personnel costs, as well as the costs of tape drives. Storing incremental backups on DASD, with a less frequent full backup to tape, is easier for the users and faster. The DASD used for backup might be located on the departmental processor itself, or it might be located on the central mainframe, with the incremental backup data sent over communications lines to the central site. With peer-to-peer communications, data could also be backed up to DASD at another department.

Centralized Backup Issues

There are both advantages and disadvantages, as regards system backup, to a departmental system that is connected to a central mainframe. With Departmental Computing, central MIS has a fear of loss of control over midrange computers just as there was with the personal computer. End users will want central MIS intervention with needs such as backup, and this can facilitate a sense of cooperation between the two groups. Users want resources that they can touch, without having the support headaches associated with mainframe resources. This is where MIS will step in. Connectivity will solve many of the administrative coordination problems that have plagued earlier attempts at finding departmental solutions.

New administrative problems will also be created with processing at the departmental level. Whereas previously departments and the central site were not able to communicate, and thus coordination of effort was not possible, now there are many more interconnected resources, and coordination is critical. Scheduling of backups, to assure that resources are used at an optimal level with minimal disruption to users, will need to be considered carefully. The mainframe at the central site can handle only a limited number of simultaneous departmental backups, while users in the departments will not be able to simply shut down their activities to in deference to the central site. With a variety of software products being used in various departments, and the need of keeping current with new releases to assure immediate restoration of data, further coordination will also be needed. Most likely, departments will want to initiate their own restores, but will rely on the central site to have the information and technical resources available to accomplish this.

With Departmental Computing, the impact of a service outage is really minimized. If all VM users in an organization are sharing one machine, and it experiences an outage, then all of these users are affected. In a distributed environment, it is likely that fewer users will be affected. If one machine goes down, the others will continue processing. The down side to this is that the disaster recovery plan needs to take into account many different levels of users and applications spread throughout the organization. Coordinating a centralized site is much easier than coordinating the efforts on one or more departments or remote sites. Users will need to be kept abreast of the procedures involved in responding to a system outage and recovering data. Technical personnel will not be available in these locations to handle these procedures. Furthermore, with connectivity between the central site and the departmental processors, if the central site experiences a service outage, the remote sites will potentially be affected. An electrical failure, or a major user error, can effect performance monitoring, system security and other functions as well as backup. The central site will need to develop contingencies not only for its own resources, but also for the functions that are performed for the departments.

Due to advances in technology, disaster recovery is becoming more an issue of providing for recovery of data after user error, rather than thunderstorms. The central site will need to be equipped with a means of restoring data for users that can be initiated with minimal involvement by either users or system programmers. This will be facilitated by intelligent system software.

Chapter Summary

The conclusions of Chapter 10 can be summarized as follows:

- Disaster recovery is a nebulous term, and refers to both the ability to recover from natural disasters as well as user error.
- System backup is an important element of disaster recovery, and native VM provides this capability through TAPE DUMP and DDR.
- The development of the disaster recovery plan can be accomplished through a five phase process, beginning with the identification of critical systems through the testing of the plan.
- Departmental Computing offers many options for handling the organization's need for system backup, and this is most efficiently handled through coordination at the central site.

Chapter

11

Tape Storage in VM

Storing data with the use of tapes is a "necessary evil" in any production mainframe environment. Users have a need to store files and programs for future reference and transfer data between computers. The disaster recovery plan also has tape requirements. With the extensive user involvement fostered by the VM environment, the use of tape as a storage medium can become a major management issue. Effective tape management, with storage alternatives, is discussed.

Using Tape in VM

Tapes have been referred to as the last great manual task of the computer age. In spite of many rapid developments, the magnetic tape remains the medium of choice for storing data. There have been improvements to tape management, including automatic tape loaders, cartridge tapes, and library systems. But organizations that are otherwise technologically sophisticated continue to rely on large operations staffs to mount and label tapes. This may in part be due to the need that humans have for being able to touch and hold what belongs to them, and a distrust of less concrete DASD. Though realtively inexpensive, tape is subject to so many potential mishaps that the comfort factor can be far overshadowed by the risks.

The use of tape involves much more than asking an operator to mount and then detach a clean tape on a tape drive. It includes labeling tapes, to maintain control over what is on each tape and to make sure that the information is not destroyed. The storage of tapes is also an issue. With many users making use of this storage medium, the physical storage of these tapes, so that a user's tape can be located when requested, can become a major logistical exercise.

Tapes may very well be of minimal use in a departmental environment, depending on the availability of DASD, as well as the disaster recovery plan. Some departments may have a need for their own tape drives, and may even arrange for their own storage. Others will rely on the central site for backup capabilities. In either case, tapes will be in use at the central site, and effective tape management, as well as alternatives, will be important.

Why Tape?

Something complicated may be implied by the term "tape," but using tapes in the computer room is not much different from using them in the living room. The owner of a casette tape player, recording music from a favorite record, is performing the same basic task as that which a tape operator does in the VM Data Center. The tape operator is recording corporate data, yet the process is much the same.

Tapes are generally considered the medium of choice for system backup as discussed in Chapter 10. Tapes provide a way of storing data in case of disasters that result from hardware error, or "head crash." Data that is no longer being actively used, but which may be needed at a later time, can also be stored on tape. In addition, past versions of a file, such as a program, may need to be stored as working copies and reused at a later time.

The kinds of tape storage needs in the VM environment can be summarized as follows:

- System backup: All data needs to be stored in case of a disaster.
- Obsolete files: Files not currently used may be needed again.
- Changing files: Past versions of a file may be needed later.

Tapes hold data much more cheaply than does a DASD, so they are often used to store mass quantities of data, thus freeing up the DASD. If the data has to be taken offline, tapes are a good portable medium. For example, tapes are used when transferring data from one computer to another. The data can be created on one CPU, dumped to tape, and then loaded and read onto another CPU.

Tape in the VM Environment

VM was not originally designed as a production system, and the use of tape has traditionally been reserved for the storage of large volumes of data, or for transferring software between CPUs. During the early days of VM, neither of these needs really created a need for tape management in native VM. The requirements were thus so ad hoc that issues such as security and storage were really not of concern. It is when the uses of VM expanded that the requirements for tape as a storage medium also expanded. The risks also increased.

The use of tape drives in VM is controlled by simple commands. When "attaching a tape drive," the user is literally defining a direct connection between the virtual machine and an actual tape drive. The only restriction is that the tape drive cannot currently be in use by another user. Once a tape drive is attached, a tape can be mounted and data can be moved from or to the user's virtual machine.

The process of using a tape drive begins with a MOUNT command. This is not a VM command, rather it is built, or "home-grown," within each VM installation. The MOUNT command basically accomplished what the user would normally have to do by hand. In order to mount a tape (place a tape on a tape drive), without the use of a command, a user would need to physically carry a tape to the computer operator and ask that it be mounted. The MOUNT command accomplishes this same purpose, and is followed by other information, including the VOLSER. This refers to the Volume Serial Number, and is a means of identifying the actual tape that should be mounted. If any tape can be mounted, then the VOLSER is replaced by SCRATCH. The density of the tape may also be indicated, as well as whether the tape is for input or output. If the tape is for output — data is being transferred to it — the operator must insert a write ring. The user may also indicate other information, such as that the tape has a "blue sticker" on it. Hopefully, most VM installations have evolved past merely identifying a tape as "the one with my name on a red label, on the bottom shelf of the cabinet on your right."

With a MOUNT command, sent online as a message, the operator then receives this message on his console, and responds appropriately. In reality, the operator might be in the process of clearing the console screen and may miss the message, or may be out of the computer for awhile. The command may have to be sent more than once, followed by a telephone call.

The series of steps that are performed by the operator after acknowledging the users MOUNT command are as follows:

1. The operator locates the requested tape and then returns to the console.
2. The operator visually compares the label on the tape with the tape the user has requested, to verify that he has the correct tape. If the tape is a scratch tape, the operator prepares a "sticky-back" label.
3. The operator determines which tape drives are available. The drives must be of the correct type (reel or cartridge) and capable of handling the tape's density.

4. The operater selects a tape drive for the user's request.
5. The operator places the tape on the tape drive (mounts the tape), with or without a write ring.
6. The operator issues an ATTACH command to connect the tape drive with the user.
7. The operator sends a message to the user indicating that the tape is ready for use.

The ATTACH command serves to attach the tape drive to the user's virtual machine. There are no "virtual tape drives" in VM; the user has control of a real device. Attaching the tape drive is followed by the manual mounting of the tape. Assuming that tapes are cataloged efficiently, and both user and operator have identified the correct tape, the user is now in control of what is done with the tape.

When finished with the tape drive, the user issues a DETACH command. This releases the tape drive for the use by another user, and the operator removes the tape ane places it back in the tape library. If the user forgets to do this, it remains attached until the user logs off from the system. DETACH, a CP command, indicates to CP to detach the tape drive from the user's virtual machine. Other CP commands related to the use of the tape drive include REWIND, which rewinds the tape, and UNLOAD, which dismounts the tape from the tape drive.

During the time that the user is using a tape, CP does not "see" a word of the data that is being retrieved from, or sent to, the tape. This is strictly a private affair between the user and the tape. There is no validation, or security, built into this process.

Though tape storage plays a major role in disaster recovery, there are also numerous disasters that may be associated with the use of the tape itself. The write ring must be inserted in the tape to enable it to be written on. This protects the tape from being written on inadvertently. If an operator accidentally forgets to remove a write ring, the data on the tape is subject to being destroyed. For example, if a user types TAPE DUMP instead of TAPE LOAD, all information on the tape is essentially "wiped out." If the operator has also given the wrong tape to the user, the result is that another user's data is destroyed.

Security is another potential problem in the use of tapes. Tapes are often labeled with information about what is contained on the tape, and if the area in which the tapes are stored is not physically secured, anyone can walk in and take a tape belonging to another user. The tape is only monitored at the time that the drive is attached and the label checked. Once a user has talked an operator into loading a tape, all data on the tape can be read, and the tape can be written on. This security hole even extends to the operating system itself. An experience user can make a tape of the operating system itself, without any security that the installation may have added, mount this copy, and then be "off and running" without any of the standard intercepts. The security officer may not even be aware that it occurred.

The use of tapes in the native VM environment can be a relatively simple process. The tapes need to be cataloged carefully, with a labeling procedure that is clearly understood and standardized so that tapes can easily be retrieved. Operators need to be conscientious about verifying the tape labels before mounting them, and users need to keep careful records concerning the tapes that belong to them. Operators may need to verify actual ownership of a tape before giving a user control of it. With minimal tape use, this is most likely an adequate system. However, with many users initiating tape commands during an average day or even heavy tape use by a data backup system, the potential for human error, on the part of both users and operators, becomes a greater possibility.

Managing Tape

The VM operating system provides an easy and readily available method for storing both individual user and organizational data on tape. What is not provided is a means of identifying tapes, nor a means of assuring that each user's data security is protected. This level of management, if needed, is the responsibility of the VM installation.

Tape Labels

The "sticky" label on the outside of a case containing a tape is referred to as an external label. This contains information that identifies the owner of the tape and what is contained on it. These external labels are supplemented or replaced by internal labels, which are recorded on the actual tapes.

The external label poses an immediate security threat, as discussed previously, as well as being a very inefficient means of record keeping. Installations using tapes generally have a labeling procedure developed. The procedure includes perhaps printing the content information on a label, and sticking the label to the case that the tape is stored in. This needs to be a very careful operation. Humans make mistakes in recording the tape's content, or labels are placed on the wrong cases. Because information is read sequentially from a tape, recovering information from mislabeled tapes can be a very time-consuming if not futile exercise.

VM sites have moved away from external labels, toward serial and internal labels. A serial label is based on a numbering system, such that numbers are created to identify tapes in a clearly understood sequence. This provides a basis for storing the tapes as if in a library, each tape arranged according to its serial number.

Serial labeling provides a basis for internal labels. An internal label is stored at the beginning of the tape itself. This is accomplished by attaching a tape drive to a user's virtual machine, and issuing this command:

TAPE WVOL1 (VOLSER)

This literally translates to "write a volume 1 label on the tape." It is followed by the volume serial number (VOLSER) to identify the tape on which the label should be written. The label is written on the beginning of the tape. The operating system is writing this label, but the user must enter the command which causes the label to be written. It is not automatic.

The potential weakness with this labeling system, in an environment where many users are actively using tapes, is that CP does not subsequently check this label when the tape is used at a later time. The user is not forced to enter a volume serial number against which this label could be checked. Also, the label can easily be "wiped out." Data can be written to the tape and the label destroyed by simply being overwritten. CMS TAPE DUMP, for example, will write over any internal labels previously on the tape.

Added Tape Protection

Depending on the needs of the organization, there are added protections which need to be included in the tape management system. These can be developed inhouse or purchased through system software available from IBM and other vendors.

In a production environment, with extensive tape demands, there are other labeling requirements which serve to make tape management more efficient and secure. The use of a dataset name in the tape label, as well as a creation date and an expiration date or retention period, facilitates the subsequent retrieval of data that is stored on tape. The dataset name basically identifies the data that is stored on the tape, with the operator being directed to restore the tape which contains the data the user is seeking. An example of a dataset name is Payroll Master. Based on this term, the operator then might load a tape with a volume serial number of XYZ001, which contains this dataset. The advantage to being able to use a dataset name in the MOUNT command rather than a tape number is that names such as Payroll Master can serve as traveling names. For example, the payroll might be updated on a weekly basis. When this tape is requested, the most recently updated Payroll Master tape should be loaded. This is an internal dataset name that is part of the internal label, and not written on the outside of the tape 's storage case for anyone to see.

Expiration dates are another consideration for effective tape management. In the VM environment, once a user takes possession of a resource like a tape reel or a minidisk, there is no inherent expiration of this possession. It is theirs forever. This is a perfectly acceptable system until the organization's use of VM moves from that of a testing or development environment to, with the addition of users, a production environment. Users store more and more information on tapes, and these tapes require an increasing amount of physical space.

Once a tape is stored on the rack, there is a fear of scratching this information. Users are concerned they might need it again, and the operations staff is afraid to interfere with important data. The staff generally has no idea who the tape even belongs to. Users leave the organization and leave tapes behind.

This eternal possession becomes a mixed blessing with tape storage. Even if users are not actively using a resource, they will keep it just in case a need arises somewhere in the distant future. They are not going to say, "I don't need this anymore, please take it back." It is simple human nature. The resource cannot be reclaimed, short of physically pinning the user down and taking it away with brute force. This is an option, but is not in keeping with the culture of most civilized organizations.

Through purchased system software the tape storage system can be made more efficient with the use of expiration dates included in the internal label. When a user stores information on tape, he or she gives (or the system provides) an expiration date. The expiration date is the point in time at which the data that the user has stored is no longer needed. At that point it may be purged and the tape can be reused.

A retention period is similar in function to an expiration date, expressed in number of days. Rather than specifying a specific date on which the tape expires, the retention period is a period of time, such as 14 days from the day the tape was cut. At the end of the retention period, the tape may be reused.

Retention periods can be included on an external sticky label of a tape, without the use of system software. However, tapes have a very short lifespan. If allowed to remain in the same position year after year, tapes stretch. This may render the data unreadable.

Alternatives to DASD

Archiving is the process of sending data off to be stored on tape, rather than taking up valuable DASD space with seldom or no longer used files. Users who understand the system backup process also realize that data is backed up periodically, with no protection for individual versions of files changing more than once between backups. Archiving is a way for the user to protect his or her investment, by sending data to tape as needed. The organization's investment in the employee is also protected.

An example of the need for archive capabilities would be a file that has been modified throughout the day, with each version containing important features that may be needed at a later time. At some point in the user's day he or she may want to go back to an earlier version of the file. These files can each be saved on DASD by renaming each version of the file, eg., PROG1, PROG2, PROG3. But soon, the user is on the verge of running out of DASD, especially if these files sit for months.

The user can depend on the installation's backup system, but for changes occurring within backups, this is inadequate. For example, if the user's installation runs a nightly incremental backup, then last night's version, if the file existed at that time, has been backed up. The only version of the file that would be backed up by the system is the version that exists at the end of the day. With the ability to archive, the user could also be assured that the various versions of the product would be available the next day, regardless of system backup. Furthermore, the data is not taking up expensive DASD, and it is protected from disasters.

Other examples of obsolete files would include information that must be stored to meet government regulations. Old personnel files might also be archived, as might information needed for the far-distant future.

Archiving is performed for and by the user, while backup is performed for the system as a whole, and initiated at the system level. Archiving is similar to backup, with data dumped to tape and, if the user so desires, manually recorded. Users may have to archive several versions of the same file, depending on its use, which necessitates careful recording of which tape is being used, where on the tape the file is recorded, and where the various versions of the same file are located. It is the responsibility of the user in native VM to manually record this information.

Some organizations develop a local system of providing archiving capability through a series of EXECs. These are small programs within CMS that help the user to archive files from DASD to tape. These EXECs must be maintained locally, because they are not part of native VM or a software product. With careful use, by relatively sophisticated users, a system of EXECs for archiving purposes can be adequate. The costs involved in technical support, however, can be prohibitive.

Archive System Software

Archiving capability can also be provided through system software. Archive system software serves as an intermediary between the user and the operations staff, so that users do not use tapes directly. The storage of data to tape occurs through the use of the virtual service machine. The user does not have direct access to a tape. The files that are to be stored on tape are sent off to a virtual machine which essentially "archives" the files. Thus, the files are sent to a "virtual tape." At a later time the user's files, as well as files sent to the service machine by other users, are stored on tape. The system software enforces the standard label on the tape, and adds the dataset name, expiration date, and any needed security information. At a later time, the user can then go through the system software to have the file returned to his minidisk.

Because of this service machine, files that may need to be archived can be staged, or sent to a storage area. The staging area holds versions of a file until they are sent off to the service machine to be transferred to tape. Though all files in the staging area are eventually sent off to tape, it serves as a temporary holding area. Thus if the user is modifying versions of the file, and wants to see one of the versions right away, it can be "pulled" from the staging area quickly, without requiring the restoration process that is required once a file has been archived. When files are in the staging area, they are still on DASD. Staging should be set up to be version limiting to prevent users from filling up the stage area. With this limitation, users are allowed to stage up to a specific number of files before being forced to actually archive them.

Archive system software provides the capability of setting individual retention periods for files, allowing the system to back up the individual files of users without having to back up the whole system. A feature in some archive products allows users to tag files for individual retention periods, such as a year or two. This is similar to the retention period in tape management, only at the individual file level. The system software can subsequently go through and purge the files that have expired, and generate a new tape with the files that have not yet expired. After this procedure, archived data that required 10 tapes may now require only 3. Users generally have the ability to subsequently query to find which files are still available on tape.

Archiving is really much more efficient than giving users direct access to tape. In addition to the potential security errors and general confusion associated with tape, archiving files requires much less space on a tape. Allowing a user to TAPE DUMP a complete 191 minidisk may require, for example, 4 inches of a 2400 foot tape reel. And the user now owns that tape reel forever. In most systems, it is not practical to allow users to share a single tape if this process is being done manually because each could then wipe out data that belongs to another user.

The advantage to system software for archiving is that it is much easier to use and thus more reliable than trying to accomplish similar goals in either native VM or through EXECs. By serving as an intermediary, the system software controls where the files are sent, and when the actual tape is written. At the same time, users have control over what gets archived while being provided a simple means of keeping DASD as uncluttered as possible. With archive system software, users can share tapes because no single user actually owns a tape.

Tape Versus DASD

Archiving provides an excellent alternative to expensive DASD, yet because this data is going to tape, there are potential drawbacks. At times, DASD itself may be the best file storage medium.

Tapes can be inconvenient. This inconvenience becomes very clear when data is subsequently retrieved from a tape. The data from a tape is read sequentially, and finding the spot at which the data of one user ends, and another user's data begins, can be very time consuming. Waste is another major problem with using tapes. Assuming 1600 bits per inch (1600 BPI), a file may require only 12 feet of tape. The remaining space on the tape is most likely wasted.

There is, however, a tremendous price break between DASD storage and sequential, or tape, storage. Data from a full DASD, costing thousands of dollars, can be stored on a $10 tape. This makes tape a very good storage medium for data that does not require expensive DASD, archived data being a good example of this. The disaster recovery plan, in addition, often requires the storage of data at an off-site location, and tape is the most convenient means of doing this. As has been discussed, because of human error, stretching, damage from weather, and difficulty in retrieving data, tape is also not without an unreliability factor. In fact, with current technological advances, DASD has become a much more reliable storage medium.

There are reasons why data may be backed up to DASD, stored on DASD that has been designated for the purpose of serving as a storage area for archived information. Though much more expensive than tape, DASD is in many ways more reliable. It is not subject to human error, or physical deterioration. It is also much faster to send data to DASD for storage than it is to send it off to a tape. And the subsequent restoring of information from DASD is essentially instantaneous and "foolproof," because the search is direct rather than sequential. It does not require waiting for a sequential search and does not require an operator who knows how to go forward on a tape to find a specific file.

Using DASD as a storage medium for system backup, for disaster recovery, is a matter of calulated risk. If all data is backed up to DASD, and a major earthquake occurs, than the organization is definitely in trouble. But used in combination with tape, DASD can streamline the backup process. For example, some VM sites are in areas where there are strong unions. Night time operators may be so expensive that it is more economical to buy extra DASD for routine incremental backups, while doing a full system backup to tape, perhaps bi-weekly. The calculated risk is based on cost. An organization may decide that a week's worth of data is worth $100,000. It may then be worthwhile to risk the loss of $200,000 in data in case of an emergency, to save the costs involved in transferring data to tape on a nightly basis. The full system backup to tape, biweekly, continues to assure that at most 2 weeks worth of data would be lost in an emergency.

When a user stores information on a disk, she is not in control at the same level as she is when using a tape drive. Users access a disk as a "virtual disk," or minidisk, while a tape drive is accessed as a real device. A user cannot write over a disk label on a real disk drive as she can when using tape. Thus, DASD is much less subject to error as is tape. With system software, files archived to DASD can also be associated with expiration dates such that they would either be moved to tape or deleted when no longer necessary.

Tape Management in the Departments

It is likely that tapes will not play a big role on departmental machines, and many departmental processors will not even be equipped with tape drives. Most departments will not have the available support staff to effectively handle tapes, nor the storage space to keep them organized and secure.

Depending on function, some departments will have a need for tape. Those involved in scientific research, for example, will often need to deal with very large amounts of data for which DASD storage would be impractical. A department of an oil company involved with seismic data is also an example. This data would initially be stored on tape. The use of tape does imply the need for a trained operator, defeating the goal of operatorless environments in the departments. Tape drives are a computer babysitting task, so adopting this storage medium has many implications. It in many cases will be more economical to invest in additional DASD to avoid the need for manual support.

In discussing the Departmental Computing environment, the example of a secretary performing a nightly backup of the departmental machine is often highlighted. Departmental Computing implies networking capabilities, and as discussed under Disaster Recovery, backup will generally be coordinated from the central site. Critical data that needs to be stored on tape can be sent up to the central mainframe. The main barrier to this arrangement is the speed of the lines. Backups, for example, transfer a large amount of data. If one line is going up from the departmental machine to the mainframe, the line is going to be monopolized by the backup data for long periods of time. Speed will improve, and it is still more efficient than attempting to coordinate the backup-to-tape of many departments. Any needed tape storage will occur from tape drives attached to the central mainframe.

Departmental machines are relatively independent of each other due to the specialized functions of each department. Thus, there should be minimal transfer of data between machines needed. When it is, this can also be accomplished through networking. With the increasing reliability of DASD, archiving data to special DASD areas will also satisfy any needs previously met through tape storage. In addition, archived data can periodically be sent to the mainframe to be placed on tape.

Chapter Summary

Chapter 11 can be summarized as follows:

- When using a tape drive, the user's virtual machine has control of a real, rather than a virtual, device. There are minimal safeguards to assure that any data currently on the tape will not be erased as more is added.
- External labels, indicating what is actually stored on a tape, encourage security violations and are also a poor means of cataloging tapes. Serial labels, with internal labels stored on the tape itself, add a measure of security.
- Users can get involved in conserving valuable DASD by archiving data to tape. Rather than storing a complete minidisk, archiving involves the storing of seldom used files, freeing space on the user's minidisk.
- Though tape is less expensive than DASD as a storage medium, DASD is becoming increasingly reliable. When considering the personnel requirements associated with the use of tapes, and the potential for human error, DASD is a viable storage alternative.
- There will be little need for tape drives in the departments, with backup coordinated by the central site, and any other storage needs met through sending files to the central mainframe, or archiving them to DASD.

12

VM Accounting and Chargeback

Resource accounting and chargeback in the VM environment provide both a means of monitoring the utilization of resources and of making users aware of the cost of these resources. VM provides information about resource use through CP accounting records, which may serve as the basis for a sophisticated accounting and chargeback system.

Accounting in VM

The concept of charging for computer resources was probably invented by the timesharing industry, whose very livelihood depended upon the ability to ascertain an accurate record of what resources customers were using, and how they were being used. As the term implies, accounting is the ability to identify the utilization of hardware and software resources, including CPU time, devices such as DASD, and software application packages.

Accounting data provides valuable input for efforts aimed at balancing system load. Knowing which areas of the organization have the greatest need for computer resources is the beginning of providing these desired service levels. This information can also be used as a basis for influencing users to make more efficient use of the times of day when the CPU is in least demand, as was discussed under Workload Balancing in Chapter 7.

Someone is paying for computer resources; they do not "grow on trees." Whether the organization subsequently charges users for their use of these resources is a matter of organizational policy. If the Data Center is also designated as a profit center, or is at least required to break even, then chargeback will be necessary to regain the costs involved in facilitating the delivery of these resources. Even if actual money is not involved, chargeback is a way of enforcing budget limits, and, as discussed under DASD Management in Chapter 8, a way of making users aware of what these resources cost. Other organizations view chargeback as unnecessary, with computer resources considered overhead, the same as electricity and telephone use.

A system of accounting and chargeback does indeed help the owner of the data more than it does the user, because those responsible for providing these resources are more concerned with cost and availability. However, if limits and even charges are being imposed on users, a comprehensive and easily understood system provides a means of keeping everyone informed as to what has been used and what is available.

CP Accounting

The Control Program generates many records that may be used as a basis for accounting. In fact, there are eight major types of records that may be generated during an average user session. Records are based not only on the session itself, but the use of real devices and links to other users. For many of these record types, more than one may be generated during the course of a session. In addition to CP records, software package usage may cause accounting records of their own to be generated at various times. The result is a number of accounting records being generated as a result of system use.

Most CP accounting records are generated automatically. However, three records, which record unsuccessful LINK attempts, successful LINKs, and unsuccessful AUTOLOG and LOGON attempts are not generated unless chosen by the system programmer as a system generation option. In the DMKSYS module, which was discussed in Chapter 4, there is a macro called SYSJRL. To activate the production of CP accounting records, the programmer indicates:

JOURNAL=YES

This in effect turns on the production of accounting records that detect and record unsuccessful access attempts by unauthorized users and all links.

The best way to think of a CP accounting record is to envision the "old-fashioned" punch card. CP generates the accounting record in an 80-column format; it has a length of 80 bytes. There are eight types of accounting records, each containing identification of the virtual machine associated with the use of the resource, and other information concerning the actual resource use. Common to each record is the userid, as well as the user's account number. The account number is limited to eight characters, and is assigned in the user's CP directory entry, based on whatever system the organization has for assigning these numbers. Generally, VM sites indicate user account numbers through a combination of numbers, letters, or symbols.

Following is a description of each of the eight types of accounting records.

Type 01 — Session record

Only one session record is created for each user session, with a session being defined as a period of time on which a user's virtual machine is logged on. The single record is created irregardless of how long the user is actually logged on, for one hour or ten hours. Some accounting system software packages cause multiple session records to be generated, but this is not part of native VM. The format of the session record is shown below.

```
1–8    VIRTUAL MACHINE IDENTIFICATION
9–16   VIRTUAL MACHINE ACCOUNTING NUMBER
17–22  DATE OF ACCOUNTING (END) — YYMMDD
23–28  TIME OF ACCOUNTING (END) — HHMMSS
29–32  NUMBER OF SECONDS CONNECTED
33–36  MILLISECONDS OF CPU TIME USED
37–40  MILLISECONDS OF VIRTUAL CPU TIME USED
41–44  TOTAL PAGE READS
45–48  TOTAL PAGE WRITES
49–52  VIRTUAL SIO COUNT FOR NON-SPOOLED PUNCH
53–56  VIRTUAL CARD COUNT — SPOOLED PUNCH
57–60  VIRTUAL LINE COUNT — SPOOLED PRINTER
61–64  VIRTUAL CARD COUNT — SPOOLED READER
65–78  (RESERVED)
79–80  CARDTYPE CODE (01)
```

Again, an accounting record has a length of 80 bytes. At the left of the accounting records shown above is the number of the actual columns needed for the accounting data, indicated at the right.

The first eight columns of the session record contain the user's virtual machine identification. This is the userid. The user's accounting number is indicated in columns 9–16.

When a user logs on, time begins to accumulate immediately. The session record is actually generated, or "cut," at the moment the user logs off, recorded as the end date (columns 17–22) and end time (columns 23–28). The connect time, recorded in columns 29–32, is the amount of time, in seconds, that the user was actually logged on. The connect time can subsequently be subtracted from the end time to calculate the moment in time at which the user logged on. CP does not perform this calculation, but it is useful for determining the shift during which the user was active, for chargeback by shift.

Users may have been idle for much of the logon session. The accounting session record also includes, in columns 33–36, the milliseconds of total CPU time actually used. An active user would have a higher number in this category than one who had been largely inactive. In columns 37–40, the number of milliseconds of virtual CPU time is also recorded. The total CPU time in columns 33–36 is calculated by CP and is based on this formula:

Virtual CPU time + overhead CPU time = total CPU time

Overhead CPU utilization is dependent on system load, i.e., the number of demands other users are also making on the CPU. Virtual CPU time is what the user's application actually requires (problem state). Overhead CPU utilization (supervisor state) includes system paging between virtual and real memory. Paging occurs the most during peak times, and individual users really have no control over this occurrence, other than to save more CPU-intensive tasks for non-peak hours. When CP is forced to read or write a page into virtual storage, "tallys" are added to the PAGE READS (columns 41–44) and PAGE WRITES (columns 45–48) categories.

Each time a user reads or writes from a disk or tape during the session, the number of records or lines of information spooled to the device are tallied in columns 49–52. The commands initiating the use of these devices are not being counted, rather the lines of information being sent to them. This information is not separated according to device.

PUNCH refers to the process of transferring a file, generally from one user to another. This transfer is generally accomplished through the SPOOL facility, with the file routed to the other user's virtual machine reader. When the PUNCH command is used, files are sent in the form of 80 character virtual cards, similar to the format of the CP accounting records. In fact, the term "punch" refers to the process of punching these cards. The session record, in columns 53–56, tallies the number of records that were transferred. If data is spooled to a printer, the accounting record reflects the actual number of lines of data that were sent to the printer and not how many were actually printed, in columns 57–60. If a user has many print files in hold status, waiting for a printer, and these files are not subsequently printed, the accounting record still reflects the I/O required to get these files to the printer queue. In columns 61–64, the number of virtual punch cards sent to the user's reader, which is an area in which files wait to be read by the user, are tallied.

On the type 01 session record, columns 65–78 are reserved for IBM use. The record type, which in this case is 01, is recorded in columns 79–80.

There is only one type 01 session record generated for a user's session. Of course, if the user logs on and off repeatedly throughout the day, a session record would be cut each time that this occurred. The session record, because of the nature of the information, is key input into accounting and chargeback systems.

Other accounting records may be generated repeatedly during the course of a user session. These are described below.

Type 02 — Dedicated Device Usage

A type 02 record indicates the user's dedicated device usage. For example, if a virtual machine had a tape drive connected to it, and then detached the drive by issuing a CP DETACH command, or logs off, a type 02 record is cut. The data in the record includes the number of seconds that the user had control of the device. If a user had control of a tape drive more than once, then a record would be cut each time the device was detached.

Type 03 — TDISK Usage

Each time a user creates temporary disk space (TDISK), for additional space, this record is cut at the moment the DETACH command is issued or the user logs off. TDISK space is created with a CP DEFINE command and provides the ability to "borrow" extra space during the user session. This temporary space disappears at the moment the user disconnects or logs off. The 03 record includes the device type, the amount of space used, and the number of seconds connected.

Type 04 — Invalid LOGON and AUTOLOG Attempt

If another user attempts either to log on or autolog the user's virtual machine, this record will be cut to record the attempted violation. Each attempt is not recorded; rather a threshold is set and invalid attempts beyond this threshold cause the record to be cut.

Type 05 — Successful LINK

The type 05 record is generated when another makes a successful link to the user's minidisk.

Type 06 — Unsuccessful LINK Attempt

This record is generated as a result of an unsuccessful attempt of another user to link to the user's minidisk.

As discussed earlier, records 04, 05, and 06 are not cut automatically, but as a result of having activated the CP JOURNAL option. Most chargeback systems do not actually cost these records, but they may be included in a security report.

Type 07 — VCNA Usage

This record indicates the use of the VTAM Communication Network Application, with VTAM referring to Virtual Terminal Access Method. Whenever a VTAM communications network is used, to transmit or receive data directly, for example, this record is generated.

Type 08 — Optional

This is a seldom used accounting record, with application for security purposes.

CP accounting records provide an excellent basis for an accounting system, with records covering the major user activities that affect resource consumption. It is the subsequent use of these records, however, that constitutes an accounting system.

Using the CP Records

When accounting records are created they are routed to a specific userid, via the spooling system. Unless the organization has provided a means of using these records, they simply "sit." VM has no standard mechanism to periodically copy records from the spool areas to a minidisk. If the individual responsible for accounting assumes that the system is also recording chargeback data, disappointment will result. The CP accounting records lump together information about resource use. Also, some needed information is not included; for example, the amount of disk space in use by each user is not included in the standard data stream. There is no provision in native VM for allocating DASD costs. Also, interactive users cannot query the records online as a means of finding out how many resources have been used and what is available. Also, spool space is subject to loss if there is a system outage, and if no means of removing these records has been developed, they can easily disappear.

Thus, even though the CP records are capturing valuable information, its use is limited if it remains raw information. These records are not providing actual cost, which is really site-determined, nor is there an algorithm provided to determine costs. Capabilities such as these must either be purchased as system software or designed by the installation.

An organization using the standard VM accounting facilities with no added provisions for resource accounting will most likely spool CP-generated accounting records to a CMS minidisk. These can later be recorded on tape to be kept as historical information. Most likely an organization that does not take the time to account for resources is charging this use to overhead, rather than allocating it to users. Even if there is no desire to change this policy, this information is a basis of estimating the future needs of the organization for increased computing resources, based on past use, though the CP records will not indicate which software packages are being used and which are not. Resource accounting information can also indicate which system resources are being used most efficiently.

Through the use of resource accounting packages, either purchased or developed in house, the CP accounting records can be the basis for a comprehensive system for both tracking the allocation of resources as well as subsequently charging for use.

The Resource Accounting System

Whether implemented in house or through system software, there are some basic considerations involved in developing a resource accounting system which protects the needs of the VM environment. It is important that the resource usage be tracked at the level needed for the organization to meet its objectives, without interfering with the capabilities that users need to perform their online tasks as efficiently as possible. The accounting system needs to be as transparent, performing this service without extensive user involvement. At the departmental level, this transparency, with the lack of onsite technical support, is even more important.

Setting up an accounting system is perhaps an interesting intellectual exercise but there are many others that are not only less complicated, and that also do not incur the potential wrath of the user community. The steps involved in setting up a system will be discussed briefly as a prelude to looking at considerations and alternatives.

Cost Allocation

The definition of resources to be costed and the allocation of these costs are important elements in resource accounting. As discussed, the Data Center may be a cost or a profit center, and the basic objectives of resource accounting will be based on this decision. If the ultimate objective of accounting is to recoup the cost of the resources, and even to make a profit, then the accounting system will be used as a basis for actual billing. If not, this information will provide a basis for decision making. Whether users are actually charged or not, the resource accounting system is a basis for budgeting and capacity planning.

There are many computer resources that can potentially be included in the tracking for resource accounting. Those that are reported in CP accounting records include session utilization resources, such as connect time, CPU-time, page reads and writes, and I/Os. The CP record related to the use of devices includes data concerning tape and disk drives. The use of TDISKs is another accountable resource, as is the use of VCNA. Information that is not yielded from the CP records, but could also be potentially accountable expenses, include the following:

- Consulting assistance from central MIS, or the Data Center
- Operating system maintenance, from a system programmer
- Administrative support and supplies
- Utilities and office space
- Performance monitoring and productivity improvement software
- Losses of resource availability, for maintenance or downtime

These costs are essentially overhead, but nevertheless represents expenses that are incurred in the process of providing information resources to users. As with other resources, someone pays for them, and overhead increases with the need to provide services to users. With Departmental Computing and the relatively autonomous units that result, the need to account for the resources of central MIS, if not individual departmental users, becomes more necessary as a means of monitoring the demands made on the central MIS group. This will be discussed further under Departmental Accounting Issues.

Costs that may be allocated vary over time. Central MIS and the Data Center experience changes in the types of personnel that are needed. For example, support functions such as application development and user training needs are greater at some times than at others. The expenditures for personal computers and associated software are variable. Thus, the means of allocating cost must be flexible to reflect the objectives and functions included under resource management. Of course, moving from a central to a departmental scheme will also result in changes in the way of allocating cost.

One method of allocating charges is through distributed charging. This involves allocating charges to jobs within an overall category. A category might include a department, or a cluster of applications. The basis of the charges is then based on the proportional utilization of computer resources and operating cost. Financial applications would be an example of an area that might be subject to distributed charging. Tasks requiring the use of accounting software would be associated with charges accrued by task. For example, the biweekly payroll run would be a chargeable item. Standard rates are assigned to computer resources, based on overhead. Below is an equation for computing this charge:

$$\text{Task distributed charge} = \text{operating cost} * \text{percent of total charge}$$

Thus, the task is being charged based on the portion of the total resources required to complete it. These costs might include both actual resource uses as well as MIS overhead. Overhead may be included in the total charge or separated out as a line item. To reiterate, native VM does not provide a means of relating resource utilization directly to applications; accounting software must be added to accomplish this level of accounting.

If true charges are to be calculated, the method of figuring rates must be more accurate than that required for distributed charging. Because distributed charges are proportional, costs can be lumped together. Charges based on the true cost of the resource must be based on rates that are clear and equitable.

Differential accounting, based on peak and nonpeak shifts, is a means of achieving workload balancing through encouraging users to make more efficient use of potentially strained peak hour CPU utilization. Typically, an organization should not be processing large production tasks or anything else that requires a large amount of resources, including payroll processing or accounts payables, during the standard work day. The greatest number of CMS interactive users are probably on the system during the 8–to–5 shift, and response time will be degraded. To discourage this, a lower cost per unit can be set for the nonpeak hours. Sites most often charge the highest rates between the hours of 8 a.m. to 5 p.m., then lower the rates for 5 p.m. until midnight, with the lowest rates occurring from midnight to 8 a.m. and weekends and holidays. This entices work groups needing central mainframe resources to schedule these jobs for processing during the less costly shift. Money is saved and the system load is balanced.

It is feasible to calculate differential rates based on time of day. Most organizations think in terms of three shifts. However, if costing is based only on the point at which the user logged off, taken from the CP accounting record, this information is not necessarily indicating the time of day during which the work occurred. The CP session record provides a session end time and total connect time from which a start time can be calculated. From this time, it can be ascertained what shift the user was in when logging on. This information can be used for differential rates based on whether the work was completed during peak or nonpeak time. The date may also be used as a means of calculating weekend rates.

Whatever the accounting method, if users are impacted by it, through true billing or monthly reports, repeatability is important. The same charges for each unit of work, based on time it was performed, need to be allocated. Once users understand this, they will pattern their behavior to stay within budget limits, or treat actual charges more seriously. Knowing what to expect, and understanding how costs are accrued, provides users with a level of control. Also, this information needs to be readily accessable to users, so that it can be used for individual planning.

Accounting Structure Considerations

Implementing an accounting structure for information resources in the VM environment does not have to result in the actual exchange of money between users and MIS. As discussed, the chargeback system is a method of costing resources. The considerations in structuring accounting are really the same, regardless of "who gets the bill." What is required to accomplish detailed accounting is software designed to accomplish this task within the VM environment.

An accounting structure is basically a hierarchy, with users grouped primarily by customer identification. Assuming that information resources are based in the Data Center, the customer is most likely a department. From this level, resources can be charged according to projects, account numbers, users, or based on other relevant categories. It is important to determine the structure that is best for the organization. For some, charging departments separately will be necessary for recouping the costs of resources, while others charge individual users regardless of department.

Figure 12-1 illustrates a resource accounting structure. This structure assumes that the resources being charged are located within the domain of central MIS, through the Data Center, rather than being consumed at the local departmental processor level.

Within each department, resources may be grouped under one or more project names. Project accounting provides a way to charge various tasks, during the same session, to different accounts. This is important when many functions cut across departmental boundaries.

RESOURCE ACCOUNTING STRUCTURE

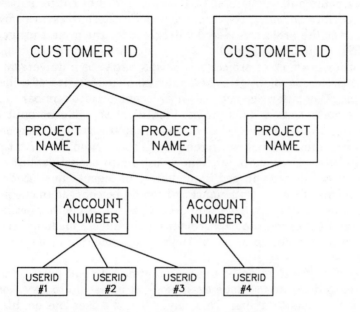

Figure 12-1 A resource accounting structure based on projects

Project accounting begins in the CP directory. Each userid in the CP directory is associated with an eight-character account number, to be assigned by the installation. Each user does not necessarily have his or her own account number; it is generally linked to the department so that each member of a department shares the same account number, or depending on job function, users in the department may be grouped by account numbers. For example, in the accounting department, personnel in accounts payable may have a different account number from those in accounts receivable. This allows the organization to track the costs associated with each of these functions.

Accounting software can allow the organization to track the use of shared resources by linking account numbers to various project names. This is done before actually beginning the work for that project, through the use of some form of a START command, followed by the name of the project. After the work associated with a specific project is terminated, an END command is then issued. Thus, if an accounts payable clerk does work associated with a specific account that has been assigned a project name, the resources involved in performing this work would be charged to that project. Someone in accounts receivable, doing work on the same project, might have a different account number but would also perform this work under the same project name. The accounting software, once the END command is issued, would create a 01 CP session record. Every time a project START command was issued a CP record would be cut for subsequent work performed since the user logged on. Resources are now distributed to the project. A record will be cut for the project usage when the END command is issued.

Another example of project accounting might be a university situation. A professor might give the students in each section of a class, for example, Computer Science 101, a different project number identifying the class section. This project identification could be built into a command which is invoked each time that the students log on, and serve to automatically cost system use to the section in which the student belongs. Even more efficient would be to assign default project numbers which are charged immediately at logon. Thus, students in Section One of Computer Science 101 would be charged to one project, while those in Section Two would be charged to another project. At the end of the term, the department would have a means of tracking the resources required to complete the assignments in each section of the course.

Project accounting can be semiautomatic. A default project number, as discussed in the previous example, can be set up to be associated with each account number. This way, when the user logs on, his charges are automatically charged to a specific project, from the beginning. This project might simply be General Departmental Use. If a user has not entered a default project command, it will still be costed.

Actual project information is included in an extension that is appended to the 80 byte CP accounting record, discussed earlier in this chapter. System software packages utilizing project accounting use a master file that is set up with the name of each project, that is in turn associated with a customer name for billing purposes. The customer is whomever is responsible for the cost, and may be the department manager.

Project accounting provides a great amount of flexibility in accounting for resources. If only using account numbers, charges all go to one number, and the organization is still left with the question of which resources are being used for what purpose. With project accounting, because account numbers can be associated with many projects, resources can be tracked accordingly.

Project accounting provides an additional level of resource protection. When charging by project, even though the project is associated with a customer, or in turn department, a userid cannot access a project unless the account number has been authorized to do so. Through the use of the master file, containing project numbers, account numbers accessing these projects can be validated. The master file invokes yet another file that relates project numbers and account numbers. When the project START command is issued, the system software checks to see if the account number is authorized to access that project.

Package accounting is another area for consideration in resource accounting. There are many miscellaneous software packages in an average organization, and it is not an uncommon situation for MIS to be totally unaware of the actual use of any of them. Package accounting is essentially a level down from project accounting in the resource accounting structure, with the use of software packages being charged either to a project or to an account number. For example, software packages can be associated with certain projects, and usage would thus be charged to the account numbers associated with those projects.

Package accounting not only provides a means of tracking usage, but it is also a means of limiting use. For example, the package access can be set up such that only a limited number of users are allowed to access the package at one time. So if eight users at one time are authorized, and a ninth attempts to execute a program, this user would be prevented from doing so until one of the others was finished. This protects the system from the demands of CPU-intensive applications.

The bottom line in determining resource accounting is to determine those resources that need to be tracked, and the level at which this needs to occur. It is important to make sure that adequate information about the use of the system is available. But it is equally important to make sure that resources are not being tracked to the point that users are frustrated, and so much information is made available that it is not digested. Resource accounting starts with a carefully thought out set of objectives, and builds from this point.

User Resistance

The VM environment provides users with high levels of control and flexibility. It doesn't take long for users to become comfortable with accessing software packages at will, using applications, and storing data at will. It is easy to view these resources as any other "unlimited" resource, similar to the telephone. As these resources become heavily utilized, accounting as a means of tracking or chargeback becomes necessary. Suddenly being required to enter account numbers or START commands, being prevented from accessing a software package due to lack of authorization, receiving a bill at the end of the month, all of these occurrences can serve to interfere with the success of the accounting effort.

The greatest resistance to resource accounting occurs when the program is first put into place. Users are threatened both by the prospect of losing privileges, as well as the discovery of misuse of resources. This can be illustrated by situations that have occurred in organizations that institute a program for tracking long-distance telephone use. Reports in the newspapers often make light of organizations who have discovered the loss of thousands of dollars through employee use of 900 numbers and long-distance calls home.

Resource accounting can shed light on the waste of resources in the same manner as tracking long-distance telephone bills. For example, an organization discovered that large amounts of documentation were being sent from one remote site to another, weekly, over RSCS lines. It was simpler for the persons involved to do this than to take the time to package the information and use the mail system.

The key to overcoming user resistance is to prepare users ahead of time for the impending changes. Any needed training should be completed before the changes are actually introduced, and the accounting procedures should be phased in as much as possible. It may even be necessary, if chargeback is involved, to phase in actual billing over a period of time. Users need to know what is being costed, the actual costs involved, and how they can control expenses. Once this is accomplished, users are more likely to cooperate with the program. System software which provides both transparency and ease of use will facilitate the involvement of users.

Accounting Software Requirements

Accounting system software should work with and enhance the capabilities of the VM operating system. The CP accounting records provide an excellent basis for further accounting, and software should help the organization to make use of this information for tracking resources, as well as chargeback and billing.

Accounting software may take a direct image of the 80-column CP accounting record and extend the length of the record before actually costing it. The record might be extended to 192 columns, for example. In this extended area, identification of project name, package name, customer name, CPU-id, serial number, and other information can be added. The start time can be calculated from the CP session record and indicated in this area. As a result, the capabilities of VM are enhanced to better meet the unique needs of the organization. Another method of generating begin time and charges is to calculate this at the time a report is run, rather than storing this information in the data.

Capabilities to consider in developing or purchasing accounting software include the ability to calculate the time that the user logged on, and then determine both the shift during which this occurred as well as the charges associated with that shift. Project accounting, with the ability to map charges and link the cost of resources to account numbers, and in turn userids or customer numbers, is also important. Reporting capabilities are another concern. Based on customer, or department, numbers, for example, detailed reports need to be available which detail the usage involved with various packages and projects.

Reports can also be used as input to the capacity planning process. Session reports provide information such as the high resource users in the system and provide I/O statistics. Looking at a report and seeing that a large amount of temporary disk space (TDISK) is being used, for example, would be a warning of potentially running out of this resource.

Accounting in the Departments

There is room for debate concerning the role of accounting in Departmental Computing. In one sense, there should be no need to account for resources that are localized within departments. Theoretically, the function of each departmental machine is more specialized, serving only the members of a work group. Thus, there is no need to track where resources are being used because the use is localized.

However, large organizations with several departments will be very interested in accounting. Central MIS will need to be able to take a global view of resource use throughout the organization to predict when and where more computing power will be needed, and to identify departmental resources that are being underused. The result of this global view is that some machines can be consolidated and others placed into warehouses to be used for applications for which they can be used more efficiently.

Resource accounting with the potential of some form of chargeback will also be necessary from the perspective of central MIS. Even the use of software that is localized in departments needs to be included in resource accounting, because central MIS will need to include these packages in overall planning. The user orientation of midrange machines, such as the 9370, promotes the use of applications, as does the increased availability of applications under VM. The central site will need to know what applications are being used, and by which departments. For example, if central MIS is arranging for the purchase and distribution of a statistical application package for 50 departmental processors, it is important to track the benefits of this expenditure. Accounting records may indicate that some departments do not need a dedicated copy of the software, and could be sharing this application with either another department or the central mainframe.

Because of the minimal technical support available at the departmental level, it would be very difficult to manage an individual resource accounting and chargeback system in each department. This will best be administered from a central mainframe, with each department designated as a customer, or as a project. This accounting structure is illustrated in Figure 12-2.

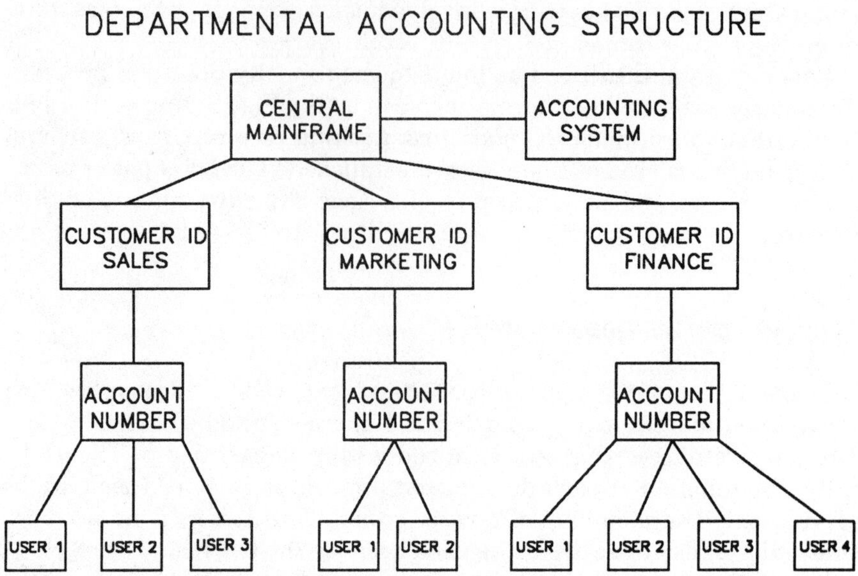

DEPARTMENTAL ACCOUNTING STRUCTURE

Figure 12-2 A resource accounting structure based on departments

The central mainframe is responsible for maintaining the accounting system, with each department designated as a customer. With this system, it is possible to track use within each department, the use of central mainframe resources as well as, with project accounting, the sharing of resources between departments. This has minimal impact on users, with account numbers associated with each department, while providing a way for the central site to monitor system use. With users sharing the resources of the central mainframe, such as a database management system, package accounting will be a major element of the accounting system.

With a centralized resource accounting system, the department is provided with a report, and possibly a bill, which summarizes resource use over a period of time. This information is accumulated at the central site, and distributed accordingly. If actual chargeback is involved, costs might include central CPU time, shared application use, and dedicated device use. Personnel resources could also be a charge, as could CPU-to-CPU communications. Charges for central MIS resources also serve the purpose of creating user awareness of the need to rely on departmental resources as much as possible to conserve the demands placed on the central mainframe.

Decentralized accounting is potentially a much more complex process than centralized accounting. The decisions that are made on an organizational level become much more complex when being made in multiple departments. Each department is a microcosm of the organization, and the issues of standardization and coordination with central MIS becomes clouded. If resources are not tracked from a central site the result can be loss of control, with the inefficiency that results.

The need for capacity planning does not disappear with departmental processors. These machines can quickly become overutilized as easily as a single mainframe. In the case of a department with one machine that services 20 users it might not be necessary to track the activities of each one of these users. However, summary statistics concerning the overall use of the machine are important. For example, reports may indicate that users overall are rapidly increasing their use of DASD such that available resources are being rapidly depleted. Accounting would also indicate times of day that the machine is overutilized and, if necessary, which users are using it. With careful tracking the necessary steps can be taken to solve problems before they occur.

Chapter Summary

The following issues were discussed in Chapter 12:

- The VM operating system provides a basis for comprehensive accounting through CP accounting records.
- The CP accounting information needs to be manipulated through software for efficient use in actual accounting.
- The major function of the resource accounting system is to track the use of resources, regardless of whether users are subsequently charged for their use of resources.
- With connectivity, the role of the central site includes that of administering the resource accounting system, with each department designated as a customer.

13

Planning for Capacity

Capacity planning is a major component of the capacity management process. The other component, performance monitoring, was discussed in Chapter 6. Though there is much overlap between these two functions, capacity planning is a key element in maintaining user satisfaction in the VM environment.

Capacity Planning in VM

As the needs, as well as the numbers, of VM users increase, capacity planning becomes a critical issue. Anticipating and preparing for future growth requires a careful analysis of historical and current use, and organizational factors, all of which combine to influence usage trends.

MIS does not have carte blanche permission to purchase hardware and software. The economic reality is such that most organizations have a budget cycle requiring extensive cost justification. The requests for increased resources must be based on hard data, with any request by MIS being scrutinized more and more by senior management. Requests for increased hardware resources must be based on justification, with demonstrated need for increased capacity. This is where capacity planning comes into play. Based on scientific methodology, capacity planning remains very much an art. The statistics are available, but knowing what predictions to make based on the number is still a very subjective process. Each organization has its own approach.

Though not necessarily an exact science, capacity planning is also not a mystery. Generally, future workload is the same as the current year's workload, only there will be more of it. Major changes in workload are the result of shifts in business conditions. For example, when a bank's business increases, this can have implications in many areas, including the use of automated teller machines, applications for new accounts, and check processing. Capacity planning needs to be aligned with these business changes and reflect an understanding of the impact on all functional areas as business volumes increase or decrease. In addition to workloads, new applications will also result in significant increases to work volumes. New applications must be analyzed as early as possible to ascertain the future impact on all areas that might be affected.

The alternative to capacity planning is to "wait until the other shoe drops," buy excess equipment in anticipation of future needs, or make educated guesses. It is not uncommon for organizations to allow themselves to simply run out of capacity, waiting for major bottlenecks to occur before making needed decisions. Crisis management results in a quick evaluation of the situation, followed by frantic fine-tuning to hold the situation together until more hardware or software can be added. These solutions hold only until the next crisis.

Capacity planning and performance monitoring are often assumed to be related, and are even confused. Performance monitoring, as discussed in Chapter 6, is concerned with the "here and now," while capacity planning is concerned with the future.

Performance monitoring techniques evaluate the current resource use, focusing on workload demands and internal operating system parameters, with the goal of identifying bottlenecks and other inefficiencies in the system. The goal of capacity planning, on the other hand, is to anticipate and be prepared for future growth. Concerns include finding the right power and size of CPU for the organization, the right amount of memory, the right amount of DASD, and to have everything working together properly. Capacity planning provides key input into hardware purchase decisions.

As the comfort factor of VM users expands, so does the need for more and more applications and resources. Departmental Computing provides solutions for the resource crunch while creating the need for even more careful analysis and planning.

Capacity Planning Issues

Capacity planning should be an application of classical economic theory in the form of supply and demand. The organization's computer system has a limited supply of resources. Departments, and in turn, users, need these resources. In fact they are competing for them. The resources are expensive, and these costs should be balanced out by productivity. But if the organization does not have these resources available, through poor planning, productivity will most likely suffer.

Thus, the resources cannot be too plentiful, but they also cannot become unavailable.

Making the most of current hardware while being prepared for near-term future growth is a dilemma that is not easily solved. The addition of only a few new users can cause system use to increase exponentially. These new users may have large resource requirements that were not anticipated. Or perhaps the organization was on the verge of needing a larger CPU, and these new users have merely served as the "final straw." Or perhaps the real devices are not arranged appropriately to manage growth (load balancing). It is clear that capacity planning, like economics planning, is a complex task, involving not only careful analysis, but educated guessing. Yet capacity planners are often criticized for having a "bits and bytes" orientation with an inadequate understanding of how the business is run. As with many other endeavors that have come into being auxilliary to advances in technology, capacity planning is also maturing.

Capacity planning in the VM environment needs to be based on an understanding of users, how they work, what their needs are, how their demands will be increasing. In this respect it should be proactive, with a focus on when the CPU will "run out of gas," with demand increasing based on an average rate of, for example, two new users per month. Each organization varies not only in terms of the demands placed on the VM environment, but also the expectations. Thus, performance objectives need to be set. What would be considered horrendous response time at one organization may be optimal at another.

The data gathered through performance monitoring is one basis for capacity planning. Trends concerning peak usage and average demand are analyzed with techniques such as analytic modeling to determine when the capacity will be exceeded, to consider the implications of potential solutions, and to determine which alternative will best solve the problem while delaying hardware upgrades. Projecting the demands on capacity into the future, so that there will be enough capacity to meet demand is really much more than a matter of CPU-size. Workload balancing in this case becomes not only a current concern but a future one as well. The plan may involve ongoing workload balancing to shift the demand around to carry out the plan. Purchasing excess CPU capability and then allowing it to be well underutilized is not efficient. It is important that the CPU be utilized at its optimum level.

Workloads in the VM environment grow. The numbers of users increase, the importance of certain applications increases. But there are also declines in numbers as well as shifts in applications use. Capacity planning needs to look at the potential for shifts in either direction and make predictions regarding changes in workload. This may at times be similar to comparing apples with oranges, particularly when attempting to analyze the demands of unrelated applications.

Generally, demand is broken down into common units, I/O or CPU seconds per task, for example. Once the impact is expressed in common units, it is possible to make more educated predictions.

Prediction, however, is a major component of capacity planning, and in this respect it does become rather mysterious. It is virtually impossible to predict what demands are going to be placed on an organization's information resources with absolute accuracy. Organizations need to do whatever level of computing that allows them to be competitive in their industry, as well as to meet individual goals. However, industries experience sudden shifts that lessen or increase the demand for information, and even in a stable industry, organizations experience their own ups and downs.

It is possible to isolate a relationship between a number of users and certain types of applications that are being put on the system, and use this as a basis for predicting CPU-size requirements with accuracy. When resources such as DASD are considered, the formulas begin to break down. DASD needs depends on user demand, and users are human beings with shifting tastes and expectations.

The MIS group in most organizations is charged with delivering timely and acceptable service to users. This involves more than simply making sure that the work gets done; response time, for example, needs to be kept below specified limits, and storage space needs to be available for new users and applications. MIS is judged by the consistency of this service. With time, the workload grows and this inevitably leads to some contention for limited resources. This makes it more difficult for MIS to meet service level objectives.

Presenting the case of user unrest is no longer a valid basis for purchasing computer resources. Traditionally, MIS has been able to wield the user as a "bat" against management, citing complaints about bad service by users, and basing purchase requests on the need to make users happier. User concerns are still very important, but basing purchasing policies solely on user concerns led to an uncoordinated approach, with each expenditure a response to a crisis.

Expenditures must result in increased productivity, and this productivity must be demonstrable before the purchase is authorized. This requirement has been an impetus in moving capacity planning from the status of isolated technical function to become an integral part of the MIS strategy. The focus of capacity planning has generally been on host-based systems. With the growth of Departmental Computing, the need, and the role, of capacity planning will expand even further.

The Focus of Capacity Planning

The basic focus of capacity planning is on three major areas:

- CPU
- Memory
- DASD

When the planning element is ignored, responding to a performance crisis may result in a knee-jerk reaction. MIS will act quickly to solve the problem with the most expedient solution, without adequately considering all the issues. A new CPU will be purchased when careful workload balancing might have solved the problem. DASD will be added when the current DASD is not being managed properly. When these quick solutions are executed at the departmental level, the mistake is thus multiplied.

Planning with regard to the CPU is concerned with processor size. The organization must decide how large the processor needs to be, based on the number of MIPS (millions of instructions per second) required to meet the current and near-term anticipated demands of the environment. This is a concern at both the central mainframe and departmental levels, since departmental machines also vary in size. If response time is slow, the problem may be one of lack of MIPS, solved only by an upgrade in CPU.

A new CPU may solve the problem of response time, or it may be a solution that is short term at best. In fact, a new CPU can also result in even more downtime. Purchasing a new CPU, for example, is associated with a long delivery cycle. Emergency delivery and installation is accompanied by cost increases. And if the equipment cannot be phased in, the system is disrupted during this process. If the upgrade is too short-term, the problems return quickly. Yet purchasing a CPU that is much too large requires unnecessary expenditures and encourages waste.

Memory concerns in capacity planning require looking at how much memory is required to support the work that the processor has to do. If memory is inadequate, throughput on any size CPU will be affected. Memory is like floor space; it is critical that every last second of memory be optimally utilized at all times. This also requires careful utilization of all parts of the computer, including the DASD, because real memory is wasted if kept waiting for DASD bottlenecks. Real memory is very expensive, and to adequately plan for memory needs requires coordination of the factors that affect performance.

It is easy to assume when facing a response time problem that there is a need for increased real memory, perhaps necessitating the purchase of a larger CPU. This may seem the most realistic solution, based on the assumption that more memory will be available to handle user demand. It is not uncommon, after making this purchase, for the poor response time to recur. If memory management is the problem, and the system is continually paging, then response time will again suffer. A closer look at how impending growth might affect memory requirements, with an analysis of how channels were being utilized, would have indicated that the solution was to add more channels, rather than more memory or a faster CPU.

Storage management problems may range from managing the data of various users to problems as far-reaching as difficulty in competing in the marketplace. If it is not available when needed, this is a critical problem. Many organizations spend more on DASD than on the CPU. There may be many controls in place for the CPU, while DASD is allowed to grow uncontrolled. The DASD component of capacity planning needs to span the whole DASD subsystem, including the control units and channels. The growth of DASD, discussed in Chapter 8, should be anticipated within the limits available through comprehensive DASD management. Planning needs to be based on a system within which users have responsibility for controlling their own DASD needs, and the organization is actively involved in reclaiming unused DASD. Passively assuming a standard percentage of growth and adding DASD accordingly is allowing DASD growth to explode unchecked.

The problem symptoms regarding DASD go beyond increased response times. Data can become inaccessable if DASD devices are overloaded to the extent that the data contained on them cannot be accessed efficiently. As a result of this congestion, new applications may require "innovative" access to the storage subsystem, with intervention required from the system programming staff to simply enable the application to work. As the DASD subsystem grows, the danger of loss of control over the contents of the subsystem increases. Ironically, data management procedures become more complex to compensate for this loss of control. As the situation continues unchecked, a crisis situation is reached, and it becomes too late for capacity planning.

In order to be used efficiently, DASD must also be organized in an efficient manner. The capacity plan needs to include options for keeping each channel balanced as well as possible, to assure that frequently accessed data, such as major shared databases, is distributed over different channels. A performance monitoring concern, distribution of workload can also be planned for if the growth areas are adequately pinpointed.

CAPACITY PLANNING ALTERNATIVES

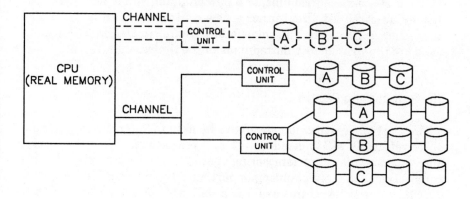

Figure 13-1 DASD may be redistributed for increased efficiency

Workload balancing, concentrating on existing workload, provides a basis for forecasting needed resources before the demand actually occurs.

The three major capacity planning concerns — CPU, memory, and DASD — interact with each other in affecting overall system performance. Unfortunately, one or more areas are often overlooked as the organization attempts a quick solution to a crisis situation. This solution generally results in a major crisis, with implications for loss of productivity, frustration, and missed business opportunities.

Channel balancing is an example of the importance of considering CPU, memory and DASD when analyzing capacity. This is illustrated in Figure 13-1.

The CPU speed, measured in MIPS, is an electronic concept, as is memory. DASD on the other hand, is mechanical, as was discussed in Chapter 8. The problem of overloaded channels was outlined in Chapter 6 under Sources of I/O Problems. In Figure 13-1, an overloaded channel is causing poor response time. The information stored on the DASD devices identified as A, B, and C is heavily accessed, resulting in channel contention. Real memory is not being efficiently utilized because access to and from DASD is becoming more and more congested.

Based on response time alone, the capacity plan might call for a near-term increase in memory, or even a new CPU. Adding more memory might be a partial solution, by alleviating the problem of memory being monopolized by waiting for the channel. Increased memory would provide a decrease in paging, so swapping back and forth between real memory and DASD would be lessened. Adding

MIPS with a new CPU would not solve the problem because processor speed is not the issue. The best solution, however, is to plan for the addition of a new control unit, or a new channel, and shift some of the heavily accessed DASD to either a new control unit or a new channel altogether, so that there is yet another "route" to DASD. These solutions are illustrated with dotted lines in the figure.

The Forecasting Process

The goal of capacity planning is to be able to determine what computer resources will be needed for 1 to 2 years or more into the future, and capacity planning forecasting methods attempt to provide this perspective. Capacity planning is particularly important in hardware purchase decisions. Hardware has a delivery time associated with it and with the addition of budgeting and approval cycles, the acquisition may require a year or more before actual delivery. As discussed earlier, any needed upgrades must be well planned and take into consideration the disruption to users that occurs when new hardware is being phased in.

Capacity planning is the process of asking certain critical questions for the organization, including: How is the system running now? What is projected? If we just grow normally, where will we be in 1 or 2 years? What applications are we bringing on? A basis for answering this question is an understanding of current workload. Any forecasting method used must be firmly grounded on quantifiable data concerning the current use of resources. This is referred to as the establishment of baseline data.

Establishing the baseline involves identifying a typical unit of work for each workload. Performance monitoring data can provide a basis for determining the work unit, with the average resources required to complete an online transaction being an example of a work unit that could be extrapolated from data collected in performance monitoring. Performance monitoring data, supplemented by that collected through system accounting, would yield the major characteristics of the average online transaction, including CPU usage, I/O, and memory. The average needs to be based on variances that might occur throughout the day. It is also important that the baseline data be collected within the organization on the equipment that is used daily.

Each organization varies in average performance, and data that is obtained from a vendor, based on the averages of samples obtained from diverse organizations, is not a true baseline for any one organization.

The forecasting method, based on the work unit, needs to accomplish more than merely summarizing data. It needs to work with an existing method of collecting data and monitor the accuracy of the forecast as new data values are realized. The forecast needs to be produced on a periodic basis, determined by the organization, or when the monitoring process indicates that a new forecast is needed. Thus, forecasting is an ongoing process, based on a method which is integrated into the day-to-day routine of the organization, and of the MIS group.

Capacity planning forecasting methods range from educated guesses to those based on complex statistical models. Rule of thumb forecasting, for example, consists of guessing, based on past experiences. Linear projection is similar to using the rule-of-thumb, with past experiences used as a basis for extrapolating trends into the future. Both methods assume that demand is constant and ignore the realities of the changing business environment.

Analytic modeling is a much more scientific method of forecasting, using data from various sources to accurately forecast what resources will be needed in the future, and the times at which they will be needed. Analytic modeling helps to translate guesses into precision forecasts.

Using analytic modeling to forecast capacity requirements allows the organization to look at the "what if" implications of potential decisions. For example, a capacity problem might be solved by more than one intervention. With modeling, the organization can ask: Do we need a bigger CPU? Do we need more DASD? Can we get by and solve the problem by reallocating what we already have? Data supplied for modeling is more indicative of the organization's entire workload, as opposed to just individual jobs. Also, applications that are not yet in the planning stages can be tested through modeling to ascertain overall effect on workload.

As a basis for analytic modeling, a baseline model is constructed. This is based on measurement data collected to describe present workloads. From this baseline, the model calculates response times and throughputs for each workload. These are then compared with the measured performance of each workload. If there is a disagreement between the two sets of figures, the input from the model is run again. This process is repeated until agreement is reached. After this validated baseline model is constructed, future workloads can be described and the baseline model changed to reflect them. Over time, changes can be introduced into the model to reflect the effect, for example, of installing a particular upgrade such as more DASD. If changes in the model have been introduced carefully, the capacity planner can guage how effective the upgrade will be.

Simulation is another method of forecasting. Simulation is based on the results of abstractly representing the computing environment and the associated workloads through a simulation language. The simulation language in turn runs a workload based on the system that has been described. After the simulation run is completed, the performance is described and results reported. Simulation tools that are generally available are difficult to use when applied to a specific environment and as a result, simulation is not as fast or as efficient as analytical modeling. Simulation is based on specific transactions, rather than overall workload, making it less valuable as a predictor of performance in a multiple user VM environment.

There are many measurement tools available for use in the capacity planning function. The basic criteria for selecting measurement and forecasting tools should be based simply on how well they are able to provide understandable and useable information. What is being measured, how relevant the unit of measure is to the capacity planning process, and where the information can be used, in chargeback, for example, are all important considerations. Capacity planning without relevant results is nothing more than an interesting academic exercise.

Capacity Planning Elements

The capacity planning function varies among organizations, based on factors that include the role of VM (testing or production environment), the number of users, and the kinds of applications. However, there are some basic elements which are common to capacity planning management. Some of these elements, including a basis for measurement, and a definition of workload, have been discussed previously. Others include:

• Objectives, with a definition of the desired work level
• The ability to analyze and project
• Adequate reporting to management

Objectives are important to capacity planning, and it is crucial to begin capacity planning by determining current computer performance objectives for the organization. If it has not been decided what the level of service should be, then it is difficult if not impossible to monitor ongoing progress. Without targets, the organization is haphazardly "tossing darts" at a moving target. Only the hardware vendors benefit from this approach. For example, a maximum response time of 10 seconds is much more difficult to plan for than is a maximum response time of 30 minutes. Based on careful performance tracking, objectives are formulated based on whatever the organization has labeled "optimal" performance.

Optimal performance needs to be based on a variety of areas, including the CPU, DASD, and memory. Each of these general areas must have performance objectives associated with it, with these objectives forming the basis for a projection of expected changes in capacity requirements. From here, alternatives for dealing with increasing demands, while meeting basic performance objectives, can be explored. Alternatives are more competently analyzed when considered in relation to the overriding question: How can each alternative meet the objectives of the organization? This concern is the basis of any capacity planning decision.

It is important that capacity planning objectives take into account the responsibilities of work groups. MIS tends to look at overall system performance, focusing on the overall workloads of the organization. Thus, there may be a lack of awareness that performance is more crucial in some departments than in others. Response time may slide in some departments without adversely affecting the tasks being performed in that group while another department capacity problems can have widespread implications. A capacity crisis in a department responsible for product production, for example, could bring many workers to a standstill as well as adversely affect the bottom line. The production department might need some level of excess capacity to ensure that adequate resources are always available.

Capacity planners have long been saddled with the stereotype of "technical wizard," and this serves to limit the credibility given to their projections. Management sees capacity planners as speaking in "bits and bytes" without a real understanding of the needs of the organization, going off with their wizard caps on and doing some kind of sorcery. It is not uncommon for management to come out of a meeting with no understanding of what capacity planning has to offer.

To effectively analyze and plan, the capacity planning group must have access to the corporate strategic plan and understand where the organization is going, particularly during the period of time encompassed by the capacity plan. For example, if management is going off on a new venture and these plans are not effectively communicated to MIS, somewhere along the line management may discover that the computer power to support this new venture does not exist in the current 2-year plan. In addition, projected market conditions must be analyzed in the process of capacity planning, to ensure that the organization is capable of adjusting to new challenges. Merely analyzing the technical elements workload demand, and making projections based on the past, will not provide the information that management needs to base decisions on. But without access to business plans, the ability of MIS to forecast is limited.

The management/MIS communication process is evolutionary. As MIS has added significant resources, the overall business operation has become much more dependent on computers. Because of this dependence, nontechnical managers have learned to understand the capabilities and limitations of information resources, and even speak some of the technical language. The next step in the evolutionary process is for individuals in roles such as capacity planning to better understand the business side of the organization and communicate the technical issues in business terms.

The users out in the departments also have valuable input into the capacity planning process. Understanding needs and plans at this level provides valuable input into forecasting future workload through, for example, historical trends in resource usage based on chargeback data. However, the relationship between MIS and users in formulating the capacity plan is even more important. Users perceive performance differently from the way MIS does. Users do not necessarily understand the technical complexities, but they do understand what is needed to perform the tasks associated with their jobs. This perception difficulty has implications for the role of MIS. If MIS is a service organization, then users feel it should be there to make their jobs easier. But users can also be egocentric in that they do not always understand their positions in the organization in relation to other users. This interferes with acceptance of restrictions that have to be imposed by MIS as a means of keeping overall capacity in check.

MIS needs to adopt an attitude that the success of the user has a direct effect on the success of MIS, particularly when dealing with potentially emotion-laden issues such as capacity. Users must be educated to understand the impact unnecessary system demands during peak hours, poorly managed minidisks, and other aspects of system use over which the user has control. Keeping costs from getting out of control is in the interest of everyone in the organization, and with this attitude, users will be more likely to see the organizational perspective.

System software and sophisticated forecasting techniques can almost make the capacity planning process look like an exact science. Almost. Capacity planning is a critical element in information management, and does provide valuable decision-making input. But it is essential that some extra computing capacity always be available so that the organization is ready and able to respond to the demands of the competitive environment. Dynamic organizations cannot predict near-future needs down to the last cylinder on a DASD. And human nature also dictates that what is available will be used.

Thus, capacity planning must be complimented by "enforcement" strategies, such as effective DASD management and chargeback, to support the capacity forecast. Capacity planning is a key element in MIS and organizational management strategy. But as with all strategic elements, it must be modifiable.

Capacity Planning in the Departments

Departmental Computing has the potential of "changing the world" of capacity planning. The issue moves from planning for the efficient use of a mainframe to planning for multiple connected machines in sites around the world. The capacity planning approach to Departmental Computing will need to be holistic, based primarily on the needs of the total system, yet balanced with a perspective on the requirements of individual work groups. Each organization will need to decide how best to approach capacity planning. With a large network, there will not be time to focus these efforts on each machine individually.

There are capacity planning experts who insist that there will be neither the time nor the need for capacity planning in a departmental environment. Capacity planning within a departmental strategy may potentially be less complicated. Departmental processors are smaller than a central mainframe, so there is more flexibility for planning. Increments are smaller, and problems can potentially be localized within the department without affecting the whole organization. Also, upgrading a large mainframe may imply adding more physical space, with the air-conditioning and raised floor requirements associated with the mainframe. The 9370, for example, does not have these physical requirements.

On the other hand, within the department a capacity problem can have dramatic consequences for the work group. For example, when running out of DASD on a large system, there are many immediate options to solve the problem. A few major files can be placed on tape storage, or some DASD can be rearranged. On a departmental machine, running out of DASD may mean that the machine is temporarily "out of business." There is less flexibility to simply add DASD, and tape may not be an option. Adding the fifteenth DASD on a large mainframe is less traumatic than adding the third DASD on a small midrange computer. If poor planning results in many departmental machines running out of capacity, the implications may be experienced throughout the organization.

Departmental Computing is modular by definition. This modularity provides a basis for an information resources strategy that is capable of changing quickly, providing flexibility for departmental and, subsequently, organizational adjustments. Making use of this modularity requires a capacity plan that accommodates this modularity from a system perspective. First from an overall system perspective, and then at the departmental levels, the major capacity factors will need to be determined. These factors include the total number of end users served, the numbers who may need to access both departmental machines and the central mainframe at the same time, the complexity of processing functions, and other overhead factors, including the operating system. A careful assessment of these factors will determine the ongoing success of the departmental strategy.

A complicating factor in capacity planning for Departmental Computing is that some departments will need more computing power than others. Buying a smattering of equipment and dividing it up among departments will not be the best solution. Some departments will have greater online needs than others. Production scheduling, for example, must be highly accurate. Thus, there will need to be some decision making on a departmental level with regard to the projected needs of invidual groups. Interconnected machines will present yet other issues. If extensive batch processing is being performed on one departmental machine, and the workload becomes excessive, it may be shuttled to another machine. This presents capacity planning considerations, with the overall batch needs of the organization being met through workload balancing options at the departmental level. Careful planning will need to begin with an overall assessment of global requirements, followed by an analysis of potential workloads, and balancing options, in each individual department.

Capacity planning with a departmental strategy involves working more closely with non-MIS departments than is necessary when the central mainframe is the focus of the organization's information resources. Planners need to understand the workloads and goals of each work group, and that means going into the departments and talking with managers and users. In essence, the capacity plan provides a link between the information systems and the business strategy, translating the organizational and departmental goals into a plan for providing the necessary information resources to meet these goals. The input of both workload balancing and accounting system software will be invaluable in providing workload and resource utilization statistics.

Departmental Computing raises a need for intelligent system software that monitors capacity, diagnoses the problem and either fixes it or sends a message to the central site to alert the technical staff to the situation. If departmental machines are going to run without an operations staff, there will need to be a means of automating the job of the capacity planner at the remote site. The systems management approach to departments, for example, implies the ability to upgrade departmental machines as necessary, even using machines interchangeably as one department outgrows a machine that will meet the capacity requirements of another department. System software that monitors the total system can make recommendations that facilitate capacity planning at the departmental, and in turn organizational, level.

Departmental Computing presents creative options for adjusting to capacity requirements through distributing the load among processors. However, to make use of these options, careful capacity planning is critical.

Chapter Summary

The following are major issues discussed in Chapter 13:

• Capacity planning is the process predicting the utilization of computer resources based on the goals of the organization.

- The major focus areas of capacity planning include the CPU, memory, and DASD. These must also be considered in projecting resource needs.
- The process of capacity planning is different in virtually every organization. Analytic modeling, making predictions based on various alternate solutions, is a common means of making capacity predictions.
- Formulating workload objectives, with a desired level of service, are important elements that must be decided as a basis for planning.
- Departmental Computing provides flexibility in solving capacity problems, with resources distributed throughout the organization. However, the need for careful top-down planning is also critical.

14

Making Departmental Computing Work

The Departmental Computing planning and implementation process will differ among organizations, based on factors that include industry group, corporate culture, and current information management strategy. However, the success of the organization's Departmental Computing strategy begins with a definition of the responsibilities of MIS, users, and department managers, with coordinated planning and cooperation among all three groups. These considerations are discussed in addition to central site management and the role of system software.

Who's in Charge?

A major benefit of Departmental Computing is the opportunity for departmental innovation. Not only do individuals not all work alike, but departments also have their own styles. To overregulate Departmental Computing is to risk the opportunity for innovation; too much control stifles creativity. But to let it develop as it may creates the possibility of lack of coordination, and MIS management in many organizations is still recovering from "PC anarchy."

Whether the strategy for Departmental Computing is based on a phased approach, with departments getting their own processors one by one or, less likely, it "happens overnight," there needs to be extensive support and understanding at the top of the organization. In the first place, large financial expenditures are involved. Second, distributing computer resources into the departments can completely change the workstyles of employees as well as the way that employees, and departments, communicate with each other. As has been discussed throughout these pages, Departmental Computing gives the members of work groups more direct control over their computer resources. As communication becomes more direct, organizational hierarchies change. This can lead to political implications which, without intervention at the top, can serve to stifle the progress of the organization's strategy. It is important that the resources put into Departmental Computing translate into productivity gains, particularly at the professional level. If the gains are outweighed by an increase in territoriality, turf building, and budget fights, then the stategy will quickly be labeled a failure.

Departmental Computing must be a very coordinated effort, beginning with the "blessing" of the Chief Executive Officer and the Board of Directors, to the Chief Information Officer (CIO), to MIS management, to the department managers, to the users within the departments. Coordination, with an understanding of the roles and responsibilities of the major groups involved — users, department managers, and MIS — is an initial step in both preventing the fear and confusion that leads to increased organizational politics and providing a basis for developing the standards which will guide the ultimate success of the Departmental Computing strategy.

Users

The ultimate test of the value of a computer system is in how well it is able to meet the needs of users. Departmental Computing implies a strategy such that the needs of work groups are met through resources located within the boundaries of their own departments. To determine the nature and extent of these needs, it is important that users be involved in the initial planning process, with the lines of communication remaining open. Information requirements in a dynamic organization are not static, and responsiveness to user needs implies a continuing dialog. An easy-to-use system, with technical considerations transparent to the user, does not also mean that users are "kept in the dark." Users need to be made aware of both options and limitations for departmental information resources.

The MIS group in many organizations has not had to be extensively concerned about users, either ignoring them completely or relegating this responsibility to the Information Center, where lack of sophistication was assumed. Departmental Computing is a more concentrated effort than merely providing users with the option of visiting an Information Center for remedial help. Many departmental users will be much more sophisticated than the average Information Center user. MIS will need to "cater" to users, assisting them in prioritizing their needs so that the required resources are available. If MIS is to serve in the coordinating role in Departmental Computing, they will be evaluated based on how well users are able to subsequently improve their productivity. MIS cannot do this effectively without a continuing dialogue with users. If MIS and users fail to communicate, MIS runs the risk of again losing control of key components of the organizational information strategy.

Users need MIS to assist in making the best hardware and software choices and in providing needed technical support. This implies understanding and agreement by both groups concerning the priorities within the department and, realizing that some level of patience will be necessary as departmental resources are phased in, balanced with the needs of the organization as a whole. Communication between users and MIS will enhance trust on both sides as each adopts a more cooperative stance.

Department Managers

Organizations are known to have turfs, ranging from MIS, with the corporate computer center, to the individual operating units, the departments. Through the central mainframe, MIS has historically been able to exercise control over all the organization's information resources (with the exception of departmental processors and personal computers). With decentralized processing, however, control is distributed. Departments will have a certain amount of autonomy as to the way in which they operate, and may even have their own budgets for certain resources. The department manager will need training and support, and MIS will be the most logical place to receive this support. However, MIS will also need cooperation from the department manager as MIS carries out overall network responsibilities. In many organizations, in fact, the department managers and the MIS manager may be equal in status, with separate but equal responsibilities. MIS will not coordinate the thrust of Departmental Computing without the cooperation of departments and department managers.

The supply and demand issue, with MIS supplying and users demanding, becomes more complicated when resources are no longer focused in a single location. With different groups reporting to different managers, all with specialized needs and, in many cases, budgets, the issues multiply. Which department is more powerful? Which manager more vocal? Each department has different goals and priorities, and one may have the impression that it needs more resources than another. Some managers will deal directly with the MIS department, while others will attempt to go a level above.

Whether focused at the central mainframe, or departmental, level, the computer resources of the organization are limited while demand from users is potentially unlimited. Department managers are responsible for facilitating the achievement of departmental goals, and advocating for the work group members is a part of this responsibility. As a result, Departmental Computing will be a catalyst for politics as department managers attempt to maximize resources and support for their departments. Competition is inevitable.

This is potentially a no-win situation. Distribution decisions will need to be made at the executive level, most likely through the Chief Information Officer, with input from others at this level. This is not a decision for the MIS or Data Center Managers, who may be equal in status to department managers. In addition, the focus of these roles is generally too narrow to have the needed organizational perspective. The individual in charge of making decisions about the distribution of departmental resources needs to work closely with both department managers and users to rank departmental needs in order of priority, both within each department and for the organization as a whole. Priorities must be based on business objectives, with decisions communicated adequately to those affected by them. It is important to develop priorities that are flexible, however. Demands within a dynamic organization change periodically, even seasonally, and to lock departmental resource allocations into an unwavering plan is to defeat a major purpose of Departmental Computing.

Department managers have always been expected, and empowered, to make competitive decisions. Departmental Computing provides them with increased information resources with which to make these decisions. Expectations concerning resource availability and support must be made clear to the managers in the departments, with ongoing communication between managers and MIS. Without communication, and flexibility, organizational standards suffer as departments begin seeking their own solutions.

MIS

End user computing has done much to change the role of the MIS professional, these role changes made clear with the enhanced status of the user in the Information Center. Increased involvement by department managers in information management decisions will escalate role changes. MIS executives are being forced to broaden their perspectives from the purely technical realm to that of business strategies and decisions.

Users have substantial input into buying decisions, and MIS is having to not only consult with users but also answer to them. It is not uncommon for the purchasing process of hardware and software to include a review with an end-user committee. For example, buying a new database management system often requires the approval of representatives of the users who will be using the system on a daily basis. Features that might streamline the tasks of MIS might not appear "friendly" enough to users, and products can be rejected on this basis. Software salespeople have long ago learned that there is more to the sales cycle than talking bits and bytes with the programmers over a few beers. Resentment of end users by MIS is a by-product of the Information Center that continues; MIS often find them to be either incompetent, intransigent, or both.

As discussed earlier, resentment of the end user by MIS was fueled not only by the Information Center but by the growth of independent departmental solutions, and personal computers. The end user learned to get along without MIS and management began questioning large MIS budgets that did not result in user satisfaction. MIS lost control.

Departmental Computing provides a means for MIS to regain lost control over all the information resources of the organization. IBM's 370 architecture, with compatibility of machines and software from the large mainframe to the PC, will serve to enable this control. Machines will communicate up and down the organization while MIS serves in the role of central coordination. This coordination role implies changes in perspectives. MIS will need to continue to evolve from the purely technical role, spearheading the planning process to balance the technical considerations with both user needs and overall business strategy. This is an admittedly precarious position and requires the ability to effectively communicate with all levels of the organization.

Networking is an important element in Departmental Computing, and the MIS group will need to develop skills in this area. Technical considerations expand from merely making sure that users have access to mainframe applications to assuring that resources are available in each department, connected with the central mainframe. An understanding of the data needs of the entire organization, with the ability to get what is needed to the remote sites, will provide new technical challenges. Departments need not only available data, but data that is usable. MIS will need to work with users to help funnel out unnecessary data, and facilitate efficiency of information in the departments. With increased computer resources, organizations often "drown" in information that is available but not useful. Users will need to be guided in understanding the specialized functions, and limitations, of departmental machines.

In addition, the data management and security requirements associated with distributed resources add new wrinkles to the responsibilities of MIS. The technical role of MIS will be tempered by other considerations, but it certainly will not dissipate.

The ability of MIS to communicate with users and department managers will need to be balanced by the ability to communicate with upper management. As a change agent, MIS needs to communicate the business perspectives with the upper management of the organization, understanding and contributing to the ongoing dialog concerning what is at stake. MIS will provide the key input into the selection of vendors and products, as well as policies concerning data access, network standards, and data structure. In fact, MIS will set the standards for Departmental Computing.

The consultative expertise of MIS will be a major factor in the ongoing success of the organization's departmental strategy. Effective dialog, in terms that management (and users) understands, will facilitate the acceptance of MIS in the pivotal role.

The Role of the Central Site

The importance of the central site in the management of Departmental Computing has been discussed throughout this book. Central site coordination provides much more than a means for MIS to retain political control of the distribution of resources into the departments. There are many practical considerations associated with the central site which add support to this type of arrangement.

Standardizing Hardware and Software

The departmental environment is generally associated with minimal system programmer and operations support needs at the remote site, and IBM has designed the 9370 machines with this goal in mind. However, making self-sufficiency a reality is dependent on careful planning before the fact. Even with 9370s, if each department is allowed to go off in its own direction in the kinds of devices that are attached to the 9370, as well as adding software as desired, the central site is going to find itself with a veritable mass of configurations that don't connect with each other. This will result in a return to the problems of the PC, only on a much larger and more powerful scale. Standards begin at the central site, controlling both the hardware and software resources that are in turn sent out to the departments.

The differences between various models of the 9370 were discussed in Chapter 3. Because there are distinct models in the 9370 series, making the choices of which models to choose that much more confusing, it may seem prudent to simply purchase a few of each, add a few devices, and send them out into the departments. Once the support requests start pouring into the central site, the folly of this approach becomes painfully apparent. The introduction of the 9370 must be well planned.

Hardware purchases are full of judgment calls and, statistical data notwithstanding, making the right decision is an art. For organizations purchasing multiples of 9370s — 20 or more — it is a good idea to consider choosing only two or three hardware configurations. The departments may have specific configurations in mind and may thus disagree with this approach, but if the central site is going to be responsible for networking and supporting these machines, this limitation will pay off for all concerned. With standards, the technical expertise of MIS can be better leveraged throughout the organization.

The design elements of the 9370 lends itself to standardization. Standards begin with the upfront planning process, through the development of prototypes. The use of the term prototype in this situation is very similar to how prototypes are used elsewhere. Prototyping a 9370 configuration begins by investigating available hardware and software options, with extensive input by departmental users. Once the choices are narrowed down, the machine configurations are tested and the software added. These combinations are then tested further, to assure that the hardware combinations are efficient and the software packages work together. At this point, one or more configurations is ready for mass production, to be "cloned" and sent out into the departments.

There are many reasons why the prototyping process needs to involve software as well as hardware. There are a large number of software packages on the market which work well with the 9370, and others are on the way. IBM has developed application packages that are easily installed on the 9370 and third-party vendors will be following suit. It is not unlikely that users will want as many software packages as the machine will handle.

The PC horror stories should not be ignored when planning for software. Even the smallest shops have been faced with the problem of different applications packages that do the same things, but do not communicate with each other. In addition, departments will be looking to MIS for software support, and maintaining diverse software packages can quickly turn into a nightmare.

The optimal approach to software is to choose a few software applications and group these packages among the three or four hardware configurations. These need to be tested as carefully as hardware, and then cloned. Problems can then be addressed and new releases distributed, with minimal disruption. Working carefully with users, MIS must decide upon the software packages to be supported and then communicate this to department managers. By releasing a list of "supported" packages, this will steer departments toward "going with the program" on software choices.

As has been alluded to, "off the shelf" software is generally much more efficient for the organization than is "home grown" software, and this applies to both applications and system software. Much of the software development process is simply maintenance. Initial development costs may not seem outrageous, but when ongoing problem solving and enhancements are factored in, the costs skyrocket. In addition, central MIS is charged with supporting multiple software copies, so not only are problems multiplied but the potential sources for problems are also multiplied.

From an economics standpoint, MIS has the opportunity to negotiate bulk purchases for departmental software. Thus, the expenses associated with off the shelf software are reduced. For departments concerned with budgets, potential discounts will bring them even closer to cooperating with MIS.

Choosing VM as the operating system will facilitate the role of the central site. As discussed in Chapters 2 and 3, IBM is positioning VM as the operating system of choice for the 9370. In addition to VM's user-oriented capabilities, VM is also a good match with the size of the 9370 CPU. To accomplish the prototyping necessary for standardizing departmental configurations, VM/SP is the recommended VM variation for departmental machines. It is a flexible foundation upon which to add whatever software applications have been chosen.

As long as VM/SP is not modified, the central site maintenance of the 9370 network should be relatively simple. When IBM sends a new release of VM, this can simply be downloaded from tape to disk and tested at the central site, based on the scenario discussed in Chapter 2. When the testing is completed, the new VM release is then be sent out to the remote sites.

Central Site Support Concerns

The role of the central site goes much further than developing configurations and providing the departments with software maintenance.

The responsibilities of MIS do not end the day the fully loaded machines are delivered to the departments. Adequate expertise must be available in the departments as each departmental system is being set up, to ensure that everything is working well and that users know how to get the most out of the system. This assumes that the dialog between users, department managers, and MIS has been ongoing since the planning process. Effective on-going implementation with results is the measure of success, not trouble-free installation. MIS is responsible for connecting the departments with the central mainframe site, and with each other if necessary. MIS will also need to have implemented a means of effectively handling ongoing support calls as they arise. This may necessitate the establishment of a support desk, as well as provisions for training users.

The coordination of the Departmental Computing effort is associated with many responsibilities. The foremost of these is to continue the ongoing dialog with the departments so that user needs are constantly reassessed and accommodated. With control comes responsibility, and to ignore the primacy of the user is to risk a return to the anarchy that has plagued personal computer applications.

MIS — the central site — can make or break the Departmental Computing effort based on its willingness to support users and adapt to the changing needs of the organization.

The Role of System Software

Automatic system management software tools play a very important role in Departmental Computing. The departments will not be housing their own technical staff, and MIS will not be adding the staff to go into each department and perform the duties normally associated with the Data Center. In order to keep the departments supported, as well as ensure that organizational standards are maintained, system software that is designed to enhance the VM departmental environment will be needed.

System software utilites have generally served to "plug the holes" in VM, helping to strengthen the security provisions of VM, for example, or providing a means of collecting and interpreting accounting data. Though some VM shops develop their own system software, it is generally accepted that system software available from third-party vendors is both more efficient and less expensive than going the home-grown route. As VM grew in popularity with users, the need for the capabilities offered by system security also grew as Data Centers looked for ways to manage the VM environment without having to add more technical staff.

In the 1980s, system software has become much more sophisticated, with features such as full-screen menus, user interfaces, and prescriptive capabilities which essentially diagnose problems and suggest solutions. The 9370 and Departmental Computing have provided further impetus to system software development, as some vendors have responded to the challenges of this market with system software that provides automatic system management with capabilities that enhance this enviroment. Software development in general has been reflecting an attitude that it is no longer acceptable to expect the user to do something that the software itself could be doing. As the demands of the market have changed, system software has become more sophisticated and complex. These developments will be of particular benefit to large distributed networks.

Comprehensive system software, providing automatic system management, helps to make the departmental machines more self-sufficient. Features such as problem correction and exception reporting, based on predefined organizational standards, provide central site expertise in the departments without the presence of personnel. The technical expertise can remain at the central site, while the system software acts as an "envoy" of the central site, maintaining each

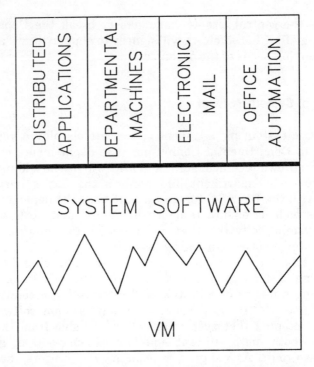

Figure 14-1 The VM foundation is strengthened through system software

departmental machine just as would human personnel. System software maximizes people resources. Site-defined options and parameters are used to maintain organizational standards, so that machines are not only maintained efficiently but also that adherence to standards is enforced.

The role of system software, serving as a buffer between the operating system and the user applications, is illustrated in Figure 14-1.

VM provides an excellent foundation for Departmental Computing. System software adds a measure of strength to the foundation, protecting and enhancing the operating system from the demands of users and their applications.

System Software Requirements

The concerns that organizations have when distributing their hardware and software resources are much the same as they are when running a central mainframe. Of these, the major system software needs in Departmental Computing can be summarized as the following:

- Performance monitoring
- System backup
- System security

These issues have been discussed in earlier chapters. Each VM environment is radically different from the others, and performance requirements are unique to each shop. Monitoring a VM machine is important to maintaining the organizational standards of system performance and adequate user service levels. If a system programing staff is not available to do this, then system software must be available to perform this function within parameters defined by the organization. Disaster, as a result of either users or natural causes, will continue to occur at unexpected moments at both the departmental and organizational levels. Managing the system backup process, as discussed earlier, is both a time-consuming and potentially error-prone process. Without available staff, the system software must be capable of automating this function. A departmental machine is much harder to protect than a mainframe locked up in a "glass house." If the departmental machine is connected to the central mainframe, and to other departments, the security of the entire organization can potentially be at risk. Security software automates functions such as directory management while providing a means of "policing" the environment.

System software designed for the VM operating system is generally based on the service virtual machine, with the software itself installed on a virtual machine of its own, where it runs in disconnected state. Described earlier, this is basically a state in which the software is not active, rather it sits idle until receiving a request from a user. The service virtual machine does work on behalf of users, without having a terminal of its own. An example to illustrate the virtual machine concept is batch processing system software, sitting idle until users initiate batch tasks. The virtual service machine in effect maintains "cool objectivity," acting on any user request not resulting in an error condition which has been predefined as violating organizational standards or a VM limitation. If an error condition is met, the request for the services of the system software is simply rejected.

Organizational standards are generally enforced through the system software with the use of a configuration file. System defaults and other site-determined parameters — basically customization details — are indicated in the configuration file. For example, the restrictions regarding password definitions, or the definitions of batch job classes, would be entered in the configuration file and subsequently "enforced" by the system software. Products without configuration files use "zaps" instead, with system programming staff entering code which in effect "turns off" certain features. This is a time-consuming and error-prone process.

The key to choosing system software for the VM Departmental Computing environment is to make sure that the software is designed to work exclusively within the architecture of VM, rather than being a modified version of software originally designed to work within another operating system, such as MVS. This assures that the capabilities of VM are in turn the basis for the design of the software; system software should not "change" VM, only make it work even better. It is also important that system software should be installable in a straightforward manner, allowing the organization clear options for tailoring it to the specific needs of the environment without necessitating modifications to VM. The dangers of system modifications, discussed in Chapter 4, also apply to those encouraged by software vendors.

In addition to being VM-based, system software for a 9370 distributed environment must include features which provide flexible, yet robust, control over the resources in this environment. It must provide for the maintenance of the central coordination that has been described throughout this book, including end-user interfaces, extensive automation, and the networking capabilities available through integration.

Chapter Summary

The following are major issues discussed in Chapter 14:

* Users play a key role in Departmental Computing, with the ultimate measure of the success of this strategy being user produc tivity.
* MIS will play a coordinating role in Departmental Computing, but this group, particularly the CIO, must become adept at balancing the technical considerations with the overall business perspective.
* Standards are a critical element in Departmental Computing, to ensure that it does not become chaotic. Limiting the number of hardware and software configurations of departmental machines, to perhaps two or three, will help to minimize the support requirements of the central site. These configurations need to be based on prototypes, with careful testing, as well as coordination with users.
* System software, with automated systems management features, compensates for the lack of technical personnel within the departments, and enforces the standards of the organization. System software should be designed to work with VM, in addition to having features that enhance the 9370.

15

Conclusions

Departmental Computing has the potential for dramatically affecting individuals and how they work within their organizations, as well as the way in which organizations function within the global community. The VM operating system is providing the foundation for these developments.

The Shrinking World

Throughout these pages, as various aspects of the VM operating system and implications for Departmental Computing were discussed, there was an underlying premise: Awareness of VM is growing and the world is shrinking. We are entering into a new era of information management.

Departmental Computing provides a means of distributing the information resources of the organization such that data can be processed 24 hours a day, at remote sites around the world. For example, the 2-hour window of communications between the United States and Europe, due to the 6-hour time difference, is eliminated because corporate data and applications are available at both locations. Information can be processed and exchanged without requiring simultaneous human intervention. Communication between the departments of organizations is also streamlined, with work groups having access to their own specialized applications and, as needed, access to the corporate data.

The world will shrink because of technological developments in both hardware and software. From a hardware standpoint, 370 architecture will provide a hardware basis for sharing applications at all levels of the organization, from the large central mainframe to the departmental midrange machine, the 9370. Capabilities will be taken yet a step further through the personal computer. The VM operating system will provide a foundation for the software applications and data that users will need as they integrate departmental resources into their workstyles. VM is the key to making Departmental Computing a reality, from the top to the bottom of the organization.

The capabilities of VM were outlined throughout the pages of *VM and Departmental Computing*. Usability, a key to the success of Departmental Computing, is the cornerstone of the VM operating system. It manages the demands of multiple users, allowing each a "chunk" of the resources such that they are protected from the potential intrusions of other users. VM is applications-oriented and, with the interactivity of CMS, it is easy to use. VM use grew in part because of the end-user revolution exemplified by the Information Center. As VM was a major factor in the feasibility of the Information Center, it is only natural that it should also usher in the next evolutionary step of this revolution. Users will take the knowledge and expertise gained in the Information Center and integrate it into the daily routine of the work group.

From the viewpoint of MIS, VM provides an optimal basis for Departmental Computing. The technical resources of MIS are limited due to manpower availability, while the user demands associated with distributed processing, based on departments, can skyrocket. The 9370 is the missing link in providing the departmental independence and resource availability that users have demanded. However, MIS cannot be everywhere at once. For MIS to regain its coordinating role in information management, three important capabilities must be provided through the operating system. It must be user-friendly to enhance user independence, it must provide compatibility with networking capabilities at all hardware levels, and it must be flexible enough to meet the changing demands of the dynamic organization. Recently announced enhancements to VM by IBM indicate that VM will continue to be the operating system of choice for Departmental Computing.

One of the most exciting current directions in VM was IBM's announcement of increased extended architecture capabilities, in June 1987. With CMS support, this provides an interactive environment for high-end systems. The extended architecture announcement was significant for Departmental Computing because it means that CMS capabilities will be available from the largest mainframe to the 9370, with VM's interactive capabilites and ease-of-use provided for user applications at all levels of the organization. During the same month IBM also announced the enhancements to NetView, the strategic network management software product. These enhancements further facilitate the ability to operate 9370s in remote sites while the staff at the central site manages the network. IBM's solid committment to VM and Departmental Computing is growing.

Trends in organizations and society do not occur solely as a response to technological advancements. People need to be comfortable with technology, to see it as a tool rather than an intrusion. In turn, their organizations need to grow and allow for both technological and interpersonal change without being threatened by it. As people change, society changes. Sometimes development seems slow, but it happens. And even something as technically esoteric as an operating system can be a catalyst.

How is technology integrated into the thought processes, and subsequently the workstyle, of the white-collar worker? This is the challenge of Departmental Computing.

Resources for VM and Departmental Computing

The additional considerations for enhancing the VM operating system, particularly in a departmental scenario, were discussed throughout the pages of this book. Departmental Computing is an important and expensive proposition, and it is critical to cover all of the bases in implementation. This will necessitate the need for consulting and educational services, as well as software which enhances and protects the natural capabilities of VM.

Below is a very brief sampling of organizations who offer services or products *exclusively* for the VM operating system.

VM/Assist Inc.
Two Roundhouse Plaza
10 Lombard Street, Suite 450
San Francisco, CA 94111
(405) 362-3310
Robert Kusche, President

VM/Assist Inc. provides system programming, administrative and educational services nationwide. System programming and administrative services are provided in a highly efficient manner using streamlined installation, maintenance, and documentation techniques. These techniques allow VM/Assist to provide full VM facility management to many VM shops at much less than the cost of full-time equivalent help. Educational services are provided in areas not fully addressed by other vendors. VM/Assist provides instruction for topics dealing with system security, capacity planning, and management, as well as certain program products available in the VM marketplace.

VM Systems Group
901 South Highland Street
Arlington, VA 22204
(703) 685-1314
Gabriel Goldberg, Director of Technology

VM Systems Group develops and supports software products that meet the reliability and integrity needs of VM. As leaders in the VM community, the company is an active participant in an ongoing dialog with other VM users through user group meetings, extensive surveys, and telephone interviews. This information is reflected in a technical newsletter, *V/UPDATE*, and an online bulletin board, V/NET. Products developed and marketed by the VM Systems Groups include V/FORCE, which frees inactive users by releasing userids and resources; V/SAFE and V/SNAP, which avoid CP abends; V/COPY, which speeds and simplifies copying CMS files; V/SPELL, adding fast, interactive spelling checking to XEDIT; V/TEMP, speeding and simplifying temporary disk allocation; V/QUEST, simplifying and automating analysis of diagnostic dumps; and V/SEG, which enhances VM's saved system and discontiguous saved segments facilities.

VM/CMS Unlimited, Inc.
161 Granite Avenue
Boston, MA 02124
(617) 288-4434
Romney White, President

VM/CMS Unlimited Inc. was formed to solve problems and provide solutions for VM systems users in the form of packaged systems and utility software, education and training, customized programming, and consulting. In addition to developing and marketing products, the company's technical experts maintain an active involvement in VM user groups nationwide. Products offered by VM/CMS Unlimited, Inc. include VM/SP Single System Image, which links multiple VM-based CPUs so that they form a sinlge system image to users; RAPID, a general-purpose facility within VM's RSCS that supports printing on ASCII printers; CMAP, which provides facilities for monitoring and analyzing CMS command activity; and FAST Checkpoint, a utility program that in the event of a system crash can speed the recovery of spool files in the VM Control Program.

VM Software, Inc.
1800 Alexander Bell Drive
Reston, VA 22091
(703) 264-8000
Richard L. Earnest, President

VM Software, Inc. is recognized as the leading independent vendor of system software developed exclusively for the VM operating system. The company's team of experienced VM experts has earned a worldwide reputation for superior product design, customer service, and documentation, with a strong record of innovation and commitment. VM Software representatives are active in VM user groups, and the company publishes informative booklets and a newsletter, *Issues in VM*. VM Software's flagship product, VMCENTER II, is a comprehensive answer to the system management needs of VM environments, with features that automate and facilitate a wide array of Data Center management functions, including DASD management, system security, system accounting, performance monitoring, and other capabilities. In one easily installed package, VMCENTER II includes automated control facilities that enhance the 9370/Departmental Computing environment. The company also offers products which complement IBM's SQL/DS relational database management system.

This list is by no means comprehensive. However, it is a solid representation of organizations who understand the needs of VM users and are committed to the growth and development of the VM operating system.

Bibliography

Adrian, Merv. "The Work Connection," *Computerworld*, February 16, 1987.

Allen, Leilani. "Performance Management and Capacity Planning: A Divergence of Paths," EDP Performance Review, January 1986.

"Baby Boomers Push for Power," *Business Week*, July 2, 1984.

Bebeau, Jon M. Tuning. "A Management Perspective," *4300 Journal*, March–April 1987.

Bowen, William. "The Puny Payoff from Office Computers," *Fortune*, May 26, 1986.

Brandt, Steven C. *Entrepreneuring in Established Companies*, Homewood, Illinois: Dow Jones–Irwin, 1986.

Cashin, Jerry. "As Systems Spread Out, Data Becomes Vulnerable," *Software News*, December, 1986.

Chester, Jeffery A. "Departmental Computing: If It Were Only this Easy," *Infosystems*, April 1987.

Clifford-Winters, Tony. *Installation Management, New Directions in VM*, Newbury, Berkshire, UK: Xephon Technology Transfer Limited, October 1985.

Colony, George F. "New Ports of Call," *Datamation*, November, 15, 1986.

Connolly, James and Beeler, Jeffery. "The Price Of Success: IBM 370 System Won't Die," *Computerworld*, November 3, 1986.

Cooper, Kim. "A Perspective On VM/SP Performance Management," *4300 Journal*, January–February 1987.

Date, C. J. "What Is a Distributed Database System," Codd & Date Consulting Group, February 18, 1987.

Diebold, John. "Rethinking Automation," *Computerworld*, November 3, 1986.

Dorsey, Jean Green. "Integration: Avoiding Mistakes," *Computerworld Focus*, February 6, 1985.

Drucker, Peter F. *Concept of the Corporation*, New York: Harper & Row, 1983.

Eddolls, Trevor. "User Mold VM in Their Systems' Image," *Computerworld*, December 8, 1986.

Ericson, Bob and Trapile, Wally. "Audit Me?" *Computerworld Focus*, February 6, 1985.

Foth, Tom. "IBM's New 9370 Series," *4300 Journal,* January–February 1987.

Gartner Group. "Establishing an Information Center," *Key Issues K–801–216.1*, Stamford, Conn., April 11, 1984.

Gartner Group. "Strategies for VM Security", *Key Issues K-031–042.1*, Stamford, Conn., April 1, 1985.

Gartner Group. "Shakeout Coming in IBM Operating Systems," *Key Issues 5PA–501–162.1*, Stamford, Conn., January 8, 1986.

Gartner Group. "VM/SNA: Panacea or Pain," *Strategic Planning 5PA–506–082.*, Stamford, Conn., July 24, 1985.

Gibson, Stanley. "Firm Predicts Explosive Growth for Departmental Computing," *Computerworld*, January 12, 1987.

Gibson, Stanley. "Screws Tighten on 4381," *Computerworld*, February 9, 1987.

Gibson, Stanley. "IBM 3090 May Endure Into 90's," *Computerworld*, March 9, 1987.

Graham, Gig, and Scott, Tom. "Don't Miss the Mark in Network Selection," *Computerworld Focus*, April 1, 1987.

Herbert, Martin, and Hartog, Curt. "MIS Rates the Issues," *Datamation*, November 15, 1986.

Horwitt, Elisabeth. "The Coming of Age of the Local Area Network," *Computerworld*, November 3, 1986.

Horwitt, Elisabeth. "User Communication in the Networking Era," *Computerworld*, November 3, 1986.

Hurst, Rebecca. "The Hunt for Distributed DBMS," *Computerworld Focus*, April 1, 1987.

Hurst, Rebecca. "Minis Reign over PC LANs," *Computerworld Focus*, May 6, 1987.

INPUT. Executive Overview, "Departmental Systems and Software Directions," Mountain View, Calif., 1986.

Johnson, David. *Performance Aspects of VM, New Directions in VM*, Newbury, Berkshire, UK: Xephon Technology Transfer Limited, October 1985.

Kador, John. "Controlling the DASD Dollar," *4300 Journal*, March–April 1987.

Kador, John. "Adding Another Layer," *Information Center*, September 1986.

Kador, John. "The DOS to MVS Transition," *Business Software Review*, February 1987.

"Key Issues in Performance Management," *EDP Performance Review*, May 1986.

Kock, Reinhard. "Contingency Planning: Where to Begin," *4300 Journal*, March–April 1987.

Kolodziej, Stan. "Departmental Computing," *Computerworld Focus*, October 16, 1985.

Kolodziej, Stan. "Departmental Computing's Political Paradox," Computerworld Focus, May 6, 1987.

Kral, Ronald P. and McClain, Gary R. "The VM Variations: Which One Is Right For You?" *4300 Journal*, June 1987.

Kutnick, Dale. *IBM's Large-System Software Strategy, New Directions in VM*, Newbury, Berkshire, UK: Xephon Technology Transfer Limited, October 1985.

Kutnick, Dale. *IBM's Office Automation Strategy, New Directions in VM*, Newbury, Berkshire, UK: Xephon Technology Transfer Limited, October 1985.

Leonard, David M. *Auditing VM/SP*, Warren, Gorham & Lamont Series on EDP Auditing, New York.

Levinson, Robert E. *The Decentralized Company*, New York: American Management Association, 1983.

Lipner, Leonard D. "Capacity Planning Methodology," Reprinted from *Auerbach Information Management Series*, Auerbach Publishing, Inc.

Lorange, Peter. *Implementation of Strategic Planning*, Englewood Cliffs.: Prentice Hall, Inc. 1982.

Ludlum, David. "Faith Required to Invest in Productivity," *Computerworld*, November 3, 1986.

Martin, James A. "Getting Information to the End Users," *Computerworld*, November 3, 1986.

McClain, Gary R., and Richardson, Deborah R. "The Real World of the Virtual Machine," *Information Center*, May 1986.

McClain, Gary R., "VM Environment Needs Flexible Security," *Government Computer News*, June 20, 1986.

McClain, Gary R., *Which VM Is Right for You*, the first in a series published by VM Software, Inc., November, 1986.

Morel, Charles P. "Looking at Micro-Mainframe Links," *Computerworld Focus*, May 14, 1986.

Mugge, Paul C. "The Computer Room in a Rack," *4300 Journal*, March–April 1987.

Mullen, William J. *Capacity Planning: Basic Elements for the Process*, BGS Systems, Inc., Waltham, Mass., 1985.

Naisbitt, John. *Megatrends*, New York: Warner, 1982.

Naisbitt, John, and Abuvdene, Patricia. *Re-inventing The Corporation*, New York: Warner, 1985.

Nolan, Richard L. *Managing The Data Resource Function*, St. Paul: West, 1982.

Packeri, Michael B. "Talking Business with Brass," *Computerworld*, February 9, 1987.

Partridge, David. *VM In Context, New Directions in VM*, Newbury, Berkshire, UK: Xephon Technology Transfer Limited, October 1985.

Prayton, Ed. "Putting All the Pieces Together," *Business Software Review*, August 1986.

Radding, Alan. "All Action, No Talk?" *Computerworld*, May 18, 1987.

Radding, Alan. "How Interruptible is Your Computer System?" *Computerworld*, January 26, 1987.

Sassone, Peter G., and Schwartz, Perry A. "Cost-Justifying Office Automation," *Datamation*, February 15, 1987.

Schneiderman, Ben. "Fighting for the User," *Computerworld*, March 23, 1987.

Shay, David L. "You Can Justify Office Automation: A Methodology," *Computerworld Focus*, October 16, 1985.

Slavin, William. "Interviewed in Viewpoint," *Computerworld Focus*, May 6, 1987.

Stallings, William. "Master Plans for LANs," *Datamation*, November 15, 1986.

Sullivan-Trainer, Michael. "Capacity Planning," *Computerworld*, January 12, 1987.

Sumner, Mary. "A Workstation Case Study," *Datamation*, February 15, 1986.

Sweet, Frank. "How to Build a Security Chain," *Datamation*, February 1, 1987.

Synnott, William R., and Gruber, William H. *Information Resource Management*, New York: John Wiley. 1981.

Toffler, Alvin. *The Third Wave*, New York: Morrow, 1980.

Tunstall, Steve. *Security in VM Systems, New Directions in VM*, Newbury, Berkshire, UK: Xephon Technology Transfer Limited, October 1985.

Vacca, John R. Life, "Liberty, and the Pursuit of Decision Support," *Information Center*, September 1986.

Vranas, Byron Jr. "Is There A Perfect VM DASD Management System?" *4300 Quarterly*, July–September 1986.

Walsh, John J. "Office Automation Is Affecting Jobs — Who's Managing Those Changes," *Computerworld Focus*, February 6, 1985.

White, Lee. "Does MIS Hold All the Cards?" *Computerworld Focus*, October 16. 1985.

Whitman, Charles P. "The Continuing Evolution of CMS," *4300 Journal*, March–April 1987.

Young, Jim. "CDAs Come of Age", *Computerworld Focus*, May 6, 1987.

Glossary

A-Disk — When users are reading or writing to a minidisk through CMS, it is generally given a filemode of A. Thus, each user's minidisk is often referred to as his A-disk.

Analytic Modeling — A scientific method of forecasting used in capacity planning, providing a means of assessing the impact of various "what if" scenarios.

Archive — A user-initiated process which serves to place seldom-used CMS files on tape as a means of conserving DASD.

ATTACH — A command which serves to attach a tape drive to the user's virtual machine.

AUX File — A control file that is used when the VM system is being updated, as with PTFs.

Backup — An installation-initiated process in which a copy is made of all information stored on DASD, so that it is available in case of disaster or user error. Information is generally transferred to tape (though backup to DASD is also possible) and stored offsite. Backup may be full, transferring everything on the system to tape, or incremental, which essentially captures only changes that have been made to data since the last backup.

Channel — This is essentially a small computer, mediating the transmission of data between the CPU (main memory) and I/O devices. The channel helps in keeping the CPU from being burdened, for example, with "stacked up" requests for data from DASD.

Checkpoint Start — In the event of a hardware failure, due to a power failure or an error, a warm start may not be possible. A checkpoint start allows for the recovery of closed spool files. This may be a comparatively time-comsuming process.

Class — Userids may be assigned a specific class in the CP directory that limits, for example, the CP commands that the user associated with the userid may use.

CMS — Interactivity is provided to VM users through this component of the VM operating system. CMS most basically functions as an "operating system with an operating system." CMS is the abbreviation for the Conversational Monitor System.

Cold Start — If the VM system is being recovered, or "brought up" with a cold start, all VM spool files will be discarded.

Control Unit — The control unit is positioned between I/O devices and the channel, and serves to manage individual devices, such as tape drives or DASD.

CP — The component of VM which complements CMS. CP creates the overall virtual machine environment, mediating the demands on the CPU. CP is the abbreviation for Control Program.

CP Command — Commands which are initiated through CP rather than CMS. CP commands, for example, may be used in directory maintenance.

CP Owned Volume — DASD that is specifically for CP, rather than users. This DASD is defined in the DMKSYS program module, and includes an area for the directory and the paging process.

CPU — This term is used to refer to the computer itself, and includes the memory and channels. It is an abbreviation for Central Processing Unit.

DASD — An abbreviation for Direct Access Storage Device, or disk drive, which actually stores data.

DDR — A CP program within VM that allows data to be transferred from DASD to tape, and vice versa. It is an abbreviation for DASD Dump/Restore.

Departmental Computing — An in formation management strategy in which the specific resources needed by specific work groups are located within each department, through a midrange CPU, while organization-wide resources are centralized on a large mainframe. The departmental processors are connected to the central mainframe to facilitate user communications and data exchange.

DES — The Data Encryption Standard, according to the National Bureau of Standards. This is used in data security.

DETACH — A CP command which indicates that the user no longer needs a tape drived, and that it may be detached from his virtual machine.

Device — A hardware item used in the I/O process, including a DASD, a tape drive or a printer.

Directory — Similar to an address book, the virtual machines on the VM system are defined in the directory. Directory information includes userids, the amount of DASD associated with each user, as well as his privilege class, and the address of his minidisk.

Disconnected Virtual Machine — A virtual machine that is not associated with a physical terminal. System software products often run as disconnected virtual machines, "lying in wait" until issued a command to perform a task.

DMKRIO — Essentially a program module, an assembler program that is part of the CP nucleus. DMKRIO defines the I/O device configuration of the VM system. RIO refers to Real I/O.

DMKSNT — Also part of the CP nucleus, in which the saved systems are defined, such as CMS. Saved systems are essentially "communal copies" of programs, to which users have access. SNT refers to System Name Table.

DMKSYS — Another assembler program in the CP nucleus, DMKSYS is used in defining options that are critical to the performance of the VM system, including the definition of CP-owned DASD areas. SYS refers to System Definitions.

DOS — DOS is an abbreviation for Disk Operating System, an older, batch-oriented IBM operating system. For the mainframe, it is now referred to as DOS/VSE, or simply VSE.

DOS Simulation — DOS application programs may be developed and tested within VM, through this CMS feature.

EXEC — Essentially a programming language within CMS providing the ability to write simple programs that consist of CMS commands and basic logic. Programs written in EXEC are referred to as "EXECs."

EXEC2 — A version of EXEC with more capabilities.

FBA — A type of disk drive. FBA is an abbreviation for Fixed Block Architecture, and DASD of this format is assigned in blocks, rather than cylinders.

Fileid — A CMS file is identified by a fileid, which consists of a filename, filetype and filemode.

Filemode — An identifier for a CMS file that essentially helps in identifying the minidisk on which the file is stored. For general use, the filemode is A to refer to the A-Disk. It may contain as many as two characters.

Filename — A name given to a file by the user. Up to eight characters in length, the composition of the filename is at the discretion of the user, and provides a means of quick reference to the content of the file.

Filetype — A further descriptive term for the file, the filetype may help in grouping files that fall into a specific user-defined category, or may identify the file, for example, as an EXEC. The filetype may also be as many as eight characters.

Fix — Software programs, including VM releases, with an error, or a "bug," may be corrected by a fix. The fix is a modification to the program.

Guest — The CP component of VM is also capable of serving as an "umbrella" in which other operating systems are managed within the VM environment. MVS, DOS, and UNIX may run as guests under VM.

Handshaking — The performance of DOS may actually improve through this capability of CP which essentially relates to the paging function.

HPO — A VM variation that includes enhancements to VM/SP that allow VM to run on larger machines. VM/HPO is also used in organizations with a very high number of CMS users. HPO refers to High Performance Option.

IPL — When the operating system is "brought up," or loaded into memory, the Initial Program Load (IPL) refers to this action.

IUCV — A communications facility in CP that basically allows two cooperating virtual machines to talk to each other (not the humans using the virtual machines but the programs running on these machines). IUCV is an abbreviation for Inter-User Communications Vehicle.

Link — The means by which users grant access to their minidisks to other users, as well as gain access to frequently used applications.

MAINT — This is userid associated with the maintenance function. IBM recommends that the MAINT userid be used, for example, when installing a new VM release.

MESSAGE — A CP command used in sending a message to another logged on user.

Minidisk — DASD space is assigned in portions called minidisks. A minidisk is a logical, or virtual, area of the physical DASD. Depending on the type of DASD, minidisks are assigned in either cylinders or blocks. The addresses of minidisks are assigned in the VM directory.

MIPS — A means of measuring the speed of a CPU. MIPS is an abbreviation for Millions of Instructions Per Second.

MIS — An abbreviation for Management Information Systems, this group is the central department in the organization which serves as the focal point of technical decision-making and coordination of information resources.

MOUNT — A command sent from a user to the computer operator requesting that a tape be placed on a tape drive. The mount command is not native to VM, rather it is defined within the installation.

MVS — The major batch-oriented IBM operating system. MVS is an abbreviation for Multiple Virtual Storage.

Native VM — Also referred to "vanilla" VM, this is the basic VM operating system without modifications, and without the enhancements offered through system software.

NOTE — A CMS command, similar to TELL, which is used to send what is generally a more lengthy online message to another user. A note is similar to a memo. The user(s) for whom the note is intended do not need to be logged on at the time the note is sent.

Nucleus — The "heart" of VM, the nucleus is loaded into memory during the IPL process. The nucleus contains the basics of CP.

Object Code — Source code that has been compiled or assembled is object code, and this code is what is actually executed by the CPU.

Operating System — This is software that provides overall management of the environment, as is provided through the VM operating system. The operating system, for example, controls I/O and the allocation of system resources.

Page — A portion of data or instructions that may be swapped between the main memory of the CPU and DASD. A page in VM is 4K in size.

Paging — The process of swapping (transferring) pages of data or instructions between main memory and DASD. Paging provides a means of more efficient use of the CPU's main memory, enhancing overall throughput.

Parallel Processing — A batch processing option in which tasks are completed simultaneously.

Password — The foundation of security in native VM, the password is a word (generally user defined) that supplements the userid in the logon procedure, and is used in granting link privileges to other users.

Problem State — A performance concept, Problem State refers to the amount of time devoted exclusively to the execution of user tasks. This can be contrasted to Supervisor State.

PTF — The IBM term given to a fix, an abbreviation for Program Temporary Fix. PTFs are distributed on PUTs (Program Update Tapes).

PUT — An abbreviation for Program Update Tape, the PUT is a tape that is periodically sent by IBM to VM installations. The PUT contains recent fixes to the operating system. PUTs are also sent for other operating systems and application software.

Queue 1 — The schedule in CP maintains three lists of tasks waiting to be executed. The tasks in Queue 1 are associated with users who are currently working interactively.

Queue 2 — This is a list of userids that need processor time to complete their current task, but are not entering more data.

Queue 3 — The Queue 3 list contains userids that will require a large amount of CPU time to complete the current task.

REXX — A CMS programming language similar to EXEC and EXEC2, but much more sophisticated. REXX refers to Restructured Extended Executor.

RSCS — A communications facility for VM that enables the transfer of spool files between CPUs. This allows, for example, users to send messages to each other. RSCS is an abbreviation for Remote Spooling Communications Subsystem.

Scheduler — A program within CP that selects from Queue 1, Queue 2, or Queue 3 in deciding which task to process next. The Scheduler acts as a dispatcher.

SENDFILE — A CMS command used in sending a CMS file from one user to another, through RSCS.

Serial Processing — A batch processing option in which tasks are completed one at a time.

SNA — The rules and formats used to facilitate communication between CPUs. Designed by IBM, SNA is an abbreviation for Systems Network Architecture.

Source Code — Original program code that has not yet been compiled or assembled to become Object Code. Generally, source code must be compiled or assembled before it can be run on a computer, as is true for VM source code.

Spool — An area of DASD that acts as a holding area for files that are being transferred, for example, to a printer or between users. Spool refers to Simultaneous Peripheral Operation On-Line.

SQL — A standard language, originally defined by IBM, that is used with relational database management systems. SQL is an abbreviation for Structured Query Language, and is pronounced "Sequel."

SQL/DS — IBM's relational database management system for the VM environment, using SQL as a language.

Starter System — A basic and relatively easily installed VM operating system, on a tape.

Supervisor State — The amount of time that CP spends in doing work such as paging and managing I/O, as opposed to specific user tasks.

SYSGEN — A means of referring to System Generation, this is the process of creating a CP nucleus that may be loaded in memory through an IPL.

System Software — Though an operating system can be broadly defined as system software, this term generally refers to utilities which enhance the performance of the operating system. System software utility functions include system security, tape management, accounting, and DASD management.

T-Disk — An area of DASD that is used as an extended work area, and that "disappears" once the user ends the session. This is a means of having a large area of DASD to work in during the user session. T-Disk refers to Temporary Disk.

TELL — A CMS command used to send a message to another logged on user, through RSCS.

Text Deck — After source code is compiled or assembled, the object code is contained in a Text Deck.

Thrashing — When system load is such that CP is being forced to page heavily as a means of accommodating heavy demand, CP may be having to use so many resources in the paging process that user tasks are not being completed efficiently. Supervisor State overtakes Problem State, and response time suffers. This is referred to as thrashing.

TSO — An abbreviation for Time Sharing Option, this is the component of MVS that provides a form of interactivity.

Userid — The identification assigned to each user, and contained in the directory.

Vanilla VM — Another term for native VM; VM in its unaided and unadulterated form.

VM — An abbreviation for Virtual Machine, this refers to the IBM interactive operating system comprised of CM and CMS. Virtual machine is the concept of each user having privileges and a storage area that simulate being in control of the total CPU, rather than sharing with other users.

VMCF — A communications facility that evolved into IUCV. VMCF is an abbreviation for Virtual Machine Communication Facility.

VMFASM — A program that transforms source code and PTFs into updated object code that is useable for the VMFLOAD process.

VMFLOAD — The program which creates the CP nucleus.

VM/PC — A VM variation for the PC/370 personal computer.

VM/SP — The standard VM operating system, designed for CPUs at the midrange, including the 9370 and the 43XX series. SP is an abbreviation for System Product.

VM/XA/SF — A VM variation providing Extended Architecture capabilities. Currently this is used as a conversion aid for MVS/XA. IBM is aggressively enhancing VM/XA to include CMS capabilities.

VSE — Another term for DOS on the mainframe, VSE is an abbreviation for Virtual Storage Extended.

VTAM — An access method that allows VM terminals to make use of the SNA network. VTAM is an abbreviation for Virtual Terminal Access Method.

Warm Start — During a warm start, after a shutdown of the VM system, all spool files are saved. A warm start is quicker than a Checkpoint Start.

XEDIT — A CMS command associated with the System Product Editor. XEDIT is used in the creation and modification of CMS files.

ZAP — A fix to object code. It acts as a patch and is applied "over" existing object code.

Index